And in the Vienna Woods the Trees Remain

ALSO BY ELISABETH ÅSBRINK

1947: Where Now Begins

Made in Sweden

Wenn ich in England s

Deinen Freund nicht böse

Tauschen? Mit bei

Nr. 117

Liebe Ott

gestriges Schreib

erst heute bestät

Vor Allem

heisst stilistisc

And in the Vienna Woods the Trees Remain

THE HEARTBREAKING TRUE STORY OF
A FAMILY TORN APART BY WAR

Elisabeth Åsbrink

Translated from the Swedish by Saskia Vogel

Other Press / New York

Originally published in Swedish as *Och i Wienerwald står träden kvar*
in 2011 by Natur & Kultur, Stockholm

Published by arrangement with Partners in Stories Stockholm AB

The cost of this translation was supported by a grant from the Swedish Arts Council.

The preface was written by the author in English for this edition.

Production editor: Yvonne E. Cárdenas
Text designer: Jennifer Daddio / Bookmark Design & Media Inc.
This book was set in Goudy and Wade Sans Light by
Alpha Design & Composiiton of Pittsfield, NH.

1 3 5 7 9 10 8 6 4 2

 Printed in the United States of America
on acid-free paper. For information write to Other Press LLC,
267 Fifth Avenue, 6th Floor, New York, NY 10016.
Or visit our Web site: www.otherpress.com

Library of Congress Cataloging-in-Publication Data

Names: Åsbrink, Elisabeth, author. | Vogel, Saskia, translator.
Title: And in the Vienna woods the trees remain : the heartbreaking true story
of a family torn apart by war / Elisabeth Åsbrink ; translated by Saskia Vogel.
Other titles: Och i Wienerwald står träden kvar. English
Description: New York : Other Press, 2020. | Includes bibliographical references.
Identifiers: LCCN 2019019275 | ISBN 9781590519172 (hardback) |
ISBN 9781590519189 (ebook)
Subjects: LCSH: Ullmann, Otto, 1925-2005. | Jewish refugees—Sweden—Biography. |
BISAC: HISTORY / Modern / 20th Century. | HISTORY / Holocaust. |
HISTORY / Europe / Scandinavia.
Classification: LCC DS135.S89 U45313 2020 | DDC 940.53/18092 [B]–dc23
LC record available at https://lccn.loc.gov/2019019275

Preface

This was a book I had no intention of writing. On the contrary, the story of Otto Ullmann, a Jewish refugee child who was sent to Sweden to escape Nazi persecution, came to me as an offer and I turned it down.

Eva Ullman—the daughter of Otto—asked to speak with me. She brought with her a trauma tied tight with string and asked for my help to unknot it. This is what she told me:

Her father was born and raised in a middle-class family in Vienna, a cherished and strong-willed child who loved music and soccer. When Hitler annexed Austria in March 1938, he was twelve years old. Like all Austrian Jews, the Ullmann family was heavily affected from one day to the next, and the persecution had just begun. Otto's parents decided to save their only child first, and managed to get him to Sweden in early spring 1939. The plan was to join him later, but until that became possible, they would write him a letter a day. Otto spent a year in an orphanage in the south of Sweden. Then, at the age of fourteen, he had to support himself and became a farmhand. Meanwhile, the letters from Otto's parents in Vienna continued to come, until the day they came no more.

In early 1944 Otto Ullmann applied for a job at the Kamprad estate in Småland and became best friends with the landowner's son, Ingvar. Later, when Ingvar Kamprad decided to create the furniture company IKEA, Otto was his right-hand man and sidekick for a decade.

Would I like to write something about this, Otto's daughter now wondered? Then, ironically, she handed over an IKEA storage box that for years had been at the back of one of her closets, never opened but never forgotten. There they were, more than five hundred letters from Otto's parents, with Hitler's profile on the stamps.

When Otto Ullmann died, Eva had reluctantly taken care of the letters but never read them. As the daughter of a Holocaust survivor, she grew up learning that there were some areas not to be tread on, some words better left unsaid, and some questions never to be asked. And she understood that at the very epicenter of silence were her father and his survival. So the letters were placed in the IKEA box, lid on, until she got the idea of offering them to me.

I said thank you, but no thank you. I couldn't. I wouldn't. Impossible. I'm sorry. The letters were of course written in German, a language of which I had little knowledge, but that wasn't the main reason. I simply couldn't stand the idea of writing about the Holocaust. The unbreakable silence within the Ullmann family was all too recognizable, it existed also within my family. And so we said goodbye.

But then, night after night, before going to sleep, I found myself imagining the letters going from Vienna to the south of Sweden, one a day from parent to child. The image just wouldn't leave me alone.

The result is this book, a story about a boy and his parents. And within the story is another, about one of the world's most famous men, the founder of IKEA, who not only was a member of the Swedish hard-core Nazi party but at the same time loved his best friend, the Jewish refugee Otto Ullmann. All in all, it turned out to be an account of Sweden before the country became a "good" one.

Ingvar Kamprad let me interview him (the result is in the book). But when I found the files from 1943 in the Swedish Secret Police Archive, stating he was member 4014 in Swedish Socialist Unity (Svensk Socialistisk Samling, or SSS), the Swedish Nazi party at the time, he declined any further contact.

And the letters? They are still in that IKEA box, waiting for transfer to an archive where they will be made available to researchers. I'm not sure I could fulfill Eva Ullman's wishes, that through words the trauma might be unknotted. But the process of research and writing managed to dissolve some of the silence and the lack of knowledge. It also defined the connection between Eva and myself—and so many others: the experience of carrying the weight of a family's pain.

A child stood outside a building in a large city. It is a time gone by. The river splitting the city was like a wound; seven bridges kept it stitched together, binding the hills to the plains, greenery to exhaust fumes. Budapest.

The boy was playing on a small square just outside his front door. His father was at work, his mother was at home in their apartment a few floors up. He had no siblings, and his friends must have been elsewhere. He was five years old, and perhaps he liked his solitude.

A passerby paused to look at him, an adult who then yelled at him in such a way that he immediately stopped playing. That word, he'd never heard it before, but the expletives, the tone, the malice were unmistakable. As was the gaze: directed right at him.

In another country, in another city with another river, with other bridges linking it together, was another child: a girl. In London.

She was already in school, involved in group games and scheming with her friends, and her greatest wish was to go to the boys' school's annual dance. So when she received a printed invitation in the mail, it made her very happy indeed—perhaps she boasted about it to her friends—right up until the moment she realized that the card was handwritten; the invitation was a fake, a forgery. Someone (the girl suspected a spurned friend behind this trap) had wanted to see her go to the dance all dressed up and full of anticipation, only to be ignominiously exposed at the door and denied entry. The girl cried tears of anger and lamented to her mother.

The mother too became angry and spoke to the girl's father; they should go straight to the headmaster, the deceiver should be punished and the daughter issued an apology. But the father would not be swayed and replied instead with a "Shush!" and "Let it be." Then he used a word that the girl would despise from that moment on and would never want to acknowledge. He added, "No, that's not what a [word] does. We don't solve problems by creating new ones; we don't cause trouble. What doesn't bend breaks."

To this day, the girl remembers the feeling of betrayal, even though by now she is eighty years old. Not to be given redress, to stand without defense, to be identified with that word; this all caused her to crack right through.

Coincidentally it was the same word (with the addition of "stinking") that the boy playing by himself had heard the stranger say. And because the boy was only five years old, he hadn't understood, and he went home, up the stairs to his mother, and asked, "'Stinking Jew': what does that mean?"

His mother said nothing about having had him baptized. She simply said there are two types of people: good and evil. And so the world became slightly more intelligible to a child. Coincidentally the boy from Budapest and the girl from

London met as adults, recognized each other's chasms, and fell in love.

Coincidentally they would go on to have a child together and pass on an inheritance of alienation—it was, after all, abundant. They allowed her to partake of that word as well, but only as an affliction. She would hear "Shush!" She would hear: "The fewer the people who know, the better." And later: "It's for the best that your children's father isn't Jewish; it'll leave the blood more quickly."

This is a history, mine.

Mutti. Dad. It's as though you never existed.
And yet I am born.

We don't know each other, but she has read my book. During our first meeting, we barely spoke. The next time, we kept each other company over a bite to eat and then went to a concert. There, in a place alien to us both, in a soundscape of distorted guitars and bass, she began to speak. It wasn't easy to hear what she was saying. But she moved closer. She was carrying something and trying to build a bridge of words so that her load could reach me.

If you asked her where she was from, she'd say "Småland," in southern Sweden. And yet she gives me five hundred letters from Vienna.

At first I don't know if I want them.

And then I can't think about anything else.

They're being stored in a large lidded box, made of stiff white cardboard and marked IKEA. One might imagine this fact is part of destiny's irony, or, if you're one to psychologize, is an expression of her subconscious. Perhaps the product of tenderness or black humor.

Otto sorted the letters. Since then they haven't really been touched, much less read. But she, Otto's daughter, still knows what they contain. One loop of twine and a regular farmer's knot separate the piles, one year from the next.

Are the letters old? Is seventy years a long time? Or is it a period shorter than a human life and of equally disputed value?

Well. In the white box they've lain, densely written, in chronological order, an epicenter of sorrow.

III

For years the memories were left to languish. As if they'd been waiting for him to take the step, into the shadows and foliage. But he'd looked the other way. Directed his thoughts elsewhere.

And then he was handed a bunch of keys. A letter arrived, an envelope containing photographs; disordered days, undated moments, silent gazes.

Of course Mitzi had taken custody of the pictures. And when everything was over she'd placed the envelope inside a larger one, on which she'd written Otto Ullmann's name, and mailed it to him in Sweden.

There he caught sight of himself. He reencountered the bright look in his father's eyes. He looked at himself as a child, anchored in his mother's arms.

Der Blade, "Fatty," is what they'd called Elise because of her soft, swelling curves.

Otto and Dad joined forces, the men against the mother, amusing themselves at her expense as often as they could. She cared for them when they had fever and fretted if they'd been out too long in the rain or cold.

Dad and Mutti divided up Otto's world between them. They'd conceived late in life, and their son became a natural focal point; they didn't let him out of sight. Anxious Elise arranged for his health and comfort. She was the one who made sure his favorite foods were on the table, that he was given new, clean, or larger clothing when the time came, and that even the slightest scratch was bandaged with care. Dad, on the other hand, had taken him out, expanded his mind, and opened up the world. The red velvet of the opera house. The boxing ring. The ballet barre. A clean backhand on the tennis court. Conversations conducted along the Danube Canal about soccer, God, and the importance of a good education. That was Josef.

The photographs from the end of the 1930s showed them as they once were, in the light of days long since gone dark. There, men in shadow-black hats stood next to women in wide, checked dresses. There was Josef at the foot of Austrian mountains and Elise wearing white socks and low shoes in the summertime.

Is this how Otto dreamed of them at night? Were they still parent-sized even though he had outgrown them long ago? Were they still forty-five years old even though they were dead? Did their love keep them present?

Josef must have made a habit of keeping a camera with him. Maybe that's why they were seldom posed and instead pictured in the midst of the everyday, strolling, on the sidewalk, in parks. City street after city street in grand Vienna was also documented in the photos; summer-saturated snapshots. The heat was apparent in their faces, in the pressure on their foreheads, in Elise's airy dresses. Otto in lederhosen, holding a cloth rabbit or carrying his schoolbag. Otto with Tant Mina's fox terrier who was forever tugging at its leash. Otto flying by on his scooter. Elise on vacation, in a lush garden in the countryside or in a warm sea, looking toward the beach. Did she dare dive in?

Josef looks content in every picture. The colleague next to him is laughing, you can see in his eyes that Josef has just said something witty. He holds his son, he plays and converses as if he knew nothing better than life with his plump wife and their little Otto.

Memories. Ideal images. The invocation of deposed powers.

Vienna was the city in the middle of Europe where they once walked shielded from the hot summer sun by an umbrella, fed pigeons in the park, kicked a ball around, had a drink, and lived their family life.

Presumably Otto's father Josef was born in Vienna, where his parents had moved after they left Iglau, a city that once was within the borders of the dual monarchy, Austria-Hungary.

Josef had three brothers and one sister. The woman who gave birth to him was one of many names rustling in a family tree where the very branches are missing and only shadows remain.

I know Josef wanted to be happy. But it's unclear if that meant he actually felt happy. I can confirm that he took pleasure in formulating long, complex sentences with successions of subordinate clauses. He eagerly partook in various sports-related challenges, where devoted athletes came together for soccer, tennis, or track and field. Josef had an eye for the subtle impact a new coach could have on the length of a runner's stride and arm-swinging technique. He was probably not sufficiently talented as a sportsman to become a professional himself, but conversant enough to analyze the movements of eleven players with a ball in such a way that the weak link in the chain could become apparent to even the marginally interested spectator, who then had enough insight into the game to draw his own conclusions about the match's result. Josef liked writing. He became a sports journalist.

One can't be sure, but it's likely that certain insights were passed down to him, insights that can indeed be verbalized, but presumably they reached him tacitly: No one can rob you of your knowledge. This too shall pass. What doesn't bend breaks.

One hundred and thirty years after Josef Ullmann was born—by which time he had long since been murdered—I speak his name.

Elise Kollmann came to Vienna from Moravia. Like Josef, she was born in Austria-Hungary, but after the First World War, she found herself in Czechoslovakia without ever having moved. She was a brunette with thick, wavy hair.

Maybe she traveled from her family home in Brno together with her sisters Margarethe and Adolfine, dark-eyed sturdy girls all three. They preferred nicknames to the ones they'd been given. So Elise was shortened to Lisl, Margarethe was called Grete, and Adolfine became Nuny.

When they got to know Josef, they called him Pepi. The four of them spent time together, became friends. And at some point, it's unclear when, Lisl married Pepi, two years her junior, and changed her last name from Kollmann to Ullmann.

Did she enjoy sports? Well, she didn't like writing in any case, she didn't think she had a talent for it. And yet she would go on to do her best, forced by future circumstance.

When Lisl was thirty-four and Pepi was thirty-two, their only child was born. On July 20, 1925.

They rocked their son Otto with the same hopes and well-wishes parents have always had. They gave him nicknames (golden boy, Wuzi, Mucki pucki), they hoped the ugly family nose wouldn't manifest, but that a gift for language, music, and kicking a ball around would. They wanted the boy to be sensitive and rational, let him dance ballet and box, and wished that both nature and nurture would yield a bounty of unbruised fruits.

He was a slender boy with dark locks, quick in body and in mind. In summer they let the barber give him a buzz cut, which accentuated his irregular features and dark eyes. Lisl and Pepi saw that he was the most beautiful of children. Their only one.

Perhaps Lisl thought that she was too old after having turned thirty-five, or was their desire to have a son so potent that when they finally got their Otto they didn't want another?

He grew up an only child, not made to compete with anything but his own need to be the best. The impulse was so clear, it never needed be said that nothing but the best would do. Pepi, Otto, and Lisl; the three of them were inextricably linked. And they wanted nothing else.

Needless to say, he was spoiled.

Like having two mothers, Otto was cosseted by Lisl and the housekeeper Mitzi. Aunties Nuny and Grete competed with each other and with his uncle over who would give him candy and gifts in exchange for hugs and far-too-wet kisses, while Pepi and Uncle Paul conducted long conversations with him about music, politics, and sport.

Otto became willful and was used to his opinions mattering. If things didn't go his way, he got angry, but it didn't take much to brighten his mood. More often than not, he got his way.

And so he grew into a loving and self-involved child, quick to give gifts because he received many, but also impatient and restless.

Indeed they impressed upon him the importance of decency and a good education, but Otto's urbanity and ability to converse was mostly due to being from a family of middle-aged, newspaper-reading, literature- and opera-loving adults who always laughed at his jokes, allowed him to box or play soccer on a whim, let him make decisions because it amused them, and because they prized him above all else. As did the kind, devoted Mitzi.

As I said, one can't be certain.

And yet I would dare venture that Elise, a woman I've never met, loved her child. And in addition to Otto studying, earning money, being popular first with the boys and later with the girls, being a good son who talked with his mother about life's difficulties and joys, who took time to ask about her well-being as well as following her advice—she only wanted one thing (try to imagine a more arrogant wish): she wanted Otto to be happy.

At the time of Otto's birth Leopoldstadt was still considered a Jewish area, even though most residents were Christian. Some people followed their faith, some diverged.

Löwengasse 49 was a simple, unadorned building. Whereas the house across the way boasted Jugendstil garlands colored "English red," and the one on the corner was creamy white with a gold clock and balconies like pearl necklaces, number 49 was planted firmly in the middle with a butcher next to the front door. Otto lived in apartment number 15 together with Lisl, Pepi, Aunt Grete, and the housekeeper Mitzi, who'd come to them from the countryside as a young girl. They lived their lives and dreamed their dreams in those four rooms, two blocks from the Donau Canal. In Austria. Not within the bounds of the German empire, not yet. Otto still went to school and Pepi still edited the sports pages of the newspaper *Wiener Tag*. After a day's work, he'd often nod off standing in the tram, but would wake up just in time for his stop. His salary afforded them a comfortable existence with evenings at the opera and Saturday afternoons watching soccer from the stands, weekend dinners with buttercream roll for dessert, and a decent wage for Mitzi.

On Sundays they packed their baskets and took the tram out to the Vienna Woods, where they wandered the paths and hillsides together with Aunt Nuny and her husband Paul. They brought a soccer ball with them and played when they came upon a clearing. If it was hot, Otto ran around shirtless. They sat in the verdant shade, reading books or planning their annual visit to the spa town Bad Ischl. They discussed their sports heroes' injuries and scores, they took a break from the demands and habits of the everyday—in short, they enjoyed spending their free time together amid patches of sunlight and the leafy rustle, under the canopy of the Vienna Woods.

The adults in the family were pleased that Otto wasn't just intelligent and musical, he also had a feel for language. Pepi asked Paul to tutor him in Greek grammar, Latin, and English. The boy, with his intelligence, might well be suited to a career as a doctor or lawyer.

It's easy to picture them. Mutti Lisl strolling with Otto, holding hands as long as he would allow. Josef was a head taller than his wife, with a solid build and a bald patch. He liked walking with his hands in his pockets, his wide pants ending just below his knee, their cuffs tucked into his high socks. Naturally, he wore white on the tennis court.

And Otto. In little blazers—one dark blue, double-breasted, one in white-and-blue stripes—and almost always in shorts. He was but a child after all.

Of course you can search for a starting point.

You can devote your life to scanning for signs in time, as though time could be inspected. You can try to arrange it in chronological order, see how various key events relate. Like a first or the last of something. The third queen, the fourth decree, the fifth truth. It's all only an attempt to create order where there is none, and then one year is as good as any.

Take 1926. Otto Ullmann, an infant with brown almond-shaped eyes, liked being bounced on his mother's or father's knee in their four-room apartment in Vienna.

At the cusp of spring, another child, Ingvar Kamprad, was born at the Hvita Korset birthing home in Pjätteryd's parish. He too was his parents' firstborn. And his story, like everyone else's, began long before then. You could just as well go back another century, to Radonitz in Bohemia.

Fanny was petite, delicate, and had fine features. Her husband, Achim, was four years her senior, taller, blonder, and heartier. Ingvar had inherited his paternal grandfather's forehead and eyebrows.

Shame must have abounded, and Fanny must have been born right into it. Her own mother. Her young mother and a married man.

That's how Fanny came to be: extramarital, extrafamilial, on the wrong side of the border. The married man got out scot-free, left a substantial amount of cash behind by way of apology, leaving Fanny's mother alone with her illegitimate child.

The money bought a tavern, and there Fanny grew up. She served, cleaned, and helped out. She got a new dad and took his name. Underneath it all, the shame stayed like skin layered on skin, a layer of dirt on what had been scrubbed clean.

And then Achim walked into the tavern. Or maybe he stormed in, hot-tempered, after a big fight with his family at the castle. He didn't want to do what was expected of him. He wanted to be with his closest friends, the dogs, in the woods. He wanted to move about freely and leave the paperwork and family tradition behind, something unacceptable for someone with his Saxon land-owning background, entirely unacceptable. He walked into a tavern, and there stood Fanny with a gaze that cut through almost everything.

At least that's how the family tells this story; they were proud people with nothing to be proud of. Affection arose.

Soon thereafter they were posing together in Herr Schmidt's atelier. The backdrop is neutral.

Newlywed? Him, standing tall with his large hand on her slender waist. Her, laced into a pale ruffled dress, turning toward him as if he were shelter from the wind. When it was probably the other way around. Fanny and Achim.

And no. She wasn't accepted by his family.

With their two young sons, they decided to emigrate. A new country, a new life, hunting grounds for him and his beloved hounds. It was the mid-nineteenth century and Achim invested in a property: 54,000 riksdaler for forest, farm animals, crops, and a storehouse of rye. Their reasons for leaving Bohemia lost their importance. Elmtaryd was the name of the farm that now belonged to them. The earth was rocky but fertile, the forest large and beautiful.

It's an old story; people cross borders, they seek new lives. The reasons vary, but surprisingly enough, are often similar. As for most immigrants, Fanny and Achim's new life meant hard work, perhaps they were met with resistance in their unknown environs; they'd probably thought that more people would speak German, maybe they'd been more reliant on advice from strong parents than they realized, and perhaps this resulted in weak finances. Whatever the case, Achim shot his two hunting dogs and then himself. Fanny was left behind, delicate but willful, with her sons and an unborn daughter.

She never remarried. Intractable neighbors moved the property lines, cutting into her land, and eventually she humbled herself and asked her German mother-in-law for help. The mother-in-law raised a fuss with the men at the Swedish National Land Survey, and the property lines were restored.

Fanny never learned Swedish, but the priest at the village church spoke German and was happy to help. In this way Fanny took charge all on her own and moved herself and the farm forward one day at a time until her oldest son Feodor turned twenty-five. From that point forward, the farm and the responsibility were his to shoulder.

Fanny Kamprad. Her son Feodor. Then Feodor's son, Ingvar. Leaders all three. A series of names that stood for strong will and the admiration for strong wills, and this notion was handed down to the next generation.

Grandmother Fanny was the person whom Ingvar would come to admire the most. More than his father Feodor. Even more than Uncle Hitler.

But does this mean it was all her fault?

III

Älmhult, 2010.

The table between us is round and glossy. We each have a cup of hot coffee from a machine. The white plastic mugs are so flimsy they have to be doubled. What a waste, we joke at the machine: two cups for one coffee.

Then we sit. Ingvar's assistant has joined us. It's okay to record the conversation. It's okay to ask questions. Everything is okay; an agreeable spirit of openness and mutual understanding reigns. Only afterward did I wonder what was okay exactly.

ELISABETH: When these documents surfaced—did you look Otto up or how did it go?

INGVAR: Yes, I wrote a letter of apology to our employees that was published in our little employee newspaper. I said it was my fault. It's a catastrophe. I deeply regret having held an opinion like that. I don't quite remember the wording, but I asked for forgiveness. And in reply, I got a letter that said: "Of course we forgive you, Ingvar," and "You mean everything to us." And it was signed by hundreds of coworkers [...]

I also wrote to friends and sent a copy of my communiqué, but I can't recall if I sent... Everything was so darn nerve-wracking then [...]

You understand, I contacted maybe twenty-five

people by phone and another hundred of all sorts who I know, and attached what I'd said to the employees and the employee response [. . .]

ELISABETH: But you don't think you called him yourself . . .

INGVAR: No. No.

ELISABETH: And asked for his forgiveness?

INGVAR: No. If I did, I'd have had his address, for instance. And I didn't.

ELISABETH: Or phone number?

INGVAR: No. [sighs] I shouldn't swear to that now. You mean I might've gotten the number from Karin and called him up? I don't think so [. . .]

ELISABETH: You maybe having contacted him . . . it doesn't sound like that's outside the realm of possibility?

INGVAR: No, sirree! [. . .] But did I? I really can't say. If I'd had his telephone number it's darn likely that I would've called him. Did I have his phone number?

III

In the presence of foreign diplomats and the press on September 15, 1935, Adolf Hitler announced two of the four Laws for the Protection of German Blood and Honor established by the Nazis during their time in power.

The conditions for existence of people defined as Jews already differed from everyone else. Their access to universities was limited, their representation among doctors and lawyers was governed by quotas, they'd been fired from the German armed forces and were forbidden to take the stage or participate in film production. But now they were being stripped of their human rights as well.

The laws had been drafted in haste during a few sleepless nights in mid-September. The planning was poor, the Nazis ran out of paper, so they had to take notes on menus. It's no wonder that the laws' wording left something to be desired, making them difficult to uphold in the first months. They'd forgotten to define who was fully Jewish, half Jewish, or merely had a speck of Semitic dust in their eye. Harder than one might think, differentiating one from the other.

But by November the lawmakers had reconsidered and made an effort to bring order to the human chaos that love and sexual attraction had created. Schematics were set. Lines were drawn. And suddenly the Nuremberg Laws were a sun-cross-clear set of rules and regulations that any dutiful civil servant could follow.

III

At Otto, Elise, and Joseph's place at 49 Löwengasse, the leaves on the chestnut tree in the yard were unfurling. In about a week the tree's blossoms would ignite their white lights.

Though the mood in the city was uneasy and fresh rumors about people being arrested and troops gathering at the border abounded, the days came and went as usual. From the parlor you could look down on the street, where the tram rattled by with its human cargo. In the morning Milos and Georg would come and hang about at the door until Otto came down, and they all would go off to school. Aunt Grete puttered about, singing, in her room. Pepi was tired in the mornings and stayed in bed as long as possible, and Elise went out with Mitzi to select the fixings for the day's meals. It was an existence that was so ingrained as to be invisible, in rooms that smelled of home from their breathing, from the dust on the bookshelves, from the ink of the newspapers, and from Pepi's aftershave lotion. Homeliness. Days of nothing special, when nothing unusual happened, nothing notable. Everyday. Something you miss only when it has been shattered.

On March 12, 1938, the Nazis occupied Austria and called it the Anschluss (annexation). Many celebrated. The Führer immediately began a grand tour of his country of birth. Three days later he found himself in uniform in the center of Vienna on the Hofburg Palace balcony. Some hundred thousand people on the square had this man and the sun in their eyes. They raised their hands in greeting, and in this way their vision was cast in shadow.

The Führer stood on Heroes' Square and declared Austria part of the Greater Germanic Reich. Now and then he was interrupted by cheers or applause. During a pause in his speech, the people—their hands still raised—chanted his name in unison. Hitler. Hitler. Hitler.

The sun shone brightly, eating away the grayness, the ordinary, everything in between, whatever was a bit of both. The edge between light and dark became razor sharp. Wherever you looked, pennants and flags were rippling and people were baring their teeth as they smiled. This was the day that the *Wiener Tag*'s sports editor, Josef Ullmann, was fired because he was Jewish.

Readers of the Swedish newspaper *Dagens Nyheter* received this news the following day: "Kärntnerstrasse, one of Vienna's main shopping streets, was on Wednesday the stage for anti-Semitic acts that recalled the scenes on Kürfürstendamm in Berlin in 1935. Young men dressed in civilian clothing with swastika armbands moved through the streets to calls of 'Death to the Jews.' On the windows of shops belonging to Jewish businessmen the word 'Jew' was painted in brown. In the evening, there was severe crowding on Kärntnerstrasse. The police are taking a passive stance to the demonstrations."

The *Social-Demokraten* newspaper reported "the rule of terror raging in Austria" and a "suicide epidemic, mass detentions."

Then Hermann Göring arrived, and fourteen days after Austria's annexation by Nazi Germany he clarified what was to come to those who might yet be unsure: ". . . here I must address the city of Vienna with a serious word. The city of Vienna can no longer rightfully be called a German city today. So many Jews live in this city. Where there are 300,000 Jews living, one can no longer speak of a German city.

"Vienna must once again become a German city, for it has important tasks to perform for Germany in Germany's Ostmark. These tasks lie in the area of culture as well as in the area of economics. In neither of them do we, in the long run, have use for the Jew."

Through the implementation of systematic measures, Vienna would be free of Jews within four years.

The Swedish press reported this, nothing was secret, everything was out in the open. Toward the summer the *Social-Demokraten* newspaper reported that "Austria's Jews are being brutally eradicated."

On June 22 the Christian daily newspaper *Svenska Morgonbladet* reported: "The catastrophe endangers 5 million Jews." The front-page article began with the assertion that if democratic states did not unite and propose a solution to the Jewish question, five million Jews in Europe would face catastrophe and death. Pastor Birger Pernow, the international Israel Mission's vice president, announced that a international meeting in Evian was being planned, and there an attempt would be made to influence the British government to take on the Jewish question.

One month later, it was indeed not going well in Evian. Nothing was decided or even improved, none of the European democratic states wanted to commit to taking in refugees. The threat of catastrophe remained, or rather, was consolidated. But Pastor Pernow would come to touch Otto's life, to intrude upon his story.

Soon.

Rehn, Elbe, Oder, Weser, Main, and Donau. Along the banks of these rivers, swimming was not all that was forbidden; crying was too. Austria had become part of the Greater Germanic Reich. In May the Race Laws were declared.

Children must have stood up during class, on the order of those who'd flung open the doors to their classrooms and strode in. Not all children, only those defined as Jewish. Without a word, without pen, paper, or book, they had to leave everything and go, with no one expressing hope for their return. From then on, their days were spent at home. The Kultusgemeinde, or Jewish Community Council, had to set up special schools where barred teachers taught expelled children, and so these became temporary havens that made space for exceptions, interstices, gatherings of people who weren't allowed to be seen elsewhere, the misfits. En route to the teeming classrooms, children might have regarded each other as strangers, wondering: Jewish? At home they looked in the mirror and asked themselves the same question.

Everyone learned the word "affidavit," and a visa became more coveted than butter.

Mutti often got angry because Dad played goalie in the doorway and Otto kicked the ball at an angle that imperiled the table lamp. Jews were not allowed in parks.

Leaving the country was not yet a self-evident notion. Pepi wasn't just born in Austria, proud of his country and in love with his city, he'd also fought for the nation. He was twenty-one years old when the Great War broke out, and he carried it with him as shrapnel lodged in his spine.

Pepi had done what the country asked of him. Why would this country, his country, want to hurt him now? This too must pass.

But through the power shift in March, the persecution of those classified as Jewish was incorporated into law and rule, and those who hadn't yet understood the scope of Nazi Germany had their eyes opened after the Anschluss. Everywhere lines were forming outside consulates and embassies.

Waiting, crowding. The few who were given the opportunity to travel.

III

Six weeks after the Anschluss, the Swedish government began to require a compulsory visa for Austrian citizens so they couldn't just slip into Sweden. Germans didn't need a visa, but for Austrians it was a necessity.

People classed as Jews were openly viewed as undesirable immigrants; the Swedish visa requirement was a defense and a hurdle. But this didn't suit the Nazis, who wanted to empty Greater Germany of so-called non-Aryans. And as though Europe were a game board with pieces that had to be knocked off, Germany quite simply decided to invalidate the Austrian passport and replace it with a German one so undesirables could more easily leave the country.

This move had an effect. As early as August 8, the Swedish consul in Vienna reported that Jews were inquiring about traveling to Sweden with their new German passports, and of course he couldn't lie and say it wasn't allowed. The information caused concern in the government's department for alien affairs, the Swedish Aliens Office: "Those hundreds who upon inspection have been denied an entry visa, as well as those who could be granted permission to emigrate, since coming into possession of German passports, will be allowed to enter Sweden and remain for three months."

The people responsible for this in the Swedish government realized that when those fleeing made it into the country, it wouldn't be possible to send them back to Germany. Sigfrid Hansson, the general director for the Royal Board of Health and Welfare, analyzed the situation:

> Thus, the protection against undesirable immigration from Austria is eliminated, and with it the applicable visa requirement that the "Austrian passport" had constituted for some time. In view of this, and taking into account the diversity of visa applications for more permanent residence in our country, which have recently been coming from Austria, as well as the circumstance that "non-Aryans" who leave Austria can be understood to face reprisals upon returning to their home country, the question arises whether it is called for to introduce measures, for Sweden, to stem uncontrolled immigration.

Under no circumstance did Sweden want to grant them entry. And so there were three ways to go. Keep the current system and kick the persecuted out after three months; intensify each applicant's inspection so that undesirables could be turned away at the border; or instate a visa requirement for German passport holders.

None of the alternatives was easy to implement. But Magnus Hallenborg, the head of the Swedish Ministry of Foreign Affairs, mulled this over, wrote a pro memoria, and did in fact clear the path for a fourth way: "Best would be if German assistance could be counted on."

A sentence that would lead to the letter *J*.

When the Swedish government found out that Jewish renters in Nazi Germany were being forced from their homes, robbed of their bank accounts, jewelry, and possessions, that unemployment was followed by homelessness and that those driven away from the countryside were amassing in Vienna, the unease intensified. Suddenly there was talk, not only in the Nazi street demonstrations but also in the government corridors, about a refugee invasion and the risk of having a Jewish question also in Sweden.

Director Hallenborg took inspiration and guidance from Switzerland, with whom Sweden shared a view on refugees of Jewish descent (that is to say, aversion). In Switzerland negotiations with Germany had begun, and the Swedish government was following them attentively. Switzerland was threatening to instate a visa requirement for German passport holders to force Germany to take responsibility for the flood of refugees that hatred had unleashed. Now the question was how Nazi Germany would react.

In Vienna Pepi was at home, out of work but full of time to think.

And this too would pass.

This sentiment had always followed him. It had been passed down from one generation to the next for centuries, so that it was to hand in each fresh moment of joy, fear, or sorrow. As though it were engraved in a ring, as though time were a circle, and however you twisted and turned it this was the one answer to countless questions: this too shall pass.

It wasn't lost on Pepi that the situation could get worse before it got better. People he knew had taken their own lives. The anxiety was apparent in his friends' faces, the fear of tomorrow.

Indoors, the children paced in restless pallor, in spite of the sun and heat outside. After three months he'd finished thinking. In June he approached the authorities of Vienna's Jewish Community Council, in order to fill out the paperwork for emigration assistance.

In early September 1938, Swedish negotiators presented a proposal from Director Hallenborg, suggesting Sweden introduce visa restrictions in consultation with the German authorities "for the category of German citizens not considered desirable in Germany." They weren't desirable in Sweden either.

The German negotiators countered with a different proposal: Germany would only issue German passports to those who had first been approved for immigration by the Swedish authorities. But the Swedish government didn't want to agree to a solution fraught with disadvantages. The proposal made it possible for people outside of Germany to find their way into Sweden unhindered. Further, a passport that was only valid for entry to Sweden would make it impossible for a refugee to leave the country. Finally, such an arrangement would give Germany far too much power over deciding who was to be allowed across the Swedish border.

The negotiations were drawn out, but the flood of refugees would not be stemmed.

So the Swedish government disseminated a secret circular to all the ports of entry in the country. From September 9, 1938, forward, only Germans with recommendations or those Germans who were frequent travelers could cross the Swedish border. The rest would be evaluated on a case-by-case basis. If there was reason to believe that the foreigner could not return to Germany, he'd be turned away. Only those who could leave Sweden were allowed in. And because Jews were only issued exit permits from Nazi Germany if they pledged not to return, the matter was resolved for the time being.

Sweden's TT News Agency reported that "stricter immigration control had now been introduced because of increased emigration from certain European states." And that was that.

Sweden and Switzerland shared roughly the same needs at the same time, and they conferred. It had been indicated to the Swiss that the Germans would pay any price to avoid a visa requirement for their citizens, so the Swedes counted on the same applying to them, and subsequently both countries threatened to instate a visa requirement if no solution was presented. It had the desired effect.

On October 5, 1938, the German negotiator informed them that he had prepared a proposal for Switzerland. A few days later, the situation was summarized for the Swedish authorities in a secret pro memoria:

> 1. With the German government's issuing of a regulation that German citizens, who are non-Aryans, will receive specially marked passports, the possibility emerges to introduce control over Jewish immigration on Sweden's behalf without necessitating a universal visa requirement...
> 2. Since the Swiss government ended the visa agreement with Germany, negotiations have taken place,

> whereby the German authorities . . . have offered a suggestion . . . On Switzerland's end, they have seen fit to accept said suggestion. It takes this form: German passports marked with the letter *J* shall not grant the right to enter Switzerland, unless those concerned can present a stamped guarantee in their passports received in advance from a Swiss legation or consulate, granting them the right to travel into Switzerland. This agreement implies a Swiss visa requirement for non-Aryan citizens.

Just a few days later Sweden sent word that here too they were prepared to waive the need for a visa for German citizens. Then it only took a few weeks of negotiations before Germany and Sweden had also reached an agreement. If the Germans did a first cull, it would be easier for Sweden to conduct the second one.

In late October 1938, Swedish passport inspectors received a new secret circular informing them that people with German passports marked with the letter *J* were emigrants, and so were not coming for a temporary stay. Those who did not have a residency permit or a border recommendation should be turned away.

J as in Jew.

III

On November 10, Elise turned forty-seven. What a day for a birthday.

Might it have gone like this?

They wished for all her wishes to come true and for a good and happy year, they wished for better times without mentioning the present, keeping them in its iron grip.

Or like this?

They gathered at night at Aunt Nuny and Paul's. Nuny had traded one commodity for another, and there it was, a real cake made of fat, eggs, and sugar. Maybe Paul and Otto sang "Happy Birthday." Maybe Pepi was miming along, still feeling shaky about her English. One might imagine Mutti smiling, Otto singing in tune, and Paul being proud of his student. And above them a chandelier: the jewel-like shimmering glass scattering the bulb's pale yellow glow. Freshly cleaned prisms, reflections' reflections, light in light, unbroken glass.

Lies and flights of fancy, plagiarism and historical fraud. November 10, 1938, wasn't just mother Elise's birthday.

Sir:

1. I have the honor to report that the anti-Jewish demonstrations in Vienna . . . assumed very alarming proportions on the night of the ninth instant and during the whole of the tenth instant.
2. The action was undertaken by the Austrian SA, most of whom were in full uniform, and the police had obviously received instructions not to intervene. A very large number of shops and houses owned or occupied by Jews were wrecked and numerous arrests took place. Yesterday morning Jewish prayer houses and synagogues were set on fire in considerable numbers; the *Völkischer Beobachter* indeed gives particulars of no less than nineteen synagogues which were completely destroyed by fire. Another in the Leopoldgasse was destroyed by a bomb, which did considerable damage to near-lying buildings. All the fire brigades of Vienna were fully employed, as at one time there seemed to be grave danger of a serious and widespread conflagration involving large sections of the city.
3. The press openly rejoices at these manifestations and congratulates the people on the fact that the Jews can

now no longer hatch plots against the State under cover of religious services.

4. In addition to this orgy of destruction, all Jewish shops were forced to close and may not yet reopen. In many cases plate-glass and other windows were broken and the shops were openly looted by the mob. Gauleiter Bürckel endeavored to give some appearance of legality to this anti-Jewish action by issuing instructions that houses occupied by Jews should be searched for weapons and illegal literature. In the course of the search numerous arrests were made.
5. The immediate consequence of these demonstrations was that hundreds of Jews formed even larger queues than usual outside this consulate general and that of the United States. On the ninth instant already at 6:30 p.m. a large number of Jews lined up outside this consulate general prepared to wait all night until the Passport Office opened the next morning. They were dispersed by the police that evening and three times again before 8:30 a.m. on the tenth. Every Jewish man was taken into custody, only the women and children being left. At the United States Consulate General the SA began beating the crowds with rope ends until the United States Consul General, unable to bear the spectacle, insisted on police intervention, which was eventually granted.
6. The Vienna correspondent of the *Times* was arrested by the SA as he was taking notes of the demonstrations in the Leopoldgasse and was taken to the police station. On revealing his identity to the police, he

received an apology and was allowed to go. Ten minutes later he was again arrested and again released. He informed me that on his arrival at the police station he observed a number of Jews cowering in corners, so terrified that they were unable even to remember their names, while an old Jew with white hair and beard was lying on the floor being brutally kicked by an SA man while the regular police looked on.

7. This morning the public manifestations have ceased, but arrests continue to be made. The Jewish population is terrified, and I am besieged with applications for help and by persons wishing to relate their experiences. I fear that several British subjects have suffered damage, and individual reports on these cases will be transmitted as soon as full particulars are available.
8. Last night Vienna presented an extraordinary spectacle, with fires raging all over the city. Jews were being hustled along the streets, cursed at and assaulted by crowds of hooligans whose pride it is to belong to one of the greatest and most civilised nations of the world.
9. The anti-Jewish demonstrations were not confined to Vienna. Thus a synagogue at Linz was burnt to the ground. The synagogue at Salzburg was wrecked and its contents thrown into the street. Jewish shops were also looted. At Hallein and at Bad Gastein the Jewish hotels and pensions were sacked, including the Hotel Bristol, the Kurhaus Cecilia, a further "Kurhaus" and a large villa owned by a Jew.

D. St. Clair Gainer.

The same day British consul general Gainer in Vienna sent the secret report to his government, *Svenska Dagbladet* published a testimony from the aforementioned correspondent employed by the *Times*. *Dagens Nyheter*, too, reported: "We have been informed that many [Jews] have fled to the forests outside Vienna to avoid arrest. No official arrest numbers have been released, but it is thought to be at least 10,000. The Jews will most likely be taken to the new Austrian concentration camp in the Mauthausen quarry. A number of arrested Jews have been furnished with tools and sent to the destroyed synagogues to clear up the fire sites. On Thursday morning, twenty-two Jews in Vienna took their own lives."

All of Germany and Austria: a pogrom, a word for suppressing, exposing, bloodily persecuting people, applied to Jews in particular. It was common for the political powers that be to sanction violence. It was common for the police not to intervene.

No one knows how many people were surrounded and forced to their knees to scrub Vienna's streets. It's no longer possible to know what Otto, Lisl, and Pepi and their friends experienced on that particular birthday of Lisl's. They saw smashed shop windows, heard the shards crunch beneath their feet. And then? Women and men being pushed into their shops' broken windows, placards hung around their necks bearing the words SAU-JUDE, passersby being encouraged to spit on them.

All that can be known is that when Otto, much later, compiled a timeline of significant moments in his life, he wrote: "mom's birthday," followed by "the night of broken glass," and finally "protected by the doorman and others."

III

There had been a time when the rotated swastika was a secret he'd mostly only sensed, and it belonged to others. Take a few of the teachers at school, for instance. They'd worn a pin with the symbol hidden in the folds of their coats, so that it was visible only if they lifted their collars. As long as that political idea was forbidden, they kept their collars down. But now the pin bearers and their symbol were everywhere and no one was hiding anything anymore. Otto had seen their words turn into actions.

His father and mother first spoke to each other, then with him, long fretful sentences tangling together behind closed curtains, slowly ruling out all but one or two exits; get him out first, then themselves and then they'd reunite, unclear where. It wasn't easy. What did they know of the ground on which they stood, everything was moving, shifting. A good friend no longer answered when addressed, a good neighbor now averted his eyes. One second went by, one country annexed another, what had been hidden by folded-down collars became visible to each and every one and then nothing was as before.

Otto was against emigrating. They had spoken about Canada, Palestine, America. Too far. But here he was barred from going to school, they reminded him. He wasn't allowed to play soccer, they said. He wasn't allowed in the parks, they reiterated. He didn't have a right to higher education, they cried. And he replied: What would he be without them?

It was only for a little while, they said. Until the next step was taken. Until the day they could pick him up and settle down elsewhere. Together.

He didn't want to settle down elsewhere. He liked the good old days with the good old friends, life at home with Sunday dinners and classes with good old Paul in English and Greek, days like the ones he'd been living until now, where the future was untouched, still unwrapped like something on a wish list.

Had Elise and Pepi been overprotective? Maybe he thought he was still free to walk in the city parks with a paper bag full of old bread, that everything was as it was before, as it had always been. That he could stand there with outstretched arms, smiling at the heavens, the fat Viennese pigeons flocking, pecking at the crumbs in his hands and flying around his head.

But they were without means. Signs were put up in the city to mark which zones were to be clear of children like Otto, of people like them. NUR FÜR ARIER was meticulously painted in white on every park bench in every park. Aryans only. Locked out. And yet shut in.

Otto gave in. He didn't want to, but he understood. And now the door to Sweden had opened a crack. The language was supposed to be quite similar to German, Aunt Grete said.

So the steps to salvation were taken, one at a time. Preparations began. But which roads were open, which options were avoided and which did they seek out? Why not the Jewish Community Council, why the Christian Swedish Israel Mission?

Maybe someone gave them good advice during the autumn. Or, as Swedes were lighting candles and baking the traditional saffron buns for St. Lucy's Day, Pepi and Elise read a notice in Vienna's Jewish newspaper, *Jüdischen Nachrichtenblatt*, published on December 13.

> SHORT-TERM STAYS IN SWEDEN
>
> One of the aforementioned plans for short-term stays can become a reality in Sweden. The Swedish government, under certain conditions, offers residency permits to persons who have arranged further emigration to trans-oceanic countries. With regard to affidavits that grant entry to the United States in the near future, the Swedish temporary residency permit is dependent on whether the person has relatives in Sweden and if said person can guarantee that those relatives or others will stand for their subsistence. Distant relatives are also eligible for entry to Sweden, and the guarantee of support will be determined by the circumstances. It should be emphasized that the temporary residency permit in Sweden will in no way ensure an entry permit to the United States more quickly than if one were to remain in Germany.

A straw of bureaucratic nature, but a straw nonetheless.

II

It's still there, the building that became a portal to another life.

Many Viennese had made their way there even before that November night: to Seegasse 16, to the Swedes. Nothing was actually new. What was coming was already on its way. There were witnesses. Some of those who'd been taken away returned from Dachau and Mauthausen to tell their tales. Not all were believed, but it was enough that a few were listening for knowledge to spread. Abuse and plundering often happened out in the open, the injuries and deaths were testimonies in and of themselves. Both exile and suicide had gone on for a long time.

But then darkness fell between November 9 and 10, when the Nazis wanted to mark a new beginning of a new end and mustered thirty hours of free-flowing collective hate.

Two days after the so-called Kristallnacht it was decreed that people classified as Jews were to be excluded from German economic life, in accordance with the Nuremberg Laws. Those who'd been employed were out of work, those who'd had assets were now poor and those who'd never had much went without, as usual. All who despaired sought comfort.

The Council's good Christian pastors and sisters did what they could, but the confusion was too great, the wishes were too many, the needs of those seeking help were too heartrending: the kinds of things that happen when people think they're like everyone else but are mistaken.

The Swedes weren't prepared. For over fifteen years, they'd been evangelizing in Vienna's large Jewish community, where some held fast to their old faith and others only to the customs, but the vast majority hardly believed at all. For over fifteen years, missionaries from Sweden had lured lost souls to services, baited with goodwill and instruction, hooked with baptism. They'd organized summer excursions to the countryside for city dwellers without money, arranged old-age homes and soup kitchens. And now: this? Order couldn't be imposed on the work, as led by Pastor Göte Hedenquist. Neither the flood of people nor their tears ceased.

When Elise Ullmann made her way to the building on Seegasse in late autumn, the waiting room was full. People sat around pell-mell all day long, waiting, out on the steps and on the street. She noted less pleasant characters, those who sometimes acted like security guards though no one had asked them to.

Two young men, Austrians in service to the mission, scuttled around like dizzy chickens, saying one thing to one person but something else to another, about why the days were passing and much was said but nothing got done. One of them tried to organize the visitors and send some to speak with Pastor Göte Hedenquist. They might be waiting from early morning to late afternoon, masses of people who all wanted to meet the pastor but weren't given the chance.

A visiting Swede noted that "many fine people never dared make their way there. Ten or so more or less dirty individuals had appointed themselves as doormen, so when you appeared, an entire staff bowed their heads like tree tops in the wind."

Here sat Elise. Did Otto have to come along? Or did he stay home playing cards with his friends Ernst Utas and Georg Werner, who'd also been forced out of school?

Seegasse 16 had long been the address of the Swedish church in Vienna. In 1938 the work was led by the Swedish Israel Mission, whereby Swedish priests collected Jewish souls for Jesus. The work was rooted in the firm conviction that the Jews had committed the most heinous of mistakes at the start of time by not understanding the Savior and participating in his execution, and they'd been punished ever since. But now the Christians had the benevolent duty to help open them up to the true faith.

Without officially belonging to the Swedish state church, the missionaries still couldn't be differentiated from it—they were ordained, and a number of church officials and bishops were deeply engaged in the project. On the Israel Mission's board at home in Sweden, the bishop of Visby was the chairman and Archbishop Erling Eidem supported the endeavor wholeheartedly.

Mission stations were where the need was considered the greatest, as in Bratislava and Casablanca. But most important of all was the station in Vienna. In no other place did such a steady stream from the target group pass through.

At the start of this story, in the thirties, around 190,000 people of Jewish ancestry lived in Vienna. Many had lived there for several generations. Others had just arrived—coming from burned-down synagogues, dodging bodies hung in trees, from the memories of children with crushed skulls or slit throats lined up on the floor of the village school.

Some had beards, others were clean-shaven. Some observed the Sabbath, many Christmas. And they continued to flow in, particularly from the east: from Russia, the Ukraine, Lithuania, or Poland. For on the clay fields they'd dreamt of asphalt, trams, and electric light. Or they'd simply wanted to live in peace. Fleeing poverty and persecution, they moved from the periphery to more civilized, central parts of the world. You could become something in Vienna, merchant or student. You could leave the group. Be your own person. Hide in the crowd.

Some forgot their Jewish heritage, wanted to forget it, did everything they could to forget, wanted to be like everyone else, and the word for them became "assimilated." Others preserved their heritage, prayed in one of the many synagogues and hallowed Fridays with prayers of peace. Others just stopped by, perhaps to listen in on some of the foreign languages that flowed into the city like tributaries into a river, before they themselves flowed on with their dreams of the future.

Many of those on the move might have been open to Jesus. For others the Savior was a door leading to a reassuring Christian majority, which they opened and walked through. Vienna was a hub, a pause, an escape route. In short, it was a good place for conversion.

But then 1938 arrived.

The tides turned. The winds turned. The currents turned. The persecutions began to catch up with those who'd fled them. Ever more people were looking for a way out of the country. Away.

The Swedish Israel Mission was quick to adapt and organized an emigration operation. And so emigration help became the new way to lure, bait, and hook souls. They traveled from hatred to a sanctuary, stopping over at Jesus.

Whereas Swedish missionary work created satisfaction among the missionaries themselves and perhaps joy for those who partook in Christianity, it caused the country's new masters, the Nazis, nothing but headache and rancor.

Directly after Austria's annexation by Nazi Germany, meetings of the Swedish Israel Mission were banned. A few days later, uniformed men bearing weapons stormed the space at Seegasse 16 on the pretext that the Swedish Pastor Hedenquist and his colleagues were hiding weapons in the basement. Furniture was smashed to pieces and threats were shouted. The pastor was handed a crumpled paper when the men went their way; scribbled on it was a promise that the damages would be reimbursed. The signature was illegible, but someone noted the car's registration number, and the men could be traced to the Gestapo building a few blocks down.

It would turn out that the cause of the attack was on the sign above the door to the house: SCHWEDISCHE GESELLSCHAFT FÜR ISRAEL—the Swedish Society for Israel. The Gestapo had come to the conclusion that the operation was Jewish. After that weapons were drawn, and in this way the Swedish mission on Seegasse was given a taste of persecution.

This violence caused fear. Pastor Hedenquist spoke with the Swedish press and with the Swedish consulate in Vienna, and asked his boss, Israel Mission director Pastor Pernow in Stockholm, to come immediately. Together they met the leader of the Blackshirts, Adolf Eichmann. And the whole matter was in fact resolved. After Swedish diplomacy assured the Nazis in charge that the mission was being run by "Aryans" in connection with the Swedish church, operations could resume. If the name was changed, said Eichmann.

A new sign was put up over the entrance: SWEDISH MISSION STOCKHOLM, MISSION STATION VIENNA. The Nazis lifted the meeting ban and the pastor in charge, Göte Hedenquist, summarized the situation by saying that then everyone could exhale and was making plans for continued operations in the harsh climate that now reigned in Vienna.

As a matter of fact, those in power had realized how the missionaries could be of use to the Nazis. In individual conversations with Göte Hedenquist, Hauptstürmführer Eichmann declared that he was actually a friend of the Jews, that he wished only to hurry along their emigration, and thus he supported the mission's emigration work. At least for now. Could he please be given a list of all the Jews who were now calling themselves Christians?

There was no such list, Pastor Hedenquist replied, because the church didn't differentiate between Aryan and Jewish members. Then Adolf Eichmann offered the pastor an office in the building where his specially founded emigration office was being run. It was an order the Swede didn't dare refuse.

He obeyed and chose a few young men (the fairest, with high foreheads and blue eyes?) who were classified as half- or quarter-Jews according to the Nuremberg Laws. They dressed in black riding pants, white shirts, and black ties, all to blend in seamlessly inside one of the Nazi headquarters, and with this the Swedish church opened a branch within the Gestapo.

Whether or not this was with God's help is unclear, but the young men were trying for a miracle. Those who at this time wanted permission to leave the country usually had to wait many bureaucratic months and go through sixteen different authorities to clear their documents. Through the Israel Mission's select administrators at the Nazi emigration office, the same paperwork was cleared in just over a week. In total the missionaries were able to pilot around three thousand people out of Nazi Germany.

It was to Pastor Göte Hedenquist, to the waiting room in the building at Seegasse 16, that Elise Ullmann came. In December the disorder from October had been configured into a clear structure. As one of the missionaries reported to the Stockholm headquarters:

> At reception, the hall is pleasantly adorned with a table covered in a cloth, flowers and water glasses. A pleasant young boy stands by the door and Sister Anna-Lena in her habit receives you. She fills in fine, freshly printed forms with the specified information, and with these in hand, you proceed to Göte, who is on his own in the office. There nothing more can take place but a two-minute-long conversation with each and every one regarding the nature of their errand. The errands are divided into three categories: matters of the soul's well-being and those to

whom Göte should tend, relief errands, and emigration errands.

Elise was guided courteously, blessed by Adolf Eichmann himself, and given a two-minute audience. Without understanding it at first, she had found a gap in Vienna's reality that fit her thirteen-year-old son. She was referred to the mission's department C, for emigration.

III

One person who had the most information and had it first, who received the most inside reports of German and Austrian events, one of the people drawing conclusions, was the Swedish priest and pastor at the mission, Birger Pernow.

Pernow was a tall man with a sharp profile and a small chin, and he would go on to work hard and in a self-immolating way to save Otto Ullmann. He was ordained as a priest in the Swedish church but was completely devoted to conversion and his job as the director of the mission's operations. He had no trouble speaking and writing in both German and English. Through this work he'd accumulated such exhaustive knowledge of the Jewish people that he acted as an adviser to the Swedish archbishop Eidem on Jewish matters.

The good Pastor Pernow. Even before the pogroms of November 9–10, he, along with others with close contacts outside of Sweden, had seen the signs for people of Jewish heritage, the gradual shackling to estrangement, the accumulated contempt. An ever-growing threat. How certain people were set in opposition to others. Already in June 1938, he described the situation in a few letters: "The situation in Vienna is so awful words can hardly describe it . . . Therefore it is both a good deed and a Christian duty of love to try to save as many human lives as possible, or else they will meet their demise . . . For this reason we have had discussions with the general director at the Board of Health and Welfare and his closest circle and they are willing to offer a limited number of Jewish-Christian girls positions as domestic servants here as well as allow an even smaller number of Jewish-Christian children to come here." And "I hardly need mention that the situation down there for all non-Aryans is completely unbearable and thousands are facing starvation and ruin."

"Antichrist" wasn't a word the faithful used lightly. But after the November pogrom, they did. The Nazis hadn't just crossed a line, they had dissolved it. But it wasn't the information about the people who were thrown from windows because they weren't quick enough to reach the door that caused the strongest reaction among certain Christians. Neither was it the knowledge of all those who'd ingested poison or jumped into the Donau, their skirt pockets heavy with stones. It was the question of baptism.

Pastor Birger Pernow still was not aware that Otto existed, neither was the thirteen-year-old aware of the pastor. But soon a list containing Otto Ullmann's name would land atop the pile of papers on the pastor's desk in his office at Idungatan 4 in Stockholm.

III

The Swedish archbishop Erling Eidem loved Germany. Just like the rest of the upper class and much of the Swedish middle class, those with higher education, who could recite poetry and prose by heart, those who took pleasure in the sublime works of German composers in concert halls and operas. The pared-back Christianity that shaped Sweden had been born in the German Martin Luther's *Theses*. One might even ask what Sweden would have been without Germany, its intellectual life, its resounding language, and the close contact between the peoples.

The ardent devotion that the archbishop represented—the pietism—had also been hewn from the German longing for purity, a form of Christianity simpler than Lutheranism, a more intimate encounter with Jesus, without even a church or parish. A faith in which only the heart and Jesus were invited. Truly, Archbishop Eidem's entire world originated in Germany. Or in his own words: "I know deep down that I have always loved and will until my dying breath love the German people."

But this matter of Nazism had called his love into question in a way that the archbishop couldn't have foreseen. Not only did the Nazi regime wish to "Aryanize" the church in Germany by excluding all "non-Aryans" as well as forbidding priests from getting married to them. Perhaps that was expected, and no surprise. But this simple racist act carried with it something greater and more shocking.

Throughout time, baptism had been the standard. Those who had been folded into the Christian community were to be considered Christians. Baptism wasn't a garment that could be worn or discarded. Once converted, once baptized, forever Christian. But the Nazi fixation on blood, heritage, and biology robbed Christianity's most central ritual of its meaning. They weren't going to let some water dribbled on someone's head matter. "Faith" as a term lost its relevance. Customs, the definition of God, rituals, or even assimilation and secularization—it all meant nothing. A Jew was a Jew was a Jew. It was under the skin, in the nucleus of a cell, in the soul's constitution, in the inheritance passed from gene to gene. The Nazis rendered conversion meaningless. Antichrist.

Right should be right; for most who called themselves Christians this wasn't really a problem. But the Swedish archbishop took issue. Erling Eidem supported the minority who couldn't accept the knives piercing the Christian heart, the fifth of all German priests who founded the Confessional church in protest. He supported them, but silently.

Might the Swedish church have had good intentions, but were reluctant to get on the bad side of Chancellor Hitler? Might the Swedish church have tried, via its highest-ranking representative, the archbishop who loved Germany, to set the chancellor straight?

The answer is yes.

In 1934 Archbishop Eidem visited Germany to get him to listen and ideally end his demands for Aryanization. He'd met the chancellor on May 2, 1934, to reason with him, to get him to understand that the church couldn't allow itself to be guided by race laws and so on.

But Hitler wouldn't listen. Instead he talked. Uninterruptedly. In fact, he yelled at the Swedish archbishop for forty minutes. Afterward, Archbishop Eidem, who didn't believe in politics, but in dialogue, noted that his attempt had been "a complete failure."

And four years after his meeting with the dictator, he was deeply worried about the Christians who because of their unlucky Jewish provenance might meet with misfortune. It's likely that he conferred with his adviser, Pastor Pernow. What should one do, and how?

Neither man believed in open polemic and public criticism. It was more likely to do harm, not just to the church's reputation, but to Sweden's and Prime Minister Per Albin Hansson's sensitive task in these insecure times. Faith and politics were separate, and would remain so. But careful action was called for. So those christened could . . . the children . . . Yes, at least them. Let the children come to us. For two years anyway.

And so Archbishop Eidem presented a secret initiative to a committee that put Pastor Pernow in charge of an investigation into the possibility of rescue, and the archbishop personally wrote a letter to the general director of the Royal Board of Health and Welfare.

Uppsala, October 17, 1938

Mr. General Director Sigfrid Hansson, Stockholm
Revered Mr. General Director:

A small committee, overseen by Pastor B. Pernow, has requested preference from Mr. General Director, in order to inform themselves about the possibilities for the Royal Board of Health and Welfare to grant entry and residency permits for a number of Christian, so-called "non-Aryan" children and adolescents from Germany.

I would very much like to have attended this audience with you in order to put in a good word on this matter, which is close to my heart. Since for the time being it is not possible for me to be present when Mr. General Director can receive guests, I offer these simple lines as a respectful and warm plea that Mr. General Director lend his interest to and, if at all possible, engage with the committee's request.

With the highest regards,
Erling Eidem

The archbishop's letter was more than respectful. But then Mr. General Director Sigfrid Hansson was among those who held the most power over the country's borders. Who was allowed to enter, who was kept out.

Just a few days later, on Wednesday, October 19, 1938, the general director, using black ink, had jotted down a note in his little wine-red pocket almanac: "Germans? Pernow, 10 a.m."

III

It wasn't easy. But it could be done.

First, you removed the extra leaves and pushed the dining table together so it was as small as possible. Then both the table and the chairs were moved to the wall on the right. After that, the door to the bedroom was opened wide, and that's where Pepi stood in the goal. Otti backed up all the way to the kitchen to get in position. It was best when Elise and Aunt Grete were out running errands, to spare the players from hearing their complaints each time the ball bounced against a mirror or the glass-paned hall doors. A bit of a challenge, landing a clean shot on the shiny parquet floor, but it could be done.

For those brief moments that the ball was in play between Otto and Pepi, it was indeed possible to forget what had been lost on March 15. It wasn't just the last seventeen years of Pepi's working life, his income, pension, and position as an editor at a liberal, respected daily newspaper. Pepi's passion for opera had earned him the role of the newspaper's music critic, and the family had spent night after night in Uncle Egon's loge in the opera house on Operngasse. And then there was the company of professional sportsmen, the game, the thrill, the sport. All gone.

Otto could whistle the great arias and enjoyed them, but not being able to go to practice echoed painfully through his thirteen-year-old body. Soccer: forbidden. And with it, what

was part and parcel, the game, the friends, the struggle, the victory disappeared too. Days of anticipation before a critical match, hours saturated with the smell of liniment, the dream of a critical pass. Exhaustion soothing the body.

As the editor of the sports pages, Pepi had received free tickets to all the important games. And of course he'd bring Otto along. For hours they'd sat together on the bleachers, analyzing the game. Could all this simply disappear? The answer should have been no, but here they were in the hall, kicking the ball toward a doorway. The smell of sweat spread, and for a moment even they forgot to avoid thinking about the state of things.

III

During the 1930s there were a few people who mattered in the management of Sweden's borders and what was called the "Jewish question," and they were all officials tasked with turning the content of laws into practical, executable decisions.

A few were diplomats, but others were employed at the Royal Board of Health and Welfare. But all were influential in their way. And Prime Minister Per Albin Hansson's cabinet let them be. His was not a government of meddling ministers. Officials could solve problems and arrive at decisions largely on their own.

How did these people look upon those of Jewish descent?

Mr. Torsten Undén was the Swedish minister in Otto's hometown of Vienna, a post that today would be called minister counsellor.

As early as 1934 he'd expressed his thoughts in a letter to cabinet secretary Carl Hamilton. Undén found Hamilton's outlook on the "Jewish question" to be naive, and to illustrate he recounted a conversation with an unnamed person, described as "clever." This person had pointed out that there were good reasons for other countries to be reluctant about taking in German Jews: "Have not all people, as soon as they have understood what this concerns, defended themselves with fist and foot against the rising immigration of Jews?" And more: "Jews are like garlic in food. They do no harm in small quantities, but when there are more, the entire dish stinks."

The Swedish minister Undén supplemented his anonymous source by stating that "In Sweden one has no idea what the Jewish question in fact means. So one is inclined to take a sentimental view, but you can be assured that if we granted entry to several hundred Jewish families who would propagate, as is the custom for this race, then the next generation will curse those who didn't know to stop the immigration in time, and the generation thereafter would not see anything remarkable in employing harsh methods in defense of the original inhabitants. One doesn't need to be an anti-Semite to realize this."

In 1936 Sweden let in a number of German refugees, but only for a short time. Temporary stays were conceivable, but not emigration. The same year the Royal Board of Health and Welfare wrote a statement explaining some of their immigration policies. Many of these emigrants "could not and probably would not in the long view be able to adjust to a Swedish environment. In this respect, it does not concern mere adaptation to commercial practice and such, but usually racial and ethnic characteristics of a more indeterminate nature."

In 1936 the Board of Health and Welfare was also the referral body for proposed changes to the Aliens Act. The two people who authored the Board of Health and Welfare's position on the question were the general director and another official who would go on to have a large influence on the question in the war years, director Kurt Bergström. According to them the Aliens Act would create a barrier against foreign labor and against, "from a racial or other perspective, difficult-to-assimilate elements."

And additionally, they concluded that only "real political refugees" should be permitted to enter Sweden, that is, those who were at risk of being punished in their country of residence because they'd committed a political crime. But a "foreigner, who cites a feeling of discomfort with the political regime in his country of residence," could not be regarded as such.

In their reply, the Board of Health and Welfare thus formulated the position that would prevail throughout the war. Those who were "uncomfortable" with the Nuremberg Laws couldn't be defined as political refugees and thus entitled to Swedish protection. And in any case, it would be best if the officials were allowed to judge this in peace and quiet on a case-by-case basis. There would be many.

Like a looming storm, it seemed to hang over all worried Swedish officials—the Jewish question. And as though the Aliens Act were only a rickety roof, as if six million Swedes could be seriously injured without storm protection, the officials devoted all their strength to plugging holes, trussing, and reinforcements.

Another official who landed in the midst of the deluge of refugees was the envoy Folke Malmar, on legation in Prague. He had neither particularly great power nor any crucial influence over Swedish refugee policies, but his letters to Stockholm suggest possible opinions held by the Swedish Ministry of Foreign Affairs. A few weeks after the Anschluss the Swedish diplomat felt concerned for his country and wrote to the Ministry of Foreign Affairs' director general of legal affairs.

Prague, April 4, 1938

> The rats are leaving the sinking ship. On our stairs "non-Aryans" are standing in lines to hear about the possibility of coming to Sweden... The other day Minister Eisenlohr said to me in his wry way: "Well, now all the Jews here can come to Sweden."... Perhaps this is cause to hear what our Swedish Jews' position is on the question, for it will be them first and foremost who will bear the consequences of an impending invasion... Certainly all share the reasoning of M's in our most recent conversation: "Once I set foot in Sweden, no one shall manage to be rid of me."

In October, the same Folke Malmar cautioned against a too-generous Swedish policy: "First, a benevolent reception of Jewish immigration, administered with compassion for those cast out of other countries, and feelings of pride for being able to offer sanctuary, then a rising sense of unease, escalating to an acute reluctance, and now finally the fourth stage, disaster in the form of vituperation, persecution, even bloodshed, the flight of the persecuted to other countries, where the problem was never experienced or already forgotten."

He also portrayed the hysterical mood that prevailed in the Jewish population after all the anti-Semitic demonstrations, and said that the Swedish legation was the most vulnerable of all embassies and consulates in Prague: "The building is full of Jews, crawling from the entryway to the stairs, all the way up to the third floor, where the chancellery is housed. In the office, the legation's domestic officials work in a sea of gesticulating arms, persuasive words and insults, crocodile tears."

But the director general of legal affairs at the Swedish Ministry of Foreign Affairs calmed him: "Naturally we are very restrictive as concerns Jewish emigrants. We are well aware of the danger of rising anti-Semitism but have seen small signs of it."

The director general expressed one of the main arguments for the restrictive refugee policy that would shape Sweden in the coming years: the refugees themselves were creating this aversion against them. He drew the conclusion that the fewer refugees there were, the less hatred of refugees there would be.

The diplomat Folke Malmar would not be convinced and wrote to Kurt Bergström at the Board of Health and Welfare, "I have now taken my position. From October 1, no visa, no so-called border recommendation has been issued to any Jewish emigrant. Other solutions are not possible." He asserted that if he made "a single exception, all would be lost," because the rumor would spread "on the wings of the wind." Malmar also continued his correspondence with the director general of legal affairs at the Ministry of Foreign Affairs:

> If you have plans of starting a Nazi movement in Sweden or if you think that anti-Semitic manifestations are a necessary and enlivening contribution to the street life, hitherto lacking in our calm and somewhat boring country, yes, then I can understand the immigration policies that you wish to follow. Otherwise not, for I cannot believe that you have been under the impression that you could contribute to solving the Jewish question in Central

> Europe by opening the gates to the additional Jews who could on the whole be thought to be accommodated by us.

Folke Malmar in Prague never was reprimanded for his actions. And maybe he started issuing visas again. A few weeks later, in any case, he formulated a letter to the Swedish Ministry of Foreign Affairs with views on which refugees were most suitable for Sweden: "I think it wise to keep to refugees of the Social Democrat group. They are for the most part physical laborers. Intellectual refugees seem to me to be a particularly difficult problem in a country where the language is unknown to them; deprived of possibilities for political and general public activity, their destiny must be more than regrettable. The Communist refugees I have seen here seem to no small extent to represent the half-intellectual proletarian type that seems so terribly disconsolate and impossible to fit into an organized society."

If a person of Jewish heritage wanted to come to Sweden, the Swedish government required the refugee to have close relatives in Sweden and to be either elderly or a minor so that he or she would not pose a threat to the job market, and that the refugee emigrate to another country as well as having economic guarantees for their residency period in Sweden. Those who were fleeing Germany and wished to settle in Sweden were given a permit "only in exceptional cases."

Was this generous or restrictive? What did the officials and people in power think? Director Kurt Bergström of the Aliens Office offers a clue in his reply to a letter from a concerned citizen during the fall: "It's clear our job market is at present an object of very strong 'penetration' from the German-Jewish side. To illuminate how we have until now conducted our policies in this category, I herewith enclose a reprint of *Social Announcements*, in which we have made a statement that accounts for our tax collection district since the establishment of Hitler's regime. Hence it should be clear that we can hardly be seen to have been lax and to have left room for venturesome immigration."

In his private diary, Sigfrid Hansson, general director of the Board of Health and Welfare, wrote that "it's not possible to oblige the unfortunate Jews to any great extent" because "anti-Semitism is lying in ambush in our country."

III

Without Otto or any who loved him having an inkling, a process began on Wednesday, October 19, 1938, that would reshape Otto's destiny. Lines, sketches for his new future, were drafted in a room in Stockholm. There Sigfrid Hansson, director general of the Swedish Royal Board of Health and Welfare, was being swayed by Pastor Pernow's arguments and Archbishop Eidem's appeals.

Under certain premises and special conditions, one might consider certain solutions. Sensitive questions. This matter of allowing Jews across the border. No papers were written, no memoranda. Sigfrid Hansson would confer and ponder, perhaps with his little brother, the prime minister. But in secret.

Director General Hansson had spoken with the pastor before. In the summer Pernow had already reached out to him about entry permits for some ten young women from Vienna who might find positions as housekeepers in Christian circles. And they could be allowed in, according to the Board of Health and Welfare director general, but it was risky. The impact on the job market and so on. In the fall, Pastor Pernow kept running into officials from the Board of Health and Welfare. Progress was incredibly slow. But in the end, the pastor zeroed in on the problem and could offer advice to others who shared these concerns:

> I've come up with a suggestion, based on my experiences, having applied for our girl. I signed the application myself. I omitted all the favorable recommendations, especially in relation to her education. Our girl had appended so much of that sort. I heard from the consul in Vienna—and so too the Board of Health and Welfare—that he believed girls with that sort of education will only be housekeepers for a month before they move on to other jobs, office work and the like. So the girl had to remove her school documents... Now hear this: after eight days the application was approved! Don't you think the problem could have lain in these school documents?

This was the only way for the threatened women to cross the border into Sweden. The girls' grades from university and high school, their intellectual ambitions and education, were undesirable. But if the Board of Health and Welfare's officials could be assured that they weren't looking to enter the Swedish academic world or were even eligible for office work, it was easier. Housekeepers, that's it.

The reasons were spelled out by special-interest organizations and unions. No employee reading his mail at the Board of Health and Welfare in Stockholm could be mistaken about what working Swedes thought about foreign labor.

> Stockholm, September 14, 1938
>
> To the Board of Health and Welfare, Aliens Department, Stockholm:

> ...We harbor hopes that the Board will consider this, our proposal, and so offer us the help of which we are now in so desperate need, for our profession in its current form is being gravely threatened by what is for us disastrous competition from foreigners, particularly those who have immigrated from Central Europe, who due to recent political events, have ever more frequently sought opportunities to earn their livelihood in Sweden...
>
> Signed by twenty-eight dance teachers and eight rhythmic instructors

And so now the Swedish Israel Mission's director, Pastor Pernow, wanted to bring one hundred children into the country. Children only. Perhaps not as threatening to the fur merchants, painters, and retailers, but a sensitive matter nonetheless.

General Director Hansson had ample opportunity to consider how he would balance the demands of the workforce, the general indisposition toward the Jews, and the growing number of inquiries about protection, entry, and work permits.

Only a few months prior in a reply to a written comment regarding permits for larger groups of refugees, so-called "contingents," he'd let two of his closest colleagues formulate his position, as well as that which guided the Board of Health and Welfare:

> The refugee is perhaps welcome in the country, only insofar as regards his right to visit, but it is uncertain whether he will be as welcome when he arrives as a job seeker. In some places it is thought that residency permits should be

> granted to refugees but work permits should be refused. This opinion has not been shared by the board; it can hardly be considered humane to condemn a refugee to years of idleness...
>
> Upon issuing a work permit, the board will strive to connect refugees to fields of work where they will not present a too-worrying competition with the Swedish workforce...
>
> All this has meant that a trickle of foreigners, chiefly reliant on their own initiative, have hitherto been able to be absorbed by the Swedish workforce relatively unnoticed.
>
> If a quota system were to be instated, the situation would take on a different form. To begin with the contingents, even if small, would surely draw attention to themselves. Furthermore they would not in the same seamless manner be absorbed by the workforce.

No big groups then. Only those who could be introduced into the workforce in a way that didn't compete with Swedes. A slow stream of foreigners unnoticeably absorbed. This was the tune the Board of Health and Welfare was singing.

So when Pastor Pernow got the general director to agree to allow in a whole one hundred children—baptized, yes, but of Jewish heritage—he'd certainly given Sigfrid Hansson something to think about.

He and Pastor Pernow would go on to find a way to avoid the contingents, and still allow the children across the border. But first the pastor had to solve some practical problems. Where the children would live, for one. Through a plea in the

Christian press he sought homes that could take in a child, if they were of the evangelical faith.

> With regard to the general acuteness of the Jewish question we see it as our duty to issue a plea to the Christian consciousness... We know and understand that our little country cannot take in an unlimited number of refugees. Yet we wonder if all that can be done has been done for those who are in need. In any case we see and feel it to be our imperative duty to distance ourselves from the mentality that has found its expression in those who are persecuting the Jews. We acknowledge every human's dignity and every nation's national significance through Christ and Christianity, as best we can.
>
> We would wish to see a collective Nordic relief action with a Christian foundation come into being. But in anticipation of this, one must see if there isn't something immediate that can be done about the matter.
>
> Among Australia's Jews, as everywhere among these people, there are also evangelical Christians. If Jewish or Christian congregations would take it upon themselves for a set time to guarantee room and board for a set number of refugees, then couldn't one offer them asylum here? With goodwill something should be able to be done. We feel compelled to issue this appeal: do what you can! Do as your Christian conscience urges!

III

Someone made a judgment. Someone took notes. Someone described Otto in hopes that he'd be chosen. Someone transferred the notes onto a registry card: "Father: editor and Mosaic. Mother: Mosaic."

This matter of "Mosaic" was the key to it all. But Elise, Pepi, and Otto ate pork. They celebrated Christmas with a tree and trimmings. They prayed to God when life felt hard and thanked him when life was good. If these prayers were directed to the Father, Son, and Holy Ghost or to the one whose name shan't be uttered, it's no longer possible to say, the one split in three but all-knowing, the other whole and all-powerful. Maybe it's not important. Down below in the human world Elise, Pepi, and Otto were Mosaic, end of story. A position rather than a faith, a well of darkness out of which it was impossible to climb.

The boy. Thirteen years old. Thick dark hair, something puppyish about his physique.

The identifier "Mosaic" is the first note about Otto Ullmann on the registry card, which constitutes the first document in his file at the Israel Mission. After that it says that he hails from an "intellectual environment." Then his schooling is described, three years of humanities education, with the addendum "is interested in language." And "adaptable."

The saviors' definition of someone who should be saved.

Nothing about his plans to study medicine or law was mentioned and maybe that was just as well. To be given permission to leave the sprung rat trap that was Vienna, one had to be practical. Besides, anyone could see that a Jew who can't walk on the grass in the city's parks can't go to university. If he can't do business, then he can't retain his property, if he can suddenly be taken into custody and sent away, then higher education is no longer a realistic option for the future.

Is that why someone supplied the Swedish Israel Mission with notes on Otto using language that suggested that ballet and Greek lessons were already a dream gone by? Now he was to "learn handicraft," as well as "be interested in gardening work."

However it was, the plan worked. Otto was chosen and was to be put on a train from Vienna via Berlin and onto Sassnitz. And then the ferry to Trelleborg.

On the registry card, with the scant details that remain of Elise and Josef Ullmann's attempt to save their child, there isn't much else. Only three more sentences, three shards of information. "Parents wish to go to Montevideo." Followed by the less hopeful "Arrival uncertain." And then a sentence, placed last, but even so, perhaps the most important, perhaps what had in the end turned the tables in Otto's favor. The family "is closely related to Protestant pastor."

The Swedish Israel Mission had good intentions, of course, wanting to save Jews. But not so much from Nazism as from their Jewishness, not so much to save their lives, but to save their souls.

Otto was indeed strong-willed, but he was also well spoken and used to conversing with adults. In other words, well bred. This would play a significant role in shaping his fate. There were certain conditions, and Pastor Birger Pernow in Stockholm outlined them in letter after letter to his colleague Pastor Hedenquist in Vienna—he who was charged with determining who should be saved:

Stockholm, November 19, 1938

> . . . Regarding the previously discussed relief action for children and youths, we have now come so far that the matter has been left to [us] to attempt to realize, and the authorities are well disposed to the matter. Therefore you can without hesitation begin to assemble a registry of children. These should preferably be Jewish Christians or Christian non-Aryans, aged 7–15, whose parents shall emigrate to transoceanic countries. Preferably the parents' departure should be secured and they should as soon as possible after at most one to two years commit to reuniting with their children. Exceptions to this can possibly be made in individual cases, it is the authorities' wish that most children not remain here in the future. That the children be selected with care need hardly be emphasized.

Stockholm, November 25, 1938

> ... The children must be well bred and well behaved, so that we by no means are introducing any difficult or unpleasant elements, for that would damage both the cause and the perception of our mission. The authorities insist on the condition (at least officially) that the children shall after one to two years return to their parents.

Stockholm, December 9, 1938

> ... However, upon closer consideration I must decline your request regarding the possibility of taking in Catholic children. In the appeal we have specifically requested homes for Jewish Christian children, and we must observe this as closely as possible. It would certainly be cause for surprise, to say the least, among our friends if they were to receive Catholic children, thus we must refrain from that entirely. So, primarily Jewish Christian children, but to some small extent the unconfessed and the Mosaic. Specifically, a few Jewish homes have also been offered.

Pernow's plan was simple. He saw the threat of catastrophe and wanted to save those who were worth saving. The converted. If they were well behaved. And had respectable parents. Who promised not to seek entry to Sweden. And who committed to picking up their children after completing emigration from Austria.

By and large a digested version of his idea, the Swedish

government's demands, and the Swedish archbishop's quietly formulated wish.

In all likelihood Archbishop Eidem and Pastor Pernow nourished the same wish to do good. They also shared the opinion that public criticism of Hitler and Nazism could damage Sweden's political maneuverability—and anyway words unsupported by action were meaningless. In any case, Birger Pernow and his Israel Mission became the Swedish church's long arm, reaching all the way into closed, Jew-hating Vienna. With Archbishop Eidem behind him, he went all the way to those who kept watch over Sweden's borders and asked for entry permits for seventy-five children between the ages of four and fifteen, as well as twenty-five youths.

Pernow really made an effort. Fair enough. If you're saving one hundred children, what does it matter if you only choose the ones who are well behaved? Those who have been baptized? Choosing only those children whose parents were respectable? Parents whose emigration papers were in order (but not to Sweden, absolutely not to Sweden). Someone had to be chosen, so Birger Pernow chose. It wasn't just the conditions, organizing, and logistics that he handled. He decided child by child, youth by youth, who was to partake in his relief action. This is laid out clearly in letters exchanged by his Christian colleagues: "... For Enny M, Bronislawa H, we have not yet passed them on to the Board of Health and Welfare because Pastor Pernow has not yet approved them ... Regarding Leo L, Pastor Pernow does not wish for him to come here. It simply isn't good to send such a spoiled boy who is uninterested in physical labor to a farmer."

Did Pepi and Elise understand the significance of Otto's good behavior, that this was among the most important criteria in deciding whether he would be saved?

And then the next question: Would it have mattered? A door to Sweden and the Swedes had opened, but those blocking that door didn't want to let in any Jews. Out of the public eye Pastor Birger Pernow had in fact negotiated his way to a border crossing as narrow as a forest path. The magic word to whisper to the guard was "Christian."

The American and British legations in Vienna were stormed by people seeking entry permits. It can be assumed that Pepi and Lisl, Grete, Nuny and her husband Paul, were among the crowds, referred to as "lines," outside the foreign legations during that wet, temperate Vienna November. Even the Swedish Embassy had to contend with swelling currents of despair.

One did what one could to resist it.

Two weeks after the November pogrom, Erik Drougge, the secretary at the Aliens Office in Stockholm, wrote a letter to the Swedish consul in Vienna. Actually it was in response to a question the consul had asked a few days prior. But with this letter, only a few lines long, posterity is given a sudden and unintended glimpse into Swedish foreign policy, as it manifested after people in the center of a European capital had been persecuted, abused, and murdered by their neighbors.

Stockholm, November 26, 1938

Dear Consul:

With regard to the letter dated the 21st of this month I herewith have the honor of reporting the following.

Over the past weeks the Aliens Office has been subjected to a veritable besiegement. Because the immediate

> hiring of additional personnel would only make our work more difficult, one has tried to move forward as best we can with those already in place. As such, the possibilities for civil servants to more closely examine the office's measures have become scarce, and so "gaps" arise easily in the question about explanatory notes on authorizations and such. Meanwhile, we're waiting for the worst of the storm to pass, since there is a general awareness spreading about a series of rejected applications.

The Swedish attitude toward those seeking protection is laid bare for a moment that lasts as long as a sentence: "Meanwhile, we're waiting for the worst of the storm to pass, since there is a general awareness spreading about a series of rejected applications."

The Swedish strategy. To quickly reject those many first applications and then trust that a rumor would spread about Sweden: it's a country that says no.

After that letter it's perhaps not strange that the general consul in Vienna soon needed guidance again. He'd been visited in person by Pastor Hedenquist from the Swedish Israel Mission, who asserted that many Jewish children had the right to receive entry permits to travel into Sweden. The consul wrote back to Stockholm, this time to Director Bergström at the Board of Health and Welfare. Under what conditions could he allow a visa for these children? And how many? Are orphans given priority?

The board's reply reiterated the prerequisite that children be baptized, as if the consul could check that. Each condition that the government had laid out and that Pastor Pernow had accepted was enumerated. An agreement had been entered into, and the rules of the game were set.

Stockholm, December 7, 1938

> Mr. Consul:
>
> In reply to your note . . . I have the honor of reporting the following.
>
> The Swedish Israel Mission, in this country represented by a committee with Pastor Pernow as its secretary, has received a provisional commitment from the Board of Health and Welfare for a number of baptized children of Jewish heritage to be given residence permits.
>
> The commitment regards certain children of parents, who according to the Israel Mission have bindingly arranged for emigration to transoceanic countries and are having difficulty bringing minors with them during this early pioneering time. In order to clear the emigration hurdles that children can pose, these children will for a short time, at most one year, with the Israel Mission as an intermediary, be temporarily cared for in Swedish homes.

The letter concludes: "Pastor Pernow has spontaneously emphasized that only well-behaved children of parents of good reputation will be admitted."

Pernow had been clever and convincing when his child relief campaign received the bureaucratic blessing from Swedish authorities.

In a letter from the Board of Health and Welfare you can almost hear the pastor's voice in the background, singing a sort of soft, low harmony along with certain sentences. Such as "parents, who according to the Israel Mission have bindlingly arranged for emigration." Or "at most one year." The word "temporary." Emphasizing the absence of threat, that which will pass with time.

Yes, the Swedish government and the Swedish church had united, Director Kurt Bergström wrote, Birger Pernow humming along in the background, his echo reaching all the way to the consul general in Vienna. In short, a foreign policy position had emerged.

Looking back now it's not easy to distinguish whose needs held the most sway. Was it the children's, those who according to Pernow faced certain demise? Or was it the needs of those in Sweden who in Jesus's name were opening up their homes? At the end of December Pernow sent new instructions to his man in Vienna, Pastor Hedenquist: "The exchange of the Pollack children for Gerhard and Ernst will face no hurdles. Should you have a few more (perhaps five at most) whom you'd like to send along, that should be fine, but then preferably four to six years old, for a number of requests have been made for those that young."

The idea of Pernow's and the archbishop's relief action was to save Christians from the Jewish fate. It was hard to accept that those who'd chosen Jesus were still suffering God's judgment and punishment for the Jews' stupidity in not accepting the Messiah two thousand years before. But, truth be known, their need was a joy for the pastors and the Swedish church. For every soul that needed help, the chink letting in light grew larger. When the pastor tried to influence the Swedish government, it wasn't so much for the sake of the children but for Jesus. One hundred saved souls. And so it's not hard to see why baptism became one of Pastor Pernow's conditions. Without it, no passage.

Children en route to Sweden were being baptized as though on a conveyor belt. Still, a number of the children whom Pastor Göte Hedenquist in Vienna had chosen for the journey to Sweden were not among the faithful, neither this way nor that. Some of the youngest weren't even aware of their Jewishness.

Thirteen-year-old Otto's attitude toward a Christian baptism can no longer be determined. Because time had been short, the ritual had been pared back to the essentials, a quick caress of the hair so that it was wetted with the holy water, and then a few words. Done.

In the good pastor's eyes baptism was a door, a passageway from the one to the other. "Mosaic" on one end and Christian on the other. And that's how it should be, if you fully and truly believed in baptism as the way into the Christian community. But still the baptized children weren't called Christians. According to the pastor and the Swedish church they were Jewish Christians.

None of it mattered for what lay ahead. The only thing that would come to mean anything was the fact that Pepi, Lisl, and Otto happened to have been born among people who'd allowed their hate to proliferate unchecked. They found themselves in a confusing transition, when a tradition called anti-Semitism shifted from an old form into a new. A venomous snake shedding its skin.

As long as the hate was tightly entwined with faith, religion, and customs, conversion offered salvation. Depending on the time, country, and community, a Jew could become Muslim or a Catholic or a Protestant. The minority could weather the majority's threats by adapting—and that's what had happened since time immemorial. What doesn't bend breaks.

But something happened with genetic material when it was discovered. Nothing was as before. Being a Jew was suddenly deeper than faith and spiritual life, deeper than the question about rituals in the temple. Being a Jew became an inherited trait and could be identified as a set of genes. With this view of the world and people, converting to a religion could be seen as comely, like fixing your hair, an adjustment in accord with the reigning etiquette. But beneath the surface, the Jew remained. Hatred left faith and made its home in biology. Therefore, baptism doesn't make you Christian.

So it was perhaps no surprise that the pastor received angry letters, anonymous and signed, from Swedes offering sharp criticism of his children's campaign. Many came from those active in the Swedish church:

> Through newspaper ads it has come to the attention of the Swedish people that you are heading the charge of the importation of Jewish children to Sweden...
> [Can] we, considering our responsibility to the next generation, import such material...?

> Esteemed church council member and churchwarden for thirty-four years, L. Dahl in Backaryd.

But Mr. Dahl in Backaryd was sent a reply. Birger Pernow answered all correspondence, such was his nature. "It is sad to note that the great word of God, which you have heard for thirty-four years, has not had a greater impact on you in that you are now writing thus of the 'import' of 'such material,' insofar as it concerns a matter so serious as arranging for a period of refuge, shelter, and protection for small, helpless children, who are innocent victims of a blind and meaningless hatred that knows no bounds."

Rural Dean Granqvist in Söderala was another of the church's men who protested the children's campaign. In his reply, Pernow argued clearly and plainly: Yes, the Jews had only themselves to blame for incurring the wrath of God. But wasn't the punishment a bit harsh?

> It is completely right that the problem of the Jewish question is Israel's induration and that this induration brings God's judgment on the people. But the judgment alone does not lead to salvation. He who suffers must also be able to hear the call of God. Now this judgment is afflicting Israel's people with unprecedented severity. But then it is the Christian community's and so the Israel Mission's duty to show the judged the way to Christ...
>
> As concerns our relief measure, it is certainly not intended to curse our own country, and I do not think it will. What we have in mind with our recently disseminated appeal is simply to offer a temporary sanctuary in

our country for a hundred children and youths until something can be arranged for them elsewhere in the world. The situation is such that if they are not rescued as soon as possible, they will perish . . . But what is to be done must be done soon, for here is true and present danger.

And so the decision took shape: around sixty children and twenty-five youths from Vienna were to be allowed into the country, and in a later phase another fifteen or so children from Berlin. Altogether one hundred, all prenegotiated and approved one at a time in deliberations with Pastor Pernow and the officials at the Board of Health and Welfare. In the corridors, they called it the "Pernow quota."

On January 3, the Swedish Israel Mission handed in the final register of Viennese children to the Board of Health and Welfare. Name after name in alphabetical order. After each name was the child's birth year followed by the child's faith. No other details, just name, birth year, and religion. Forty-five children were baptized in the Evangelical faith. One was Baptist. Four Catholics, two Anglicans, and seven were Mosaic.

Name and religion.

One week later, on January 9, 1939, General Director Sigfrid Hansson, Director Bergström, and Wiman, the official in charge, sat at the Board of Health and Welfare in Stockholm with the full list before them. All the children were granted the right to reside in the country for six months. The children's names, in the same order, were repeated in the Board of Health and Welfare 's decision, same names, same order, same list.

With one difference.

Swedish authorities didn't take the matter of baptism into account. Whether or not most of the children were baptized was unimportant, so such details weren't included in the record. Instead, all the children had been categorized in the same way, each and every one was defined by the unmistakable letter M.

Maybe the Swedish church thought they were saving Christian children, but the Swedish government knew that they were actually Jews. M as in Mosaic.

Twelve handkerchiefs seemed essential when moving to another country, but two suits were plenty.

Then Elise packed a vest for Otto, four shirts, five pairs of pants, twelve pairs of underwear, as many stockings, and three pairs of socks. There were also a raincoat, a toothbrush, soap, toothpaste, a laundry bag, shoelaces (four), six pairs of gloves—no, five in the end, and a tracksuit. Everything carefully marked with Otto's initials. Ten sheets of letter paper and envelopes already addressed home were included.

The rescuers at the Israel Mission had distributed a clothing checklist. Under the heading "miscellany," Lisl wrote the number 17. Photographs from home, perhaps. An inexpensive fountain pen. A belt. A box of candies for the evening. A toy dog of indeterminate breed, with dark, curly fur and a red collar.

At the bottom of the page, on a line where the mother was to sign, was her name in black ink. Since the new year, Elise had also used the name "Sara," just like Aunt Grete and Nuny. In the same way Otto, Josef, and Paul had been unceremoniously renamed so that they, and all of their male acquaintances, were now called "Israel."

Finally everything was all packed up. A large suitcase and a smaller one that Otto was to carry himself containing nightwear and a toothbrush for the train ride. All done.

Unreal. Palpable. Definite. Temporary. The words for what was happening that fell from people's mouths were as flurried as the January snowflakes outside the window. Did Pepi, Elise, and Otto hold out their hands to catch them midflight? Did they try to ignore their melting?

Ostbahnhof. Wednesday, February 1, eight in the morning. The looks they gave him, especially Mutti's, were unbearable. Dad tried, as usual, to part with jokes.

"He's going out into the world on his first assignment as a foreign correspondent. There's snow on the ground there now. Otto will be able to go skiing and ice-skating. Report to the home office on Löwengasse. Write to us about the snow. Write to us about everything, write soon, write."

There they stood, in the midst of a fact, overseen by soldiers. The girders holding up the station's roof seemed to be barring the sky, and beneath them people crowded in dark groups that dispersed, reunited, and unexpectedly took on new shapes, like clouds of worry. The bigger people crouching among the smaller ones, and the small people hiding in embraces and tearing themselves free.

The white ceiling lights were bright enough to cast shadows, so the people's feet were black, as though each was standing in their own abyss. The abyss followed them as they moved.

Out on the platform, parents and children were being separated by the Gestapo. The train carriages' open doors enticed with a dark offer of rescue, but as soon as Otto climbed aboard he felt longing at his back. From sun to shadow.

Departure time 8:35, destination Berlin at 20:12 via Breslau, so no visas were needed. Expected arrival in Trelleborg: the morning of Thursday, February 2.

Otto stood in the window and waved until he couldn't see the platform anymore. Then the black-out curtains shut tight over the windows so that transport of Jews would be kept out of sight. Like an inky rivulet sliding across white paper, the train would take him and the other children through Germany's enemy territory, to where it ended and became a border. A night as long as a birth. In the morning they'd be ferried across the water and given new life. No one knew at what cost just yet, and who would pay, but everyone on the platform was hoping it was worth the price. Through the darkness the children would go. From disdain to deliverance. From famine to feast. From parental love to . . . well, that remained to be seen.

Write to us about everything, write to us, write.

The children were sorted by surname.

Viktor, Alfred, and Erich were to go to the children's home in Tollarp, along with Erwin, Herbert, Karl, Sonja, and Kurt. Gertrude was also going to the children's home, whereas her younger siblings Ella and Elrika had been assigned to different foster homes in Nässjö.

Ernst and Edgar were off to Alvesta.

Helga and Heinz had to be separated and placed in different homes in Stockholm. The three siblings Gerold, Gertrude, and Gerda were also to be split up and live in different homes in Råsunda, Stockholm, and Södertälje, respectively.

Siblings Ernst and Eva were to get off in Nässjö while the girls Ilse and Eva continued on to Ljusdal. Hedi and Fritz, Eva, Herbert, and Hugo were being accommodated by families around southern Sweden, just like Ernst, Gerhart, Felix, and Suli.

Peter was a last-minute addition. His name was penciled in all the way at the bottom of the paper. Each line of the list was meticulously checked off.

Otto was among those who had to get off the train first, to travel onward to the children's home in Tollarp.

New ground. Different air. New sounds. Salty wind.

New trees making other sounds in the wind. New wind blowing in other ways through the trees and through the children. They got off the train and the wind charged around them, a wind different from Vienna's.

The platform spread out before them, the wind received them and their wide-open faces. The trees received them. Just like the trees back home, but different.

Twenty-two children in winter clothes marked with their sets of initials, along with Sister Martha and Miss Sommer, climbed off the train. They walked toward the parking lot and the wind blew between and around them. The adults held the smallest children's hands. Older children held their younger siblings' hands. Each one carried a bag with leftovers from a packed lunch.

They saw the city. Not theirs, but another. Trelleborg. The name was unusual, as were the smells and the wind's way of blowing. The children held each other's hands. Thirty-six train hours behind them lay dark Vienna, as familiar as a parental embrace. Here the trees stood still, expectant against the bright morning sky. Only the wind was moving.

The pastor in his hat and coat met them. He spoke German. The children understood that it was thanks to him that they were here. Several women were standing with the pastor. They appeared wealthy and kind. The leaves leaped from their piles and sailed around. The pastor had waited by the cars. Walking toward him, the children climbed over the leaves and the wind blew around them, as if lost.

The remainder of the children's transport continued on up the country. In the archives, you can still find the permission given by the Royal Railway Board for "35 Jewish children, aged 6–15" to be offered discounted tickets.

But the trip hadn't come to its end just because Otto and the others had gotten off the train. They piled into cars and were driven to Tollarp, about twenty kilometers outside Kristianstad. There lay the house that would be theirs for a time. The name HEMHULT was painted right on the plaster in an arc of slender black letters over the main entrance. The children found out that the women who'd been at the pastor's side were part of Lund's refugee committee and that their work was led by Mrs. Eklundh, and she too spoke German. Pastor Pernow was returning to Stockholm that same day, but before leaving, he handed over the responsibility for the children's-home children to the Lund committee and Mrs. Eklundh. She was the one who would be in contact with the head of the children's home, and if there was anything of particular importance, the children could also write to her. She would make arrangements with the cook and promised to visit. She would later say that Otto had impressed her with his intelligence from the start. This connection between Otto and Mrs. Carola Eklundh from the Fredrika Bremer Society in Lund would prove to be important.

Soon thereafter, perhaps even the very next day, it was time to have their picture taken. Nine wooden chairs were carried outside and lined up for the smallest ones, and there they sat, up front: nine children whose feet couldn't reach the ground. One of them—Sonja?—hadn't managed to get her shoes on.

Behind them in the middle row stood Otto and a few other boys. Awkward, uncomfortable, not tall not short, not young not old. In the back stood those who already had a hint of beard and down on their upper lips, those who were at some distance from their childhoods, but had not left them behind. There were also three girls sitting together, looking in different directions.

A bit cold. Rescued. Welcomed to a Swedish February where shriveled rosehips hung in the bushes and thorns snatched at your hair if you came too close.

Faced with the black camera, the children did what was expected of them. They each smiled a parentless smile.

Vienna, February 4, 1939

My darling boy. We received your letter and your photograph today, and they made us very happy. We kept a close eye on your big journey, watch in hand, and believe us when we say we think of you always. And we will continue to think of you every day, and will write so as to render this distance meaningless...

We wish you wouldn't have had to leave your home, you know that. But when we couldn't think of anything but you not being allowed to swim, not being allowed to participate in any sports, not being allowed in any of the parks, that it was forbidden for you to go to school, then we had no choice but to send you away to give you a better future and a better life.

You were so wonderfully brave when we parted, so courageous that I'm convinced you will succeed out there in the world, even if I'm not there with you...

Everyone here is asking after you. Your friends Utas, Demner, and Werner visit every day, wondering where you are and what you're doing.

Today I won't write much because we want to hurry up and post this letter, so that it reaches you soon. During the next days we'll write again and we'll enclose postage.

That's it for today. A thousand greetings and kisses. May God protect you.

your dad

Poor boy, you couldn't take your English lesson on Friday. Kind regards,

Uncle Paul

Vienna, February 5, 1939

My dear boy, You can't imagine how happy we were yesterday when your first letter from Sweden arrived. We were surprised because we hadn't expected anything before tomorrow at the earliest, so when the postman arrived with the letter in the afternoon neither mom nor I were at home. Soon all of Löwengasse will have read your words, because everyone is interested and wants to know how you're doing...

Ever since the train left and we parted we've been thinking of you without pause. In the morning we said: Now he's in Berlin and later in the afternoon we pictured you taking the ferry, seeing the ocean for the first time and watching the seagulls that were probably flying around the ship. And in the evening we went to bed missing you—but also feeling assured—because now you'd arrived in Sweden, that beautiful country with the sympathetic and, above all, good people, and because now you're being given a better future than what you would've had here... I've never visited Sweden, but what I've read about the country and its people is inspiring. And the chance to grow up among such people, in such an environment, can't be valued highly enough.

You're a sensible and clever boy, I've always known that, and your way of relating to those last heavy hours of parting more than convinces me that we've made the right choice. I'm sure that you, who know how to behave, will come to follow our will and always act in a decent and correct manner. Then everything will be fine out in the big world, too, even though you don't have your father's support or your mother's help. But we will always be with you in thought, and then distance is meaningless, and our wishes are with you in all that you do . . . A thousand greetings and kisses,

your dad

Pepi was full of confidence. Someone had to be, and his usual optimistic disposition was to his benefit, now that he and Elise had been separated from their only child.

Until the day he'd been fired because of the race laws, Pepi had gone to work every day at the *Wiener Tag* on Canisiusgasse 8. Every day for seventeen years, he'd taken his seat and typed out his copy after the morning editorial meeting. Why stop now? With Otto in Sweden, the decision was made. He would write a letter a day.

. . . It is also to preserve the memory of the room in the home where you've lived for many years, and even the memory of us here, to which you will always be connected.

If you were to walk through this door today, nothing would look any different. Aunt Grete's ottoman is still in the room. The only difference is that the dip in the middle has grown deeper. One can indeed lie in it quite comfortably, but to rise from it requires certain effort. And at the wide table by the window where you used to sit with your friends and play cards or just play, I'm sitting and doing my language homework or writing to you. Your bookshelf is still in the corner, but the boy who knew how to make such a wonderful mess of it is gone. And we who are in the room are the same. Everything is unchanged, except that it's quiet—because you're not here.

The question is how quickly the linguistically talented Otto could learn Swedish, how soon he could start reading the local newspaper and to what extent the *Kristianstadsbladet* newspaper reported on what was happening. One might hope to the contrary: that he was slow, that there was nothing in the paper.

But a few days before Otto and the other children landed in Swedish territory, one of the biggest public debates about who should be allowed into Sweden and who should be kept out began. The starting shot was fired by *Svenska Dagbladet* in Stockholm, which on January 28, 1939, published a front-page story with the headline "Doctor Import Plan Rouses Opposition."

It was reported that the Board of Medicine was being given government approval to invite ten, maybe twelve, medical specialists into the country. Dentists, doctors, pharmacists. Of Jewish descent.

Sometimes you stumble on your words. As though certain ones don't belong in the same sentence. "Swedish" and "Nazi," for example. Almost none, says one. Plenty, says another, to sway opinions.

The *Svenska Dagbladet* article may have been the result of a tip, like a strand of a campaign that Swedish Nazis launched right after the November pogrom: stop Moses at the gate. But even if this wasn't the case, it would be shown that parallel forces, aiming to pull in the same direction, were at work in Swedish society. Among them were the prominent, well-educated, and well-off. Not necessarily confirmed Nazis, but together with people like this you could be united in a hatred of the Jews and a strong desire to keep the border closed.

And it wasn't just furriers and retailers that intertwined anti-Semitism with a fear of competition, not just the Swedish Trades Union Organization. It was also the National Association of Swedish Small Business Owners. The Jewish question only concerned economics and the job market, the association's representatives said, while equating refugees with vermin. A few weeks before the *Kindertransport* left Vienna, the national association held a "large public meeting about the Jewish invasion" and a resolution that demanded strict immigration control was approved.

The same day that Otto and the other children arrived in Sweden, the front page of the *Stockholms-Tidningen* newspaper reported that Swedish hospitals had rejected the suggestion of importing foreign doctors. This is also the day that the Nazi Swedish Socialist Unity party or SSS held a large meeting in Stockholm. The party leader Sven Olov Lindholm addressed 1,500 people: "When we see how many tens of thousands, in spite of everything, have been awakened to resolute opposition to democracy, class spirit, and a Jewish Empire—then with our greatest hopes we can continue the fight!"

The next day the Västmannalands-Dala Student Union asked the Uppsala Student Union to arrange a student meeting in Uppsala, where the importation of intellectual manpower would be discussed.

Sixty-five children had just slipped in across the border. It was understandable that neither the Board of Health and Welfare, the Swedish church, nor Pastor Pernow wanted to highlight the Jewish children's transport—few knew about it, there was no newspaper coverage. However, the plan to invite those ten German doctors had leaked, and that was more than plenty.

Otto had been in the country for four days when the first Nazi protest meeting was arranged "because of the planned importation of Jewish dentists, doctors, and pharmacists." On February 6, they gathered at 7 p.m. in the center of Stockholm.

Several hundred demonstrators wearing white student caps and bearing torches paraded through the capital. Afterward, the Nazis exulted in their newspaper *Den Svenska Folksocialisten*: "Monday the 6th of February was a red-letter day in the history of Swedish Socialism...On that day 450 students marched in the Swedish Socialist Student Union's demonstration against the planned import of Jewish intellectuals. On that day our student union led the charge of student opinion. Marching in our line were not only Swedish Socialists, but also students belonging to other political movements and politically unaffiliated academics...not even in our wildest fantasies could we have imagined that there would be 450 of us participating in this assembly."

The meeting finished with speeches about the "Jewish invasion" and a resolution that demanded that Swedes alone be allowed to work as doctors, dentists, and pharmacists—in perpetuity.

The demonstration was reported by Sweden's domestic media and also on German radio.

The day the Stockholm demonstration was held, another two pieces of correspondence arrived at the Uppsala Student Union. The Värmland and Gästrike-Hälsinge Student Unions were expressing their support for the suggestion to organize a meeting about Swedish refugee policies.

Uppsala's students assembled. Nazis were among them. It was covered by the press. Parallel movements, people meeting and letting their opinions merge, gathering strength from the feeling of standing united. Nothing was moving in the shadows, nothing was hiding in the darkness. Everyone was marching down the street in the same direction in broad daylight, and they were moving without hesitation toward the Swedish government and Parliament.

Autumn 1938 had been a time of hope and agitation for the Swedish Nazis. Meeting after meeting had been held to enlist members and votes. In Småland alone the party held seventy meetings. Thousands came to listen on the square in Alvesta, Bettnaryd, Eksjö, Jönköping, Kalmar, Ljungby, and Högsby. One person who came, listened, and allowed himself to be impressed was twelve-year-old Ingvar Kamprad.

III

Ingvar was a restless and inventive young man who liked sitting in the kitchen in his grandmother Fannie's wooden house, devouring her Nazi publications, or keeping silent in the background, listening to his father Feodor discuss politics over a bridge game with the village teacher. Was he a child? A young adult? Was it an aberration?

He struggled with dyslexia, with the feeling of being different without knowing why. He enjoyed the magazine *Signal*, published at the initiative of Uncle Hitler's good friend Josef Goebbels and his propaganda center. It offered large, shiny pages and pictures taken in clear light, colors sparkling like fireworks across the pages. In long articles Europe was depicted with proud troops and strong-willed people moving forward. Meetings between serious government heads took place and handsome youths gathered in uniformed solidarity. Ingvar read and was swayed.

A less colorful publication that Ingvar also devoured was the *Jordburkarnas Föreningsblad*, the farmer's union magazine. It was as important to Swedish farmers as *Pravda* was to the Kremlin, Ingvar Kamprad would later say. And it might have been there—or in *Signal*—that he found the ads with the voucher to send away for party brochures and information. Ingvar filled them out, sent them off, and got what he wanted: the Swedish Nazi newspaper *Den Svenska Folksocialisten*. Party leader Lindholm himself was the publisher, and there was no mistaking what the Swedish Nazis wanted.

The twelve-year-old on Elmtaryd farm probably also received the Nazis' voting manifesto and other promotional materials from the Lindholmers, as these Nazis were called, to be distributed in the village of Agunnaryd and its surroundings, tooling around on Mother Berta's bicycle.

Nineteen thirty-eight was an election year, and there was no doubt that the SSS was a black hole of race ideology. On the Nazis' own Richter scale of hatred, only democracy had the same resonance: "Democracy must die for the people to live!" read the rubric in their voting manifesto. And this was the goal for the party's race and population policies:

> The reawakening of the Nordic racial consciousness. Goal-oriented measures to increase the birth rate. Considerable tax breaks for those with many children and for racially desirable families as well as changes to wage and housing policies in accordance with race biology. Preferential housing loans to spouses of good genetic stock. Sterilization of demonstrably race-degenerating elements, vagrants, those with severe hereditary illnesses, imbeciles, criminals and the like. Substantial support for sporting and outdoor life. An immigration ban on Jews and other foreign race elements. Deportation of immigrants and other undesirable aliens who were permitted entry in recent years. The Jews' position under the Aliens Act.

Twelve-year-old Ingvar cycled alone those sixty miles to Moheda to participate in a Nazi meeting next to a warehouse. Youths on the square wore uniforms, they recruited members to the party, they carried flags and beat drums. Later he went to a meeting where party leader Lindholm himself addressed the audience. It might have been in Eksjö on August 14 of that year. There, three hundred Smålanders gathered to listen to the Swedish Führer, in uniform and a Sam Browne belt, with swastika flags and a greeting that began with "Heil."

Ingvar had ended up on a path that he'd stay on for the coming years. Very close by, but as if on a strange desert isle, was Otto and the other children newly arrived from Vienna, clothing marked and carrying suitcases.

III

Was Hemhult bad? Aside from the homesickness, not at all. Otto might as well have been on a weeklong outing, a field trip. It was like staying at a simple boardinghouse with only children as guests. The constant singing of psalms.

He had to rise early, but then hot chocolate was served. Only a few days had passed since they'd stepped off the train. The landscape was mild, foggy, a quiet sky. No trams passing by, no newspaper vendors shouting, no honking cars. Nary a February bird opened its beak. But they could kick a ball around outside. He hadn't been able to do that for eleven months.

To share a room, to sleep and wake up in groups, to move as a flock and to appear together—it wasn't just unusual, it was to fade into the crowd and be forced to swallow your pride. Otto did all this. He stood in line. He wiped the baseboards during cleaning.

No one wondered what he wanted anymore, and if he made his desires known no one in particular would listen. But he accepted the new circumstances and decided to master them. He endured. Lisl and Pepi were going to come—later—and pick him up. So far only five days had passed, and they were in agreement about this time being a parenthetical that would reach its end, so the next phase—one in which they were together—could begin. Remarkable: how painful the ache of longing in his muscles. For isn't that all a heart is—a muscle?

Oatmeal was hardly Otto's primary concern. But maybe oatmeal was easier to write home about.

Vienna, February 7, 1939

Dearest Otti. Your second letter arrived today and I'm making sure to answer right away. Foremost I want to say that it calmed us to hear that you are doing well. The food seems to be good and plentiful, and that oatmeal... My God, one can get used to worse things. As I mentioned, I don't like it either. It seems to be a family trait.

I assume you've already received our three letters. You can see we are diligent and don't want to give you too much cause for longing. Industrious letter writing keeps the communication going and preserves the closeness between us, with the drawback that we can't see or hug each other. But that too will be possible one fine day, and we'll box together again one day, or—to Mom's dismay—play soccer in the living room. But who can say where we'll play soccer in the future, the most important thing is that we will...

I agree with you that life would be wonderful if only you had your whole family with you. But for now we have to satisfy ourselves with the fact that our youngest got out and has found a better life than here. Egon Bock, you know, has no choice but to mill about the streets or sit at home.

I must reiterate that however much we'd want to have you here, we are so happy to have been able to give you that wonderful country, where you can once again be viewed as a whole and—most importantly—esteemed person.

One fine day we'll be together again, such is our hope, and until then we have to suppress our every wish and longing, for I am convinced you understand that what has come to pass is for the best, and that distance doesn't lessen our love one bit…

Each day we await the postman. If he has something from you, he waves it in the air so that we can see it from a distance, and waiting with us are your friends who always ask after you, your father's sisters, your mother's sisters and brothers. Since you left you have become an even greater object of interest, but don't let that go to your head. So dear boy, write diligently, as I do, write about everything you do… One thousand kisses,

your dad

Dear Otti. Your letter made me happy. And as Dad writes, distance is meaningless. We are with you in thought. Always. Write often.

your mom

Many greetings from Milos. Write soon. I'm waiting.

Dear Ottel. Full of envy, I see in your letter that you—just like an Englishman—sit down to "dinner" at five o'clock. We can't imagine such things. Tell me how your menus are composed, so that we who have so little to eat can at least feel our mouths water. By the way, do you already boast a few Swedish phrases?

Your friend
Paul

February 8, 1939

My darling boy. Today we received two letters from you, both postmarked February 6. I assume the one is from Sunday and the other is from Monday. After you wrote them, you must have received a pile of mail from us, so we can await a reply from you soon.

We were very happy to hear that you're doing well, and the letter from Monday was particularly nice and funny. You seem to be content, homesickness aside. But longing is a sickness that can't be cured just like that. It's an expression of a sense of belonging, and for people who have a heart in their body, it can neither shrink nor vanish. And if you have no complaint but your longing, then we can be content. The most important thing is that you are still together with your friends, playing and above all working and, of course, studying. Your friend Milos, who has read your letters, says that it is indeed a bit much to have to eat oatmeal and study Swedish, but I do think you can manage both…

Each letter you write makes us happy, even if it's only a few lines. To know how you're doing and that you're content is our greatest wish.

Here we are having wonderfully beautiful days. And we are filled with joy and satisfaction when we think about you no longer having to be here, but instead being able to go out into nature like a free person again, and also to feel like one. This fills us with joy, even though you are not here to give your favorite Fatty a lesson with your sharp tongue when she's done something stupid. We can't thank God enough for finding you the opportunity to get away. As you well know!

And now dear Otti, I repeat: take care. Think of us whenever you have a free moment, and write to us. One thousand kisses

Dad

Dear Otti, there is nothing left for me to write because Dad's already written everything. From morning to night I think of you, of what you're doing, and what you will do and what your days are like. We're forever waiting for a letter from you to arrive so that we can know everything. If you're working with agriculture, it is certainly very healthy, but make sure to not get sick. Today I've given your address to Mrs. Lubatz, so her boys can write to you. A thousand kisses

your Mutti

There was something incomprehensible, one riddle that Otto couldn't solve, and that wouldn't leave him in peace. Why did he and a few others get off in Trelleborg when most of the other children had traveled on? Why had he been placed at a children's home when others had been assigned foster parents?

After that first Sunday at Hemhult, the question developed a sharp edge and cut into his thoughts. Several families from the area had visited the home and the children were made to sit politely in the room with the harmonium. The adults had peeked in, whispered, and nodded at each other. And then some children had been chosen, packed up, and went home with the visitors. But not Otto.

Otherwise everything was good, almost pleasant.

February 14, 1939

My dear boy. No letter came from you today, but I suppose that's because it was Sunday. So we await a few lines from you in the afternoon or on Monday. I've read your card from yesterday, it arrived just as I'd finished writing my letter. We were put at ease by the menu and are assured that there is no risk you will go hungry.

Earlier today your mother visited the Swedish mission and spoke to Sister Martha, who accompanied you to Sweden and has since returned. She said you were very good on the trip. Splitting you up between Stockholm and Tollarp wasn't done in accordance with any specific wishes, but those who traveled on have ended up in homes as well, just like you in Tollarp. You'll stay in these homes only until you've learned Swedish, and then you'll be placed with foster parents. Until then, dear boy, be patient. Anyway, I don't think that life at the home is a misfortune. Perhaps you are bored from time to time. Write and tell us what it looks like. Sister Martha says that Tollarp is very beautiful…

Yesterday I received the family photos Engineer Honigman took when you left. I'll send them along so you have something to laugh at. You're the one who comes out best in those two pictures. Mom gives the impression of gentle suffering. I, on the other hand, have put up a handsome facade and look like a well-fed and happy citizen. Aunt Nuny seems to be afflicted by a "tumor," at which she's laughing, while my sister Grete, who is standing behind me in the photographs, appears to be in deep contemplation over some domestic task. Paul seems to have discovered something across the room, for he is glaring accusingly at the sky. And your favorite, the other Grete, has in your honor made her mouth even wider and pressed her lips together as if she were about to pronounce the M in Mucki pucki. So there you have it: the entire family.

Milos stopped by yesterday. He was a little tired because another one of your favorites, Professor Klein, had him do fifty squats. It is said to be very healthy to do so, but Milos felt it would be better to not be here anymore and to instead be doing those exercises in some other country. He has no desire to be doing squats for Professor Klein. Nothing is happening for him right now. But Diamant is leaving tomorrow, two weeks after you. He's going to stop by and say farewell.

Tomorrow it will be fourteen days since you left. When we think about it—not just now, but all the long day, in every conversation and every thought—the longing for you surfaces. Then we are reminded that you are being taken care of by good people and are safe in a beautiful country, and we see that you have the chance to grow up as a free person and work for a better future. We would like all of this for ourselves, too, but now it is still more important that you—our pride and our hope—are protected from all danger. God willing, we too will get away from here, and then we'll be able to make arrangements to see you again. But for now we must, as you know—because you are clever—have patience.

And if your homesickness gets to be too strong, think of all your friends who are still here, and longing to leave. Think about all who envy you and finally—aside from all the other unpleasantries you'd experience here—think of Professor Klein. He wasn't really your favorite. Being rid of him now might be worth a little homesickness?

Beloved Otti. I expect you to hear more interesting stories from you soon. Take care of yourself. One thousand kisses

Dad

Beloved Otti, your Dad told you about those fifty squats your friend had to do, but he didn't seem to know that they were followed by a big slap. Milos Werner did in fact deserve that slap. Yesterday he shot the moon as the second-to-last card! What is it you usually say? "A person like that using up all the air!"

warmly
Paul

Beloved Otti. Well, there's nothing left to write because your dad already laid claim to the interesting bits. I'm curious about your surprise and wonder what it can be. Each day I wait and hope you're not giving up, that you'll stay well, and I won't have to worry about your health. My treasure. Kisses and hugs

Mutti

. . . Just keep drinking that wonderful milk, my dear Wutzi. It's a very nice name, entirely to my taste and so befitting my Mucki pucki, isn't it? How's your Swedish coming along? Can you already understand a few words? Signing off, warm greetings

Aunt Grete

III

Grossmutter Fanny Kamprad. There wasn't much that made her cry. Insolent is the word.

But she cried over the Versailles peace treaty. And over her German relatives being forced to become Czech. She cried over their poverty, and maybe over life not turning out as she'd thought it would.

Ingvar saw the tears. Grandmother Fanny sent packages to her poor relatives in Sudetenland. There were many forms to fill out and her Swedish didn't take her far, so the postman had to sit at the kitchen table in the large house and help her. Then she cried. In rage.

And he was inventive. When Ingvar wrung a chicken's neck in the coop, for instance, it angered his father Feodor. But mischief wasn't all that caused his temper to rise. Feodor's moods swung and he'd fly into a rage and beat Ingvar. Then there was only one direction to run—toward Grossmutter.

To the wooden house painted gray and white, Grandmother's domain. There was safety and candy. There, in the kitchen with the publications from another larger reality, life seemed to Ingvar a little closer and farther-reaching than Agunnaryd parish.

He says himself that he was a recluse who wanted to break away from solitude, out of the echoing feeling of being odd, and into the fellowship and warmth of others. And this is why he answered that ad about the Lindholmers and started reading Nazi newspapers. In retrospect, it's not hard to see this through his eyes. A trinity had emerged that would carry him through many years: Fanny and Ingvar and Germany. Where did the love for one begin and the love for the other take over?

Ingvar's little sister Kerstin walked alongside him and took notice. When Ingvar was sitting in Grandmother's lap, Kerstin was left to stand by the door. When Ingvar was given a treat, she was given errands to run.

"They adored each other, Grandmother and Ingvar," Kerstin says today, seventy years later. "Only once did I get to sit in Grandmother's lap, and that was during a storm when she was afraid of the thunder."

Locals called them *nassar*, slang for "Nazis." Kerstin heard people say it, though she hardly understood what the farm boys in Agunnaryd were shouting at her on her way home from school. But that's how it was. Everyone knew what Grandmother Fanny and her son, the estate owner Feodor Kamprad, thought about the matter, and where their sympathies lay. No one was surprised that Ingvar went the same route.

As a loyal party supporter, Ingvar received posters in the mail. Then he'd cycle to the parish and put them up: large images of the leader Lindholm.

III

The requested student meeting in Uppsala, the debate about refugee policies, was to be held. A committee was assembled and though the participants were not at all united in their opinion, they had finally drafted a resolution on which the students could vote:

> In response to the problem of intellectual refugees immigrating to Sweden, which in these days is increasingly timely, Uppsala's students, gathered for a general meeting, wish to submit to the king a humble request that future opportunities for academic youth not be compromised by placing foreign intellectual workers in posts that could otherwise be filled by qualified Swedish men and women.
>
> Uppsala's students are following the developments with growing concern. It seems to us that in this situation it is a right and a duty, in our opinion, that the natural sympathy for the suffering of others should not lead to measures that will create hitherto unknown and dire problems for Sweden.

First, the student union leaders considered approving the text. But there weren't really any changes as a result, every word was still there and in the same order. Only half a sentence was added, a sympathetic phrase, an assurance that Uppsala's students understood the refugees' difficult situation. As if to blunt the text's edges a bit, to soften their opposition.

On Friday, February 17, the time came. About 1,500 students met in the union's tennis hall, more than the organizers had anticipated. The resolution was proposed. The only female speaker was mocked after dropping her script, and the time dragged on. Finally a vote was called. Should the resolution be adopted?

It turned out that the audience wasn't circulating one but two drafts of a resolution. One contained the student leadership's additional wording, the other did not.

Of the 897 students who remained when the vote was called, the majority voted for the text that did not express an understanding of the refugees' difficult situation. The harsher text won.

Well. Students. An easily led bunch, one columnist wrote in the *Social-Demokraten* newspaper, and continued, "To call Uppsala's students' lamentable exploit a Swedish position is an affront to the Swedish name."

Dagens Nyheter also commented on the students' meeting in an editorial: "But the refugee problem appeals to all Swedes with humanist traditions. It is painful to watch young Uppsala—such a large part of the student world there—distancing themselves from this line of thinking."

Youthful concern for their own careers—that was perhaps all that lay behind the students' absolute rejection of foreign intellectual manpower. As though the battle over those ten doctors ended there.

In Nazi Germany on February 21, Jews were ordered to hand over jewelry, precious stones, and metals to the authorities.

That same day medical students gathered in Stockholm to arrange their own meeting. They determined that the German doctors were a matter for the union—employment opportunities might be at risk—and the humanitarian aspect had to be left out of the discussion.

But it didn't quite work out that way. A recurring argument was made about the "inhumanity" of allowing German doctors in—as *Dagens Nyheter* would report on their front page on February 23: "[He] energetically asserted that it was precisely for humanitarian reasons that the 10 doctor exiles should be refused entry—the term 'humanitarian' had but to be interpreted correctly and allowed to apply to the sick in this country and to Swedish health care."

With a crushing majority—263 voted against the refugees, 18 for—the medical students in Stockholm passed a resolution similar to that of the Uppsala students. To ensure that the question was being handled in accordance with reigning objective ideals, students with Jewish heritage weren't allowed a say in the matter.

In *Läkartidningen*, a medical journal, a hot debate raged, and even though there were doctors defending humanity and opposing a country's own "self-interest," others openly declared that it wasn't about the job market for Swedish doctors or that recent graduates were having a hard time finding posts. It was about race. For instance, Axel Odelberg wrote:

> Until now our country has not had a Jewish question. Are we to adopt one? Our Swedish colleagues of more or less Semitic extraction have had the same ethical understanding as their purely Nordic friends, without any opposition,

that many of them have done our profession and our society proud. However, we know that in a number of countries, not just in Central Europe, similar good relations have not prevailed, and long before these past five years there has been a sharpening opposition. This is the heart of the matter. This is what should be discussed. An attempt to conceal that which our thoughts are circling neither benefits us nor the general public.

III

Days of rolling fog came and went. Hemhult was now Otto's whole world and the drops that clung to the branches were his closest neighbors.

It was as though the journey had given birth to him. As though he were unborn until 8 a.m. that Wednesday when he'd let go of Elise and Pepi's hands, climbed up the train's steps, and hurried to the window that opened onto the platform where they were standing. He'd stayed there, face pressed to the past, watching his childhood slowly pull away from his field of vision.

At the train journey's end, another life had been waiting, a colder light. As if Sweden were perpetually in the month of February, never turning to spring, and not one thing was reminiscent of the sun-baked stones he'd skipped across the slow-flowing Donau.

Dad and Mutti had stayed behind. Left to days during which they weren't allowed to work, left to streets where they could be arrested. Left waiting for it to pass. Home's harbor blown to bits. Now they wanted to moor their days to him. They wrote and wrote.

Otto didn't know how it came to be, but however much he longed for them—his big, safe parents—something in their embrace held him too tightly. Something in their gaze lingered too long, a tenderness that contained reproach. He read their letters and noted what they left out. He knew they were protecting him from their reality, the ever more appreciated visits to their butcher friend in the shop back home. He knew they felt increasingly ringed in. In contrast to him. So why didn't he feel free?

He and the other Hemhult children were assigned a task. They were to dig up the ground behind the children's home. It angered Otto to have to devote himself to something he didn't see the sense in. But perhaps it was to become a kitchen garden. Perhaps the children at the home needed something to do. Well, he did his best.

After a day's work in the meadow—first taking a spade to the turf, then prizing it up by leaning on the shaft, lifting, turning, and tossing the clumps into the wheelbarrow—it was easier to read letters from the others: Aunt Grete, Nuny, and Paul. The air was a little clearer, the jokes sharper. They weren't as intent on...what to say? Raising him. Was that why the ache in his heart after reading them didn't weigh on him for hours after, but felt simpler? Like a needle through the skin, eased in with a smile.

February 9, 1939

Dear Otto. Today I too am using the typewriter because it's easier and I need the practice. I'm very happy that you're being kept busy with farm work. Paul wouldn't be able to handle it because he can't bend down, and yet he insists that he'd also be able to savage a meadow.

Here everything is as it was. Today the Glasses were here for their English lessons and Aunt Hansi ate lunch with us. We had a pasta bake with ham. Dad kept his eye out for the black cat, sorry, I mean the meat, and Paul had to put his glasses on to even catch sight of it.

Gerhardt, who is most likely going to the conservatory in Jerusalem or to Brussels, wants to leave as soon as possible so he can enjoy the beautiful sunny days.

Write and tell me if you've made friends with another boy yet—I don't dare hope for a girl—and if you've already become a top pick in soccer, if the meadows where you're playing are still covered in snow, if you still have your evening candy and if the battery is still working.

Werner is visiting today to hear the latest about you. That poor dear has no chance of getting away. He's taking a re-education course, though not for card games, and for Demner a course like that would be a waste. I'll stop here and let Aunt Grete and Paul write. Until the next letter, warm greetings,

Nuny

I've already written to you once and am still awaiting a response. You won't get another letter until you reply. Warm greetings,

your Milos

Do you really understand how much we all envy you? Me, who's stuck here with your aunts, I envy you because you're rid of them. Best would be if we could send Aunt Grete away like a package without return postage. Warm greetings,

Paul

Dearest Otti. I wouldn't have anything against Paul sending me to you without return postage. That would be entirely in accordance with my wishes, I want to see you working in the meadow so very much. But you will improve and the meadow will have recovered by next spring. How did your first Swedish class go? I can't imagine you'll find your lessons difficult. Some of it is very similar to German. Dearest Mucki pucki, take care of yourself. A thousand kisses and hugs,

Aunt Grete

February 16,1939

My dear Otti. Your dear lines to me made me very happy. Through your letters to your parents—to whom you write diligently—I get to hear all the news. You know I'm so very curious.

Life in your home must be very nice. Does it gleam with all those polished shoes? Which position do you play on the team? Are you the goalie, by chance? It's more of a challenge to play on a real soccer field than in the space between the dining room and the bedroom at home, isn't it?

By the way, have the Subaks written to you from London? Their mother often asks about you. Have you already managed to make new friends out there? You don't have to use the attached postage for me. Go ahead and write to another of your friends in Vienna who want so much to hear from you. Here at home, there's nothing to tell because your dear parents have already written to you about everything and compared to them I always cut a ridiculous figure. My dear Otti. Please keep writing. Take care of yourself, may God help you.

Aunt Grete

PS. What do you say about the photographs?

A few days prior Otto had received two photos. So there you have the whole family, his father had written.

Yes, there they were. Otto, Pepi, and Elise in the one picture, and the whole family gathered as a group in the other. It all had been arranged ahead of his departure.

Care had been taken to close the curtains in one of the rooms at home and Engineer Honigman took equal care when setting up two lamps. Stark white light shining on those seven people, taking the measure of their faces and bodies and sending their highlights, shadows, and darkness straight into the camera's open eye.

In the foreground, two chairs. Lisl sits in one, dressed in black as though in mourning. Otto, hair slicked down for the time being, is sitting beside her. A thirteen-year-old still surrounded by familial warmth. In the photo he's slighted blurred, midmovement, with an unclear gaze. He was the one who, according to his father, came out best in the photo. Did Pepi ever find flaws in that boy?

Elise looks a touch distressed. A coincidence, maybe. Toothache. Or she was bad at keeping her mask on, didn't have it in her to keep at bay the thought that she and Otto would soon be separated. Pepi describes himself as having a sturdy stance, like a well-fed, happy citizen. His eyes are light, perhaps gray, there's a hint of a smile.

Otto's Aunt Nuny is standing up, facing the center of the group; the angle accents her double chin. Pepi says she's laughing in the photo. Maybe she was lighthearted by nature. She was married to Paul, seven years her senior, grizzled and gangly, who over the years had become both Otto's friend and language tutor. After all the hours spent with Greek grammar and homework, a special bond had developed between the pair, and Paul told everyone who would listen that thirteen-year-old Otto was his favorite pupil. In the photo he's looking up at the ceiling.

Otto's paternal aunt Grete looks younger than her brother, thinner and more serious. Soon, she would find a tear in the net and slip out of Vienna and this story.

Finally, there's his maternal aunt Grete with her hand in her skirt pocket, glasses, beard hairs on her chin, and something slapdash about her clothing. She was a career bookkeeper, unmarried, and seemed to have found her place as everyone's object of ridicule. Aunt Grete called Otto "Mucki pucki," happily bought him candy, pinched his cheeks, and wanted kisses.

"So there you have the whole family." It was an unfortunate picture with each family member showing their worst side. Remarkably bad. One might also say entertaining—under different circumstances.

III

The question was there waiting for him when he woke up, it followed him to sleep every night: everyone else was getting a foster family—why not him? He was already among those who spoke the best Swedish. Why wasn't he chosen? And as though they were Siamese twins, homesickness stood right beside this persistent question, constantly drawing attention to itself. The letters from Vienna were no comfort.

> *Dear Otti,... You write that you would like to be with foster parents, but fail to mention if any of the other twenty children in the home have already been placed. Can you write about this transfer, how it will happen, and how much you know, when you're to be moved and so on? We have no idea and would very much like to know more.*
>
> *In any case—if it's boring sometimes or if you're overcome with homesickness and would rather be here with us, let it be said that you have it better than all of your friends who are still in Vienna and who, except for a brief visit to school in the mornings, don't know what to do with their time. At least you get to savage a meadow by being put to work in it, here your friends can't even walk in the meadows. That's a vast difference...*

How is your Swedish coming along? We expect to receive a letter in that new language soon. If you make an effort, I'm convinced you'll learn quickly. I know you're ambitious.

Your letter mentioning a surprise for Mother has given rise to much head scratching. We're making wild guesses as to what it might be. Maybe it's a letter in Swedish? Or a photograph? Well, soon we'll find out. In any case, we're very curious. We always have been.

There isn't much going on here. The weather is bad. It's raining and windy, so being outdoors is no fun. Aunt Grete just unleashed her melodic voice and filled the apartment with song, so being home isn't agreeable either, where to go? Best would be Sweden, to you, so we could complain about her together...

Dear boy. Take care of yourself, with God's help, and send us a nice letter again for enjoying us [sic]. *One thousand kisses,*

dad

My darling child—I shall wonder about my surprise every day. Dad has already written that I'm going to the Swedes now to arrange to visit you. You know how much I'd like to see you. But I also know that you're a clever boy and you realize that anywhere but here is better for you. Every day I meet mothers who are running around, trying to send their children abroad. Life is incredibly grim. Sometimes a reunion comes sooner than we expect. Well, my treasure, a thousand kisses. Take care of yourself. Hugs,

your Mutti

The thought was soothing.

The idea of Mother's visit to Hemhult suppressed the other thoughts for a time, like a hug, an extra blanket on a cold night. And Elise, she wanted to see her son again. They'd never been apart for this long.

She wrote that she was going to the Swedes to arrange a visit to Sweden, and the tone is hopeful, practically triumphant. "Reunion may come sooner than we expect."

What was she thinking?

There are no notes left in Otto Ullmann's file about her meeting with the Swedes in the Swedish Israel Mission's building on Seegasse, a meeting that in all likelihood took place in mid-March 1939. But the man she visited, Pastor Göte Hedenquist, kept up a healthy correspondence with Pastor Pernow at the head office on Idungatan in Stockholm. This month was no exception. Children like Otto, and parents like Elise, worried him.

> As concerns the children, they write all manner of things to their parents here. Many are homesick and attempt to describe their conditions in a way that will encourage their parents to collect them, which is impossible. For that reason we have thorough conversations with such parents. But the overwhelming majority are happy and grateful, parents and children alike. One difficulty is persuading the parents not to write quite so often. Many have some money yet and nothing better with which to occupy themselves than their own kin. But surely, it will get better with time.

> What you write about us not making it clear enough to parents that they would by no means be able to come to Sweden if they have children there, does not stand. In each particular case I have personally detailed our conditions for the parents and that we expect the children to be picked up in a year's time or so, when the parents themselves have secured the means of supporting themselves in some other country.

Conditions. The pastor had in each particular case detailed the mission's conditions for the parents.

Whatever the case. The meeting at the Swedish Israel Mission had the intended effect. Lisl never mentioned visiting their son in Sweden again, not in one syllable, not in one letter.

III

Otto could get up early if he had to. He could fold his clothes at night. He polished his shoes. He made friends with Erich and Gerhardt. His heart softened at the sight of Gertrude's long dark braids.

The adults, Miss Sommer from Vienna and the old Swedish Sister Cecilia, did what they could for the youngest ones who cried the most at night.

Otto understood that this was where he had to be, for the most part. Only sometimes, when he still wasn't quite awake, could he believe that he was in his own bed back home, and that the sounds from the other rooms were in fact kind Mitzi puttering in the kitchen or airing Mom and Dad's blankets on the balcony. He could picture himself getting up and meeting Mutti and Aunt Grete in the kitchen, walking past them at odds about what should be cooked for dinner and getting irritated. How he'd stick his nose in and try to mediate (he used to try to remember whom he'd supported the day before, so as to be fair) or how he'd laugh at them.

How Aunt Nuny would be warbling in one room and Grete in another. How Dad would stay in bed, taking his time.

Then Aunt Grete would go visit Auntie Mina, and when she came back in time for lunch she always said the weather was delightful, rain or shine, and then she would sigh over her bad foot. After they'd eaten they did the dishes together, and then Dad took lessons from Paul in Hebrew or English.

And Otto himself, he pictured how he used to take his schoolbooks and his ball down the stairwell, his steps echoing on the stone floor, how with his left hand on the lacquered railing he took the steps two at a time. How he'd walked past the water faucet built into the wall on the ground floor, the nice doorman's apartment, through the tall doors with four glass panes in each, and would finally reach the front entrance, open it, and step out onto the street. As he'd always done. The butcher's shop would already be open, the trams thundering by, and high up on the house on the opposite corner sat the stone lion, keeping watch over his neighborhood. But as soon as he opened his eyes, he was back in the Hemhult children's home in Tollarp. Washing his hands before breakfast. He spoke a little Swedish. Was served more food than he'd had in a long time. Was trying to get used to the syrup bread. All was well.

III

Not far from the children's home, people were gathering around the swastika. Otto and the other children had in fact arrived in the region with the greatest number of Nazis in Sweden.

But it wasn't just Skåne, the adjacent parts of Småland were also thick with Nazis, and they too were gathering. For instance, on March 5 the Nazi party's youth group, Nordisk Ungdom (Nordic Youth), held a district meeting in Växjö. The whole thing took place at the Stadshotellet city hotel. After dinner, the lawyer and captain in the Swedish Territorial Army C. P. Ossbahr, a long-standing member in the German-Swedish Association, spoke. Then they marched to Teatertorget in Växjö, where speeches were made on the square. To conclude, a ball was held at Stadshotellet.

On the same day in Stockholm, around eighty members of the association for Sweden's young doctors gathered to discuss the immigration of those ten doctors from Germany. After being informed about the matter, they decided to task the Swedish Medical Association with communicating the refusal to the asylum seekers. The Swedish Medical Association's heads followed their members' will. Time and time again, the association rejected the proposition that the Jewish doctors be allowed to practice in Sweden.

On the very next day another meeting was held that would echo throughout the country for a long time. Inspired by the young Nazis' torch procession in Stockholm and the Uppsala students' meeting, Lund's students were now holding a meeting to protest the suggestion that those ten medical specialists be sheltered in Sweden.

On March 6, the students gathered in Lund. Just as in Uppsala, they would hold a debate before agreeing on a resolution, so that their opinion would reach the public as a single thousand-person voice.

There were three blank votes. A vast majority, 731 people, voted against the refugees. The resolution stated, "an immigration bringing with it an unfamiliar element for our people to absorb seems dangerous to us and faced with the future, indefensible."

The *Kristiansbladet* newspaper kept their column-inches free for the most important matters and then some. They didn't merely report on estate auctions and publish rows of movie ads. Domestic matters and world news abounded every day. Otto and the other teenagers could partake in Alfred Rosenberg's speech regarding Germany's Jewish question, where the Reich leader stated that the tiniest concession could be interpreted as a sign of weakness and that the question could be considered resolved only when the very last Jew had left the country. They could read about Kurt Leeser in Nuremberg, who was sentenced to eight years in a house of correction for his love affair with an Aryan girl. In late March, a large photo of Samuel Eckstein's vandalized store was published under the headline "A Jewish

Store." On a cobbled street in Pressburg people were standing and staring silently at shattered windowpanes and destruction, with a caption stating that the Jews in Bohemia and Moravia were now in the same position as their racial kin in Germany. In Elise's hometown, Brno, Freedom Square was renamed.

Otto was asked about flowers and he'd answered positively. This meant getting away from the children's home and spending each afternoon in the greenhouse with the village gardener. The old man wasn't one for talk, but it didn't matter. Otto understood his actions better than his words; his rough hands showed him how it was done.

It was easier with the gardener's boy. Otto had already exchanged a Swiss postage stamp for a Swedish one with him. There'd be more, Otto promised. They'd meet again, the boy promised in return. They understood each other, those two philatelists.

And the girls. They didn't collect stamps but Otto understood them well enough, both of them. Their father, the gardener, let them be.

Dearest Otti. Today, Monday, is a holiday here in Vienna because it's the anniversary of the Anschluss. We won't receive any mail and all the stores are closed. The weather isn't quite holiday weather, it's cold and sometimes snows. But that isn't keeping me from writing a letter so that you can stay informed...

Uncle Karl and Berta called earlier today to say that they're going to Stockholm in one or two days, probably on Wednesday... A few days ago Sophie and Uncle Kassler also went away, but to Switzerland. We're going to end up being the last ones left—apparently no one wants us. But I won't allow myself to feel slighted. It's going to work out for me one day too . . .

There's one thing I've been wondering for a while: is there a movie theater in Tollarp or is the place too small for one? Write about what life is like for you, now that you've met the villagers. Your last letter has been forwarded so all who are curious can read it, as usual. Everyone praises your lovely handwriting and your exquisitely clever way with words. Keep it up.

Now you're becoming a good gardener, a good letter writer, a good soccer player. Short and sweet, everything you do is good. So you'll also do well in life even if now and then you encounter setbacks and disappointments. Those are inevitable in every person's life. All a person needs is the drive to succeed, and having certain skills, you will.

I'm convinced you'll strive to learn new things, so that one day you'll be a grown man. But luckily that takes its time. Everything that's happening now is nothing more than a playful preparation for life's true struggle, for which you are still too young and that you so far fortunately know nothing of. But it never hurts to remind yourself that alongside happiness and joy, life's pleasant sides, are other chapters. You yourself have had to leaf through a few of those along with us over this past year.

But enough seriousness, back to fun and games. Keep amusing yourself and being happy, not least over the fact that you can be a person among other people. Don't forget those who are less fortunate. We think about you all the time and are happy that you, thanks be, are well. We await new letters about your well-being. Don't make us wait too long.

dad

Dear child. Dad is having his English lessons so I'm taking the opportunity to write a few lines. Because he's already written so much, there isn't much for me to add. Your Swedish will be up to scratch soon, seeing as you can already speak to others. Otherwise there isn't much else to say. Dad has already said everything. I'm looking forward to your next letter. Thousand kisses and hugs.

mom

III

The Swedish government couldn't help but be influenced by the student meetings and the anti-Jewish resolutions, the Nazi demonstrations in Stockholm, the debate in the press, and the medical association's rock-hard resistance to offering their ten German colleagues asylum. On the contrary. The policies were debated in the Swedish Parliament in late February, apropos a suggestion about state support of the refugees' subsistence and education, and from the speaker's chair, ideas about Jews, Swedes, and the country's borders flowed freely.

In the upper chamber, the right-wing party leader warned of "unsuitable immigration," and a fellow party member repeated a recurring theme in the debate: "We are lucky enough not to have a Jewish problem in this country, but we must also be careful not to get one."

Many harshly criticized the Swedish policies being pursued, and some were upset by the students in Uppsala. The Social Democrat Östen Undén was one: "Many Swedes declare themselves completely free of anti-Semitism, but fear that this illness shall establish itself in others and spread, with all the implicit consequences, if a few thousand Jews enter the country. I for one believe that this fear of coming anti-Semitism is the very factor that most easily prepares the way for the anti-Semitic movement."

But Prime Minister Per Albin Hansson defended Sweden's stance. "It is necessary for our country to preserve a certain restrictiveness in its foreign policy, and this has also meant that one cannot say our country has in any way been put under strain or is overstrained because of its relationship to refugees."

Among the elected, in the Swedish Parliament's lower chamber, the tone was harsher. Axel Hansson of the Farmers' League, today's Center Party: "Most fitting in any case would be to try to get rid of these refugees as soon as possible."

"The suggestion of involving our agrarian population with a race perhaps quite alien to our own does not speak to me," said the conservative Karl Magnusson.

The liberal John Bergvall countered: "I must say, the attempts at riling up a storm around the refugee question stand in glaring contrast to the reality at hand. This reality is the severely restrictive refugee policy being pursued by the Swedish authorities."

The Social Democrat Allan Vougt: "To be sure, they do not comprise a specific 'race,' but one could rather speak of a population with a shared religion and certain uniform characteristics as a people . . . In my understanding it is a misjudgment of the entire refugee question to say that the refugees are draining rather than sustaining. Refugees are spoken of as though they were paupers instead of making clear that they are almost always in a position to create new enterprises and make work heretofore unavailable."

But the Farmers' League's Otto Wallén offered a response:

> It is always at our own expense and especially at the cost of our small businessmen, craftsmen, and small tradesmen

> that we allow them to remain. We do not want the difficulties we already have because of, for example, Jews and gypsies having acquired Swedish citizenship and homes here in the country, to be exacerbated... It is not possible to sit in Sweden and judge a question like the Jewish question, but to do so one should probably have lived for some time in the states where the question has been relevant for a good long while... I'll gladly admit, Mr. Speaker, without reservation that today I am an anti-Semite... Mr. Speaker, I do not have dubious motives, but I am Swedish. I want to state my main point, a point shared by many, even by the gentlemen's constituents, whatever you may think. It is shared by people from Malmöhus County, but even more by people from the county of Norrland.

The debate concluded with a motion to support the refugees being pushed through. But the government and responsible authorities were worried, very worried. How could they ease the flaring hatred of Jews, how could opinions be cooled? How could one assure the people that the refugee policy being pursued was not generous?

The solution was to thoroughly investigate the matter. If the black newspaper headlines were shouting "Jewish invasion," then the correct response was a dry table of facts. And so it came to pass that at this time the Swedish government issued a decree calling for all foreigners in the country to be counted.

Winter hesitated but chose to linger. The children from Vienna had unpacked their bags and were becoming accustomed to the home's prayer hours.

In Nazi Germany ten trained dentists, pharmacists, and doctors who also had work experience were seeking protection and residency in Sweden. The Swedish Board of Medicine wanted to invite them in. National opinion (thousands of people, the young) was opposed. Debates, demonstrations, resolutions, and waves of opposition intensified. And so came the Swedish authority's response: count the foreigners. This all happened in February.

A census was conducted once a decade, so the authorities did have a rough estimate—but now exact numbers were essential. It was designed to create the greatest possible effect. Or, one could also say, the greatest possible silence.

As the aim of the census wasn't really to count foreigners, but Jews, a few questions were added to the usual questionnaire. In addition to name, nationality, and faith, foreigners had to answer the following questions: "Jewish father?" and "Jewish mother?"

The whole thing was complemented with this instruction: "When answering this question please note the parents' heritage, irrespective if they are of Mosaic faith."

An open declaration of what the Swedish government wanted to find out: race.

The result of the census: "Of all foreigners, 3,420 can be characterized as Jews (father, mother, or both Jews)."

And national opinion was slightly calmed, the storm stilled, the burning fear of invasion not as acute.

III

Every morning, the same feeling. His body thought it was at home and waking up began with a millisecond of calibration. The language had to be adjusted to Swedish after a night of German dreams, he was no longer the focus of everyone's gaze and affection, but was now a child alone in a group, requiring of himself to be the most capable of all the orphans.

The day stretched out before him like a shallow sea, with its chores and writing hours. For write home he did. He knew how much they expected, and his great task—in addition to doing well, being liked, and working in the market garden—was to collect events to include in the letters, things that might spread joy and impart calm. Every day Otto waded in with his net. When he sat down for an hour in the afternoon he meticulously laid out his findings: unexpected benefits like the weather, a nice environment, a found ten-öre coin, an upcoming visit to the movie theater. He counted each smile directed his way and wrote about how the physical labor was making his arm muscles swell.

Otto was given oatmeal and hot chocolate every morning. Then Swedish lessons and prayer, after that various duties and a moment for letter writing in the afternoon. They tended to the rooms, and on Sundays they dressed in their finest clothing and combed their hair smooth, for that was when the local people came to choose which children they'd take home.

The youngest were chosen first. Then the girls left with foster parents. Perhaps they were like daughters in the family, but more often than not they became housekeepers. After that the fairest boys. Otto and a few others remained. Same thing every time.

And even though you couldn't put words to what happened, everything recalled something that had already taken place. Shut out from the others, shut in at the home. As if it were impossible to be born again, even after the long journey here. Otto was only thirteen and a half years old, but he recognized this experience. He'd experienced it before. Him, something else. Born Austrian, but not the genuine article. A dark element, a different vein. And now, in Sweden. Something that begins with *u*. Un-Swedish. Unusual. Always seeing himself through someone else's eyes. *U* as in always unsafe.

III

Vienna was slowly being emptied of certain people, above all of children and the young. Those who ended up staying in Austria and Germany were mostly poor, middle-aged, or older. The men became forced laborers and more and more families relied on welfare from the Jewish Community Council because they weren't allowed to work. People were driven from the countryside and into Vienna, where the Council was forced to feed twenty thousand people each day. Another ten thousand were given money for food.

Pepi, Elise, and Aunt Grete barely dared be seen outside. Instead they sat at home and did nothing, something, anything at all, thinking about everything they didn't want to be thinking about, weaving dreams from future threads, patching up the everyday with fantasies, hiding the flaws with daydreams.

> *Dearest Otti . . . There's nothing much happening here at home. Aunt Grete still has those holes in her vest. She believes the item of clothing to be an artifact of cultural heritage, and therefore it should not be mended. Otherwise she sings and caws with her usual enthusiasm. Only her German is losing its shine, since along with you, her opportunity to mix in Viennese slang has gone. In other words, she's a fine specimen. Incidentally she's decided to start shaving daily because her beard growth has*

accelerated—obviously in pace with her longing for you. This exceptional beard growth is, by the way, a trait she shares with other female family members. They're forever standing at the mirror plucking out hairs.

Write to my sister Grete in Taborstrasse. She is sick and always asks after you. Surely you can take on this task, can't you?

Your friends still stop by occasionally to ask after you, but also to play cards with your uncle and teacher, I suspect... That poor Milos. You can imagine what he's in for!

Diamant was supposed to have traveled to England yesterday, but at the last minute something was not in order and it all had to be pushed back a few days. The entire journey is taken using one and the same travel document and a few people in the group hadn't arranged for all of their documents. Now it's supposed to be done by Saturday, and then they'll go.

Speaking of documents, what about your passport? Do you have it with you, or is the home keeping it for you? You must take special care of that document because you'll need it for your next journey.

Now I've written too much again. The others want to write too, so I must stop. Stay handsome and keep your chin up, and write soon. A thousand kisses.

dad

Dear Otti. The best is always saved for last: I only need to write a few words because you already know you're all I think about. Take care of yourself and keep your spirits high. What is Edlauer doing? Are you still friends? Does he also play soccer? Dear sweetie pie. A thousand kisses.

Mutti

Lisl and Pepi kept returning to that same point in their restless worry. Every night, before they went to sleep, they met in a shared space of memory: the moment they let go of Otto's hands. The morning of February 1 was set in relief, and they cautiously approached it: the fraction of a second when they actually let him go. Then they'd watched how he walked out onto the platform, bag in hand, how he'd ascended those three steps and walked along the train's dark aisle. His half-adult body and their endlessly strong love.

Together they re-created the scene. The platform. The pigeons. The lunch bag. Otto's gaze. The guards in uniform. Otto's hand. The heaving train. The dark aisle. Their reluctant parting. How they wanted to send him away. The mission's Sister Martha looking friendly. The lamps. Otto's gaze. The shadow beneath their feet.

They opened the door to farewell, walked through it, pieced together what they each had seen so that in the end they pictured the same image and recalled the same memory. With a common will and a shared flow of love they could conjure their son for one flickering moment, like a hologram, a secret. And it kept their spirits high.

III

He'd arrived in Sweden on February 2. Just over twenty days had passed since then. What is it they say? One human year is equal to seven dog years?

Here, in the Skånish calendar, each day was a year. Twenty days were equal to twenty years: refugee years, a child-without-parents year. The days moved slowly but reached far.

Had he known any another place? He could hardly imagine it. And yet memories of the city, streets, and trees in a park charged through his mind like dreams after an uneasy night. Had he ever heard anything other than the square language foisted on him during morning lessons? That sometimes yielded, opened up. That he was expected to understand.

He and the other children in the home spoke German together. It sounded clear and cozy, like the pigeons cooing in the trees in the courtyard back home. It didn't matter what they said, or even how. Just that they were. They sang the Viennese song and it calmed them, grounded them, reminded him of old rooms with soft rugs where there was no border between thought and speech. But the grown-ups in charge didn't let him disappear in there. He grew tired. Mutti. Where are you?

But then Otto started to hear rumors: the sisters and pastors at the Swedish Israel Mission never intended to place him or the other boys in foster homes, there would never be a school with continued education. There was a shortage of workers in the countryside and Swedish farmers needed people. The boy who was saying this seemed to know what he was talking about, and his certainty shredded Otto's calm. He discovered that the mission had systems in place to lend out Jewish boys as manpower and that they had to do the hardest work without so much as being given a place to live. They had to sleep in stalls and sties together with the animals.

In pencil, he wrote an angry letter to Mutti and Dad, the people who'd sent him to this children's home, to stand in line to brush his teeth and to wear work overalls. The people who thought he'd be given a warm home and a sterling education. Who pushed him out of the street he grew up on, the warm spring walks through the city, the lessons in Latin and English with Paul, and into Skåne's slushy winter's end, early spring. Who had been dumb enough to allow themselves to be fooled.

February 24, 1939

Dear Otti. Today your letter from February 22 arrived. It was no fun at all to read because you were in such a mood. Most of all I think it's unfair to suggest that the Israel Mission tricked your mother. People don't do that here. Something different may have been decided in Stockholm that we are unaware of in Vienna, but for them to say one thing and know another to be true—that simply isn't the case.

Now to your big "accusation." . . . The purpose of placing you in the children's home has been made clear even to you. Here in Vienna you wouldn't have been able to do anything: neither study nor becoming anything at all. Out there you have the opportunity to gain knowledge and learn a trade, it doesn't really matter what kind. You'd need to study even if you get placed with a pair of foster parents one day. And you will, no matter what it says in your letter... You're very upset over a possible placement with a farmer. That your hard work will be exploited is, needless to say, not true. But still, reflect on this in peace and quiet: all, or more rightly said most, emigrants are forced to work on farms in their new country. Everyone must conquer the land in some way, but to do so one also must have knowledge. Say you become a "farmer"—and you would be a handsome one—then you'd have to learn everything you need to know.

If you think that boys your age in England are walking around doing nothing, you're mistaken. Either they have the language skills to attend school, and so are sitting at a school desk, or they go to farms to learn about working the land. That's what it's like in England, that's what it's like in Holland. In Palestine. And that's how it might be in Sweden, too, without necessarily having to worry about being humiliated... Learning the farmer's trade from the ground up will surely be interesting, and because you and your friends are not strong men and neither are you experienced, you won't be given the hardest tasks...

We're going to consult with the mission once more and I'm also going to ask Dr. Schwartz to turn to his acquaintances in Sweden on your behalf. But one thing is certain: in Sweden too, no matter who you are, you must work. No one can take upon themselves the great responsibility of allowing a fourteen-year-old boy to go unoccupied. So don't sulk, it won't be as your trusted source has said.

Surely the Swedes don't do that. They don't exploit children. You have to stop thinking that. As I said, what we've heard here is that you will be placed with foster parents and there's no reason to doubt these assurances.

So my dear boy, chin up. An Ullmann can't be crushed that easily. One can become despondent, as can we all, but then your will must guide you: the will to not let yourself be crushed. At present, there is no reason for you to suspect danger. Thankfully you're enjoying a free and beautiful life, and so shall it continue, no matter the work you're assigned.

I'm certain your next letter will contain better news. I'm signing off now, because a flood of letters was posted to you yesterday and you'll have more than enough to read. Everyone hopes you'll endeavor to answer them all—what a bother it is to have relatives! One thousand kisses.

your dad

Dear Otti—we've received your letter. And dad has already explained everything. I know my child and know that he is clever enough to realize that out in the world only his best is wished for. Right now you're imagining all the terrible things that can happen, but if you think about it you'll soon realize that things don't always turn out as you fear.

Once you've learned a little Swedish you'll most likely be placed with foster parents. Until then it's only natural for them to want to keep you occupied, and you can be sure the work won't be too exhausting for a boy of thirteen and a half. Don't be impatient and don't lose your temper, I hope your next letter will have a different tone. Dad and I would give anything and do any job we were offered, if we had the slightest chance of being where you are.

You'll receive some post today or tomorrow. And answering it all will give you plenty to do. If I can, I'll send you stationery. A thousand kisses.

Mutti

Dear Otti. Ernst and Utas say that anything is better than Greek grammar. Warm greetings.

Paul

Who is a fool, who has been fooled? Without knowing it, both Otto and his parents were right, even though they held opposing positions. The idea of placing Otto and the twenty other Viennese children in a children's home was for them to then move on to private homes, and maybe also attend elementary school, if their stay in Sweden dragged on.

But the journalist Josef Ullmann should have put more trust in his correspondent son's sources. The truth was that most of the private homes that contacted Pastor Pernow about the children wanted only girls. They wanted cheap child care and domestic help, preferably combined with gratitude and a small appetite. And the demand continued to exceed the supply. Pastor Birger Pernow and his colleagues at the mission received letter upon letter like this one: "Brother! It is going well with our Jewish girls in Ljusdal, and I think they are getting on well. Now there's a woman in Ljusdal—a forest ranger's home—who's wondering if they too could have a Jewish girl—around the age of twelve or thirteen."

Foreign, dark, teenage boys, big in appetite, small in muscle power, were undesirable. Thirteen-year-old Otto and his parents couldn't know that they'd landed in the midst of this worry. But just a few weeks before Otto sent his bitter letter to Mutti and Dad, Pastor Pernow himself had expressed concern about the matter in one of his many letters: "If only I could receive applications from 8–10 homes, preferably for boys, the entire question could be considered solved. The sad fact is that all homes with the exception of circa 10 are requesting girls, wherefore it seems to be rather difficult to place the boys."

Sometimes he found solutions. Sometimes they disappeared before they could be realized. In one of many letters from good Christians in January and February 1939, Pernow received, among other things, greetings from Fjugesta: "Regarding a Jewish boy. When Dr. Karl F wrote to me, I thought I might have use for a young man in the barn. He who now occupies this position had intended to move in the spring. Upon inquiring how long he means to stay, I found he'd changed his mind and has now decided to remain until fall, therefore I am not in the position to oblige your request. As far as placing Jews in this region goes, the outlook is not good."

What the farmer in Närke had expressed applied not only to his region—thirteen-year-old Otto in Skåne could also have confirmed that, and his savior Pastor Pernow in Stockholm would have concurred. The sentiment applied to the entire country: for placing Jews in any region, the outlook was not good.

Otto did his best. Smiled, learned the words, kept himself neat and tidy. But no foster parents chose him, no school of higher education was opening its doors. Instead the cold water chapped his hands. He was shown behind the greenhouse, where there were large empty pots to be cleaned, pitchforks and snow shovels. That's what an apprentice is for. His arms ached. And in order to learn, he had to follow behind the rough old man's slow hocks like a child.

The private lessons he'd had, the plentiful homework he'd obediently completed in the evenings, his quick intellect and gift for language—everything seemed for naught. But he knew anger wasn't part of the rescue plan, that the words he was expected to repeat were "thank you." So just as he collected stamps, meticulously organized in an album, he arranged his injustices, suffered, and seethed.

February 25, 1939

My dear child, having read your latest note I understand that everything isn't going as you want it to. I can relate, and I know you well. If you were here, we'd talk through it in peace and quiet, but now I'm writing to you instead.

You know, darling, you happen to be in a free, healthy country that has hospitably taken you in and in a truly noble fashion has done everything to offer you children a free life. This is apparent in all your letters thus far. Now you've become impatient. Why? Because you imagined being with foster parents, and that's not possible at present. Here I've been told that you must learn a little Swedish first, otherwise you won't be able to communicate.

I'm convinced that you've already rediscovered your good humor, and all this was because your friend's down-heartedness rubbed off on you. Don't ever let yourself be influenced by other people. If you think about it, you'll realize that you have it better than all the children who have to stay here. Demner just said that he'd really like to be in your position, and would very much like to work with a Swedish farmer. You know that Dad and I, if we were out there, would take the hardest work upon us even if we were unaccustomed. Unfortunately we live in a time when life is not good, but thankfully our bodies and souls are in good health and will endure.

You are a clever boy. I know you. You are honest and fair and you're going to realize that they mean well. In other words, your next letter will once again be full of humor. Then we'll be delighted along with all the others who read your letters. Because Werner also wants to write, I'll end here and kiss you a thousand times.

Mutti

Dear Otti—I've heard you got it in your head that you don't have it good, but I can only tell you that I'd be happy if I had what you have. Let me tell you, there will be no trip to England for me, apparently. I'll probably have to start school because I haven't passed eight classes. Milos says that there are only a few students in school now. Professor Klein is very nice!!!!!!!!! I don't think it's fair to leave when you still have debts, either. That's it for today, with warm greetings.

your devoted Georg

Dear Mucki pucki. Today you only get a thousand kisses and greetings.

Aunt Gretel

You don't know how good you have it. You don't have to play cards with Werner and Milos. I get so irritated. Warm greetings.

Paul

There is no room left for me on the page. Greetings and kisses.

Aunt Nuny

Otto felt sorry. He thought about everything that had been at home being elsewhere and how what was called "home" here, the children's home, was alien. About how when he changed places, the words changed, too.

Sometimes he forgot what he was supposed to keep in mind. Like the tailor he'd visited almost every day on his way home from school and who'd always chatted with him about the results of that day's game and practice, how the day after the Anschluss that very tailor had put swastika flags on his motorcycle. How smug he was, waiting for Otto's reaction, and how he'd laughed. At him. Not with him.

Otto wasn't convinced that the boy who'd told him the lay of the land was wrong. But he didn't want to cause trouble. All they could do back home was lie awake at night and worry. He decided to solve the problem himself.

Otto wrote a short letter to Dad and Mom, Aunt Nuny and Paul, Aunt Grete and his friends, because he knew they'd all read his previous letter and would read this one as well: his prayer for forgiveness.

February 27, 1939

Dear boy. Saying that you would endure anything for our sake has moved us deeply. But believe me, the only big sacrifice we and you have made is parting. All else is meaningless considering that you were able to trade this monotonous and, to you, completely worthless, yes utterly harmful, life here for an existence in a better country, where you have everything.

Surely all is not as you wished it would be. But under the circumstances the old saying "There's no place like home" does not apply. Because nowadays, it's better to be anywhere but here—and you must tell yourself this, again and again…

In your letter from the 25th, you describe what happens when foster parents select children. But at the moment you all still seem to be there, because you're speaking of twenty children? If foster parents care about appearances, you will surely be singled out, because if you take care of yourself you'll certainly be able to compete with the other children . . . A thousand kisses.

your loyal dad

Darling, your letter made us very happy. I know what a good, solid core my boy has. By the way I'm curious about your surprise. A thousand kisses.

Mutti

Dear Ottel—you asked if I'm still working as a teacher. I can't complain that I lack students. My youngest pupil is little Löwi, and my oldest, as of tomorrow, will be Reichsrat Mazarek, who is seventy years old and practically deaf. I don't know if you've met Mr. Bernstein, he now sees me for two and a half hours, and says that studying is his greatest joy (just like you). I'll finish here, because your father can hardly contain himself before his next English lesson. Warm greetings.

Paul

Dearest Mucki pucki. It delights me to hear of your diligence. What a shame I can't watch you work. A thousand greetings.

Aunt Grete

Those Sunday afternoons with farmers choosing their manpower were never quite the same again. As soon as they could, Otto and his friend Gerhardt left their room. They interrupted the grown-ups. They picked their noses, kept their hair mussed. They made sure not to be chosen. Soon they'd turn fourteen and in no way did they want to be farmhands sleeping among the animals.

III

Pastor Pernow was in constant epistolary contact with his colleagues in Vienna and with all the families who requested, had, or wanted to exchange foster children.

In the remaining documentation of the pastor's laborious work, schooling is hardly mentioned. The idea was, of course, that children were only to stay temporarily. Moreover it was understood that these children had been saved and therefore were indebted. The youngest were allowed to go to school, but the older ones, from thirteen years of age upward, were to do right by themselves. In a Sweden suffering from a shortage of farm workers, the country's large southern agricultural region became their new home, physical labor being one way to reciprocate.

The children from the home in Hemhult weren't only going to learn Swedish; skilled people were also brought in to instruct them in, for example, horticulture and flower arrangement. Otto learned how to make bouquets and corsages, which he sent to Vienna as gifts along with the promised surprise.

Dear Otto, Just as you can only write letters twice a week, I've decided to write you on Wednesdays. That's why I'm only now thanking you for the boutonniere. I like it very much. Even Mrs. Hanse is enchanted—and that's not bad, because she is very good at assembling bouquets. I've chosen the black-and-white one because it fits better with my coat and dress.

In your latest letter I can see that you've developed an interest in girls. Three declarations of love—that's a bit much. Is the girl good-looking at least?

Many greetings and kisses.
Aunt Nuny

He was in love again. But chosen he was not.

III

Sudety, Kraj sudetów, Sudenteland. Beloved countries have many names.

Bohemia, Moravia and Silesia, Saxony and Bavaria were relics from a time before national borders, when the world was instead divided into regions of land, of language, of culture. As long as the grand Austro-Hungarian monarchy reigned, they were all part of the same German-speaking sphere. But after the Great War, after the Treaty of Versailles…

The maps of Europe became useless when the borders were redrawn. Hungarian speakers landed outside of Hungary's borders, Romanian-speakers outside of Romania's, German-speakers outside of Germany's. Order?

No order.

Chancellor Hitler knew how to speak so that those on the other side of the border wanted to cross over. But they weren't going to leave the land they'd cultivated, their fertile native soil. Instead he was going to make sure to move the border. A state with limited space is doomed, survival is only possible with expansion, that was the logic. Make a bid for the East. Long for the East. Take, fight, push east. *Drang nach Osten.*

Like unseen air currents, ideas about land, country, nation streamed forth, finding the gaps in people's senses. Some, such as Herren Hess, Himmler, and Hitler, acted as wind catchers and kept it blowing, guiding its direction.

The farmer was worshipped. He was the nation's soul and marrow. Living a sound life. He could tell the difference between what was important and what was not, between well-established village life and the disorganized big city. The farmer was a man, and he tilled his land. Watered by beads of sweat, blood mixing with earth, and the fruits that burst forth were as if born of his strong body.

When Hitler was in prison struggling with his book, he wrote: "Never forget that the most sacred right in this world is the right to that earth which a man desires to till himself, and the most sacred sacrifice that blood which a man spills for this earth."

So, the Sudetenland: almost three million German-speakers who according to the peace treaty following the First World War were now a restive part of Czechoslovakia. Three million people who wanted to see Germany expand across the border and claim them as their territory. They pinned their hopes on Chancellor H.

Intrigues and plans were puzzled out in secret rooms. One Nazi by the name of Henlein was to represent those three German-speaking millions, to turn to the Czechoslovak government and demand independence for the region as well as the freedom to practice Nazism. If they said yes, then the Sudeten Germans could be part of Germany. If they said no (of course they were going to say no), well...

Chancellor H coolly counted on France not going to war over this snippet of land, and that it didn't want to stand alone against Germany. He was sure that Great Britain wanted peace at all costs. He knew that Mr. Chamberlain actually thought the wish for unification was reasonable and guessed that the British prime minister trusted him when he said that was all he wanted—for Sudetenland to become German. After that, nothing more.

Chamberlain returned from Germany with his faculties of sight intact. No doctor's examinations exist that might attest otherwise. And yet he was blind. He stepped out of his airplane at Heston Aerodrome on September 30, 1938, brandishing a document. That very morning he'd spoken with Chancellor H and secured his signature on an agreement stating that Germany's unification with the Sudetenland would be peaceful. The prime minister waved the paper in front of cheering crowds and the press, and then repeated the performance later that day outside the door at 10 Downing Street.

"I believe it is peace for our time."

The next day the chancellor's troops marched into the Sudetenland.

It was a day of joy, of celebration and coffee parties. At least in the gray-white wooden house, known as "the big house" on Elmtaryd farm in Agunnaryd, near Älmhult in Småland. Those celebrating offered the guests wheat bread, cakes, coffee and cream. No one had ever seen Fanny Kamprad this excited, she was never usually this generous. Something quite special must've happened, that was clear, despite her heavy German accent. Finally her Adolf had made good on his promise, what she and her relatives over there had hoped and prayed for those many impoverished years. Finally he'd made sure they were no longer scattered, like strangers in another country, finally they were one with their nation—and that, if anything, was well worth the very best coffee party. Grossmutter Fanny's prayers had been answered.

The leaders of Great Britain, France, and Italy had chosen to believe Chancellor H when he promised not to lay claim to any other part of Europe. They'd agreed to his annexation of the German-speaking part of Czechoslovakia. They'd believed him when he promised that he would thereafter respect Czechoslovakia's borders. Five months had passed since then, five months and one coffee party, and now the chancellor didn't give a damn about these promises.

On March 15, 1939, German troops occupied the rest of Czechoslovakia. The Western part was declared a German protectorate and incorporated into the German Reich. Slovakia, the eastern part, became a self-governing state allied with Germany.

That same day Pepi wrote to his son. It was 10:30 in the morning, one year to the day since he'd lost his job as the sports editor at *Wiener Tag* because of the blood-tie statutes and the race card's intricate line work, borders drawn between human and human.

March 15, 1939

Today we were disappointed and saddened because there was no mail, but we hope some might arrive later. By the way Mrs. *Edlauer didn't get a letter from her son either—that is to say, it probably has more to do with the mail. I'm not sure either when you receive our letters.*

At present, tensions between Czechoslovakia and Germany have arisen again—maybe you've heard about it over there, too, and according to the mailman the trains aren't as regular as before... I can only hope that it will all blow over and we'll be able to continue being in uninterrupted contact...

We can think of nothing but the delayed post; we hope you are still healthy and no other circumstances are causing the hang-up of your letters. We know you take care of yourself, not just for your own sake, but also for ours, because we don't want to have to worry about you in these difficult times when so many terrible things are befalling us...

In a few weeks Josef Ullmann would turn forty-six. He sat at the wide table by the window. It was snowing outside and the day was so dark he considered lighting the lamp. He noted that it was frightful and cold. In the middle of the room was the ottoman with the indents in the center of the seat cushion that the whole family blamed on Aunt Grete. In one corner of the room was still Otto's bookcase with its adventure stories and schoolbooks, their order undisturbed. And yet Josef wrote to his son that everything was as usual. Perhaps he refused to believe anything else. He called the annexation of Czechoslovakia "new circumstances." And then the incantation that would be drowned out by more than a thousand news reports: "I can only hope that it will all blow over."

March 16, 1939

Dearest Otti. Your letter finally arrived today and eased our worry. Because of the new circumstances, of which you over there are probably already aware, train services are somewhat interrupted for the time being. In addition, snowstorms and snow obstructions have led to delays. But the important thing is that your letter has now arrived, and once again we are put at ease...

It really is lovely, what you're doing right now. Gardening work is excellent. To begin with it will do your body good, not to mention its practical value... How long do you work? I'm assuming you're only there mornings, or do you also work afternoons? Do tell us about it in your next letter. What do the others at the home do? Do they not work? We assume that everyone is kept a little busy. Whatever the case, gardening work is a good thing.

Have you already made the acquaintance of many Swedish boys? I see that you've had good contact with them. In any case your Swedish will get better if you socialize together...

Mutiny on the Bounty *is indeed a big movie. I'm sure you found it very entertaining. The actors and the scenography are excellent. Surely you'll go to the movies more often now, which is a nice change for you. Did you all go together?...*

Keeping homesickness at bay is no easy task, neither should you. If you spend years living in one place, with your family and your friends, knowing each tree, each house, each stone, well then you can't simply throw it all away like trash and say that it's over. Neither can you forget all the happy moments. Remember the happy days you've shared with us, with God's will they will soon return, but you also have to think sober thoughts. This soothes the pain of separation.

But you're familiar with these thoughts: the impossibility of young people living here and becoming anything, the impossibility for us to develop and get somewhere in this world. Your having to leave us behind was painful, but necessary. And right now, in these days, we are twice as happy that we managed to give you a more beautiful country, where you might not be with your parents and friends, but you are a free person and are finding yourself in a community in which you are liked. What a big difference there is between your life out there and the life your friends have here! This difference alone—you can go to the movies, whereas they are not allowed—shows how unfavorable the living conditions are here.

So continue to think about us, as we think of you daily. Think about how at the moment it's better to not be where we are. We will be reunited one day. We just have to bravely suppress the feelings closest to our hearts, namely our longing for each other, and tell ourselves that the separation was necessary.

And even with a sea between us, we will not forget each other, we will always think of each other until the day we have a shared home and a shared life again. Maybe then we'll be living in a little house in a foreign country and, thanks to the skills you've acquired, you'll be able to tend to our garden.

In other words—the most important thing now is to endure! And you will, because I know you. Dearest boy . . . a thousand kisses.

your loyal dad

The most important thing is to endure.

Seventy-one years after that day in March when Pepi finished his lengthy letter—seventy-one years after he sat at that wide table where Otto had sat so many times and written, played cards or games—I read his words and wonder if he was addressing his thirteen-year-old son or himself.

This too shall pass.

That same dark and snowy morning, the day after Germany occupied Czechoslovakia, Paul and Aunt Nuny wrote to Otto, as well. They did what they could to leave out the violence and reality of the world.

My dear Ottel. You can't imagine how happy your letter from the 13th made us, which because of certain political events arrived after some delay. It is a true joy for you to be introduced to one of the finest professions, where you can be out in the fresh air all day long, be close to nature and watch plants grow from seeds to fruit day by day.

As for me, unfortunately I have only a theoretical interest in gardening work but diligently read articles in the English publications that cover it. So I have recently read that it is of the utmost importance to vegetables—so that they may grow—that their seeds be sown during a waxing moon.

Don't think that everything you've studied has now become superfluous. You simply don't yet know what use you will have for it later. Aside from that, your studies have made you into an intelligent young man who stands apart from others his age.

You, you lucky duck, get to go to the movies, something forbidden to us here. Moreover you can see such high-class films as Mutiny on the Bounty. *Unfortunately, we have missed that one.*

Of your friends, only Werner and Milos stop by. The latter has learned to play cards. Poor Ernst must still suffer Latin and Greek, and some days I only have time for him in the evening because I'm busy giving English lessons during the daytime.

My dear boy. Today I've been able to devote a little extra time to you. Even if I don't write often, you can be sure that I have preserved my love and loyalty for you and that I haven't forgotten you, and will never forget you. With very warm greetings.

Paul

Sweet and dear Otti. Dear because it is for you that I am affixing a 40-pfennig stamp on this letter, so you can have a complete set of stamps.

Ever since Paul received your letter, he has gone around with a long face. First of all because he isn't allowed to go to the movies and secondly because you are busy working with flowers in the greenhouse, while he has to try to teach people English. Until now you've only had us to tease—I'm glad you now can tease the flowers as well.

Tant Hansi and her husband have been living with Mrs. Reiner since April 1. Eva Rakover is leaving for England at the end of the month. Otherwise there is no news. The weather is miserable, but even when the weather is fine I'm always at home or nearby. Greetings and kisses.

Aunt Nuny

Now the Czech Jews were being persecuted as well. Anti-Jewish laws stripped them of their rights as citizens. Their property was confiscated. Synagogues vandalized. People of Jewish heritage were harassed, attacked on the streets, and arrested.

At home in Löwengasse 49 the everyday rolled along in a manner both ancient and new. Everything had changed yet everything was the same. People maneuvered in the gap between the two. The rest of the family tried to put out of their minds that the boy, their Otto, was elsewhere. At least that thought could be controlled. Sometimes. But daily life. Too much had happened, and now nothing was happening; they couldn't decide if this was a good or bad sign. They paced around the rooms. They ate little. They took short walks to the post office around the corner. They returned to the house. They paced around the rooms. They waited for the mailman.

Pepi wrote: "You know how it is. In the morning you hear sounds from Aunt Grete's room, then in the kitchen, where our 'ladies' converge to talk about the shopping list or proclaim that they do not share the same opinion. Then unfortunately I must get up, even though I would so very much like to stay in bed. The rooms are cleaned to song, and with Aunt Grete and Nuny's wonderful voices it can sound very good indeed."

Otto used to partake in this kitchen discussion, but now his voice, which had "always chimed in," was missing. Instead the adults tried to shoulder the child's role, all alone.

Pepi would then take a seat at the table in front of the compact black typewriter and write letter upon letter. Each day to his son, and then endlessly to friends, acquaintances of acquaintances, contacts he'd made through his work as a journalist. If there was an opening, he wanted to find it.

Elise darned socks. Nuny was always there, sharing meals, the aimlessness, the eternal conversations about who had gotten their children out and who had failed, the daily accounting of who was packing their suitcases and how they'd discovered that loophole. Paul was the one who still had a job because many people who were waiting for the possibility of leaving the country now needed to learn English. Now and then Otto's old friends, Utas and Milos, came over for a hand of cards. And so others in the vicinity came to visit, visits during which parents read letters aloud to each other, compared the children's handwriting, ways of expressing themselves, and experiences. Was England better, was the food more abundant in Sweden, how hard did they have to work in Palestine? What was it like in Shanghai?

Mitzi was forced to quit as their housekeeper and find other work because Jews were not allowed to employ so-called Aryans, but still she visited faithfully each day. As though everything were as usual. Lisl and Pepi could no longer afford to pay her salary, and so their roles shifted. Mitzi was now the one who had more. She could move about freely. Her ration card provided her with more and better goods. The card was not pale pink and patterned with hundreds of printed red letters that formed the word "Jew." She was the one who could walk into stores where they were forbidden to shop, and she was the one who shared the food packages sent by her parents in the countryside. She was no longer the one who was grateful.

Otto might have been getting used to things. His days were filled with the children's home's routines and rules, although the line for the outhouse was shorter now that there were fewer children. He did an apprenticeship. He knew that he could only make the best of the situation. The market garden was large and had an endless number of pots that needed the old clay and roots scrubbed out of them. Changing the soil. Planting bulbs. Three hours in the morning and two in the afternoon.

"Discontent" was not the word for it, but neither was "content." There were his memories of the streets, trees, and family in Vienna, and in contrast there was the tangible fact of his daily life in Skåne. Only one of the two could be obscured.

March 23, 1939

Dear Ottel. As always it made me very happy to hear that you're doing well—which comes as no surprise if you get to go to the movies with girls, who presumably are attractive. Does the girl understand you when you speak English? Do you understand her? So in other words, you cultivate flowers in the morning and girls in the afternoon.

Milos and Werner still visit us, and as far as Milos's ban on playing cards, we've found a solution. We play anyway.

We are all very curious about how you will fare as a tap dancer. I think you shall be quite the sensation. Farewell for today, dear boy. Think of us. Greetings.

Paul

March 23, 1939

Dearest Otti. Today the mailman walked right past our door again. It makes us a little sad, but we aren't worried because we know from your letters that you don't always have time and energy, and that you can be too tired to write. But I hope that we will soon receive your lovely letters again, they bring us joy. Wherever they are shared, they never fail to impress because you write with such humor, intelligence, and so well. The only occasional criticism I have is that your letters are not detailed enough. But if you had a bit more time, surely you'd fix that, wouldn't you?

There is nothing new on our end. Yesterday Helleberg, Burchi's dad, took his farewell. Today he travels to Switzerland and then on to England. When Harry Schein is leaving, I'm not sure. He hasn't said anything to us. I presume you're not particularly interested in him, but he may well contact you once he's out of the country . . . A thousand kisses.

your dad

As a younger boy Otto had picked up chestnuts from the ground in autumn and filled his pockets with them to bring home to Lisl. She'd put them in a bowl on the dining table; they were heavy, shiny, and just as cool as the ground on which they'd lain. It was always the same. The very next day they'd lost their shine and begun to wither. And even though he knew that the wrinkles were, in a way, lying in wait beneath that shimmering hull, it was impossible to imagine them. Like imagining hunger when you are full. Or your parents being powerless.

One of the head gardener's daughters was also thirteen years old. She and her sister helped make his workdays more tolerable.

March 25, 1939

. . . Today I will tell you about a milestone. You are now in possession of our fiftieth letter. That's how long you've been gone already. But time flies by. I must say, I've been the more diligent one. I've written every day, whereas you've been leaving plenty of "air" lately. Today we waited in vain for the mailman again . . . We hope that he will arrive with a letter from you during his second round or in the afternoon.

Not receiving any mail is rather unpleasant. One so wishes to know what that dear Wuzi is up to, if he really has lost weight or if that was just an empty threat. One wants to know if work in the garden is a pleasure heightened by the presence of the head gardener's two daughters. If the cinema is nice and how the people in Tollarp relate to handsome boys from Vienna—you are among them. One so wishes to know both this and that, but one hears nothing, for mail has been so scarce... Have you really had so much to do?

Hurrah! Just now, around 11:30, the mailman arrived with your letter from the 23rd, which says at least that you are healthy.

Poor boy. You're tired. I understand. But surely it will get better once your muscles have real strength. We don't want to feel sorry for you because we imagine that everything you're doing will be useful to you at some point in the future. Do tell us right away if the head gardener is a younger or older man. Because he has two daughters around your age he must be like me, is he not? Perhaps you could send us a photo of the entire garden and its contents. That is, including Wuzi? Is that possible?...

Harry Schein is still here. The transport has been delayed again. But he is hoping to get away this March...

Dear boy. Mom is already at my side and wants to write. She is forever scolding me for taking up all the space, but as far as I can see she's doing just fine with what I leave her. It doesn't really matter if I happen to write a bit more. A thousand kisses.

dad

March 28, 1939

Dearest Otti. We're not expecting any post today because there never is any on Tuesdays. But you will have your daily dose even if there isn't anything to say. The weather is bad, it's raining but warm. It's the kind of weather that justifies staying indoors . . .

Today, at this very moment, Harry Schein is with us. He has procured a Swedish visa and is not waiting for a transport, but will attempt to travel alone. He thinks he can leave Vienna in the next days. I'll keep you posted. In any case, once he's gotten out, he'll surely write to you. I've already mentioned that he's going to Uppsala . . .

We hope your workload has not increased. Three hours in the morning and two in the afternoon isn't that much . . . You know we'd prefer to have you here, but now all the young people are wishing themselves away. And the parents wish to find a place overseas for their children. Nothing is happening here—and I mean nothing at all. For people your age it's destructive, they can do nothing, are left to rot and ruin. You couldn't have it as good here as you have it there. And that is why we satisfy ourselves with thinking of you. For the moment it's all we can do. We are happy that at least someone in the family has it better and can perhaps make something of his life . . . Now we have only one wish, and that is to see each other again. But that time will surely come. Be happy and healthy. A thousand kisses.

dad

Dear Otti. Tomorrow I shall be happy again if your letter arrives. Everyone is gone but Egon and Kurt, only the parents remain. But something will come for us one day.

We just have to be patient. My treasure. A thousand kisses.

Mutti

April 1, 1939

My dearest boy . . . We're sorry to hear that work has tired you out so, and hope you aren't overexerting yourself. It's not something you're used to, but we hope that the fatigue will yield after a while. I'm sorry I can't help you, but as you know that's impossible for now. We must hope for better times . . .

Harry Schein has already arranged a ticket to Uppsala and will travel to Sweden on his own in the next few days. Of late, that poor boy has been standing in line for hours at the district office on Seitenstettengasse to procure the ticket, and he was starting to look drawn. But he is energetic and managed in the end. He intends to travel early next week.

III

How familiar and yet strange it was to read about life back home, that all was as before. Only without him. Otto received reports of how Aunt Mina's fox terrier was playing with his old heavy rubber ball, the one he used to call a soccer ball, and how the dog went bonkers when the ball landed on his snout.

How could this continue without him? How could he be here at the children's home next to the beech forest, surrounded by dark brown fields and gravel roads somewhere far away from trams and exhaust fumes—how could he be here without everything over there grinding to a halt, losing its dimensions, becoming shadow play and silhouettes?

Longing for the dog overcame him, longing for the ugly bowl, for the rug's snarling fringe, for Mutti's irritation when he made a mess—no, don't think about Mutti, just the dog, how the water splashed when it drank from the bowl in the stairwell and how Mitzi would wipe up after it—no, don't think about Mitzi.

The letters that arrived every day were both a lifeline and barbed wire, reunion and farewell; first they made him happy and then he grew tired and he simply couldn't fit it all in. Aunt Mina's fox terrier wasn't something he wanted to read about at all, that's how much he longed to lie on the floor running his fingers through her rough fur.

Dearest Otti. Tomorrow is mail day. Then I shall be waiting for the mailman first thing in the morning. Otherwise it's really rather boring here, and I wish I could have one of your unruly days, so that things would be a little more lively. One day you will be so well mannered that you won't be able to irritate me anymore. That's how times change. I'd very much like to scold you again, but that time will come, and I look forward to it. Then, we won't have enough time to fill each other in on all that's happened. Dearest. We are hoping for mail tomorrow. Many greetings and kisses.

mother

April 5, 1939

. . . Tonight Harry Schein will travel alone to Uppsala. He has noted your address and will write to you from Uppsala when he arrives. Then you will have at least one of the lot up there. He is very happy to finally be getting away, and looks terrible. But I'm convinced he will recover up there.

III

In 1939 the chancellor made a total of twenty-four long speeches, roughly two per month. April was no exception. On the twenty-eighth he stood before a uniformed Reichstag and spoke in response to a letter from Franklin D. Roosevelt, in which the American president made a plea for nonviolence, nonaggression—well, nonwar.

Chancellor H: "Finally, Mr. Roosevelt asks that assurances be given him that the German armed forces will not attack, and above all, not invade, the territory or possessions of the following independent nations. He then names as those coming into question: 'Finland, Lithuania, Latvia, Estonia, Norway, Sweden, Denmark, the Netherlands, Belgium, Great Britain, Ireland, France, Portugal, Spain, Switzerland, Liechtenstein, Luxembourg, Poland, Hungary, Romania, Yugoslavia, Russia, Bulgaria, Turkey, Iraq, the Arabias, Syria, Palestine, Egypt, and Iran.'"

The collective laughter from the crowd of men in the German Reichstag increased with each country that was named, it filled the Reichstag building in Berlin and spread with the speed of ether to every living room and kitchen where the radio was switched on.

Today the Führer gave a speech. Whatever the case, we are happy that war has not broken out. How terrible it would be for us if we couldn't correspond with you. But at the same time we're happy you aren't here in these critical days. Whatever happens, you are probably safer abroad, safer than here at least. And whatever happens, we trust you, and that you will manage until we see each other again. One must consider life's every eventuality, for one can never know how things might develop.

The edge of the winter melted into spring. Otto picked cowslip in a glade, pressed and sent them home, a flower for each and every one, with hope that they'd bring luck.

When it got warmer, the children from the home went down to the creek. They shielded each other with towels when they changed, just as they'd always done at home, one holding the towel around the other as their clothes came off. The water received their pale bodies. The surface was broken by breast strokes. Afterward, biscuits and bottles of juice from the basket.

A handful of children in the water one summer's day, the children in the sun afterward. The scene could easily be described as a happy moment on a good day. No wonder sadness followed.

Eyes shut, Otto lay on the creek's bank, the sun bright and hot above him, coloring the world beyond his eyelids pale red. If he kept his eyes closed, listened to the other children's familiar Viennese dialect, pushed away the thought of the past year, recent times, the train journey, the starving back home, the farewell, what happened on Mom's birthday—then he could find his way to a day gone by on another bank, only a year ago, but also an eternity away.

How could he write about the hot sun, the green Vrams Creek flowing past? How could he get them to understand what this was like, feeling grief alongside joy?

Vienna, May 26, 1939

My dearest boy. Yesterday I left the house after I'd written to you and then we received your letter which rendered the content of mine in part superfluous. I was only able to read your lines in the evening and so wanted to reply posthaste.

First and foremost I want to thank you warmly. Not just I, but everyone here at home along with the others who read your letter were touched. You conjured the memory of the Otto we hold so dear. Not just a good boy, but also a boy full of emotion. And—as I always write—we miss you. As I read your words, my longing becomes almost unbearable, I'm not ashamed to admit it. But then I read about you bathing in the creek, about the sun, about the pleasure of being able to eat fruit, and then I am once more calmed and gladdened that in these dire times there is still so much you can do that others your age cannot . . .

At first it might seem unpleasant to wake up as early as six in the morning, but now it's already the end of May, and it's light outside. When one has gotten used to getting up early the fresh morning air has a better effect than one might first imagine. Needless to say this is no comfort, and I do feel very sorry for you, you poor thing, who must get up so early. But I hope you've already grown accustomed to it. Tell me how things are. What is it that you do in the mornings? Work only begins at nine a.m., isn't that so?

Don't reproach yourself for not having written to us for a few days. We may have worried, but now that we know the reason why, we have been put at ease. We completely understand that you are tired. We also do not want you to be sitting inside writing during your free time, when the weather is fine. But we have a suggestion. When you have much to do, write us a card. A few words will suffice, as long as we can hear that you are doing well. We'll understand that you have lots to do, that you are tired and didn't have the energy to write more. Think nothing more of it. We are grateful for your latest letter, which travels from hand to hand. Even Mr. Götz will receive it—perhaps he'll use it in his book because it is so good—and we look forward to the next one.

As I said earlier, on the one hand I long for you intensely and am sad that you're not here with us; on the other hand, I'm happy. For when I read of you eating fruit and tomatoes and so forth, then I can only say that you have it better out there, across the border. There is hardly any fruit here and if you find it, it's too dear. Neither are vegetables easy to obtain. You, and everyone else who has gotten out, have unimaginable advantages compared with life here...

When I read your memory from that lovely time we all bathed in the sun together in Ischl, I am deeply moved. Back then there wasn't even the thought of parting and sending you away to a foreign place. But today we realize it was necessary: We wanted you to be well, for you not to experience this discomfort, all the degradation and pain. You know that.

It was especially good that you were able to get to another country right at the time in your life when you became such a handsome boy, both attentive and clever—but also vulnerable in thought and emotion and sensitive to indignity. A new country, yes, and alien to you, but with people who are so good and decent that it doesn't feel alien.

And however sad it is to have to say this, it must nonetheless be repeated: We hold you too dear and love you far too much to be so egotistical as to keep you here in Vienna.

We're happy you are a free person, and I'm sure the time will come for us to be reunited. Hopefully we will lie in the sun next to each other again and delight in life.

You've made new experiences, you've arrived in a foreign place and become independent. If it so happens that you think about the moment we said goodbye, there at the Ostbahnhof, I can only say that we do, too.

We cried from the pain of parting, but there was joy in our hearts. And as we cried and waved you off, we said to ourselves: there he goes, our sweet boy, to a better country and a better future. And hopefully that's how it will be. We wish for nothing today but to see you very soon again and that you will remain in good health. So take care of yourself, when you eat fruit and when you swim. A thousand kisses and greetings.

your loyal dad

PS. Grete is enclosing stationery for you, so that you can write to her sometime, too. She hasn't changed at all. She's just as batty as before.

III

The letters between Vienna and Sweden came and went like white windows. The adults looked out and saw everything they were missing. Otto caught glimpses of a life remarkably like the one he had until recently been living, but that no longer was his. Pepi insisted on calling Aunt Grete "a silly goose" and allowed himself be provoked by her clothing, noises, and facial expressions. He took his daily walks, but kept close to his home street, and he continued to write letter after letter to his network of contacts, searching for someone who could function as a financial guarantor abroad and get them each their affidavit. Waiting gave way to irritation. First he directed it toward Grete—who else—then toward Lisl. She barked back, but that didn't help anyone.

So dearest boy, today I've written another earnest letter, presumably because it's so beautiful outside, and I can so keenly feel the benefit of you no longer being here. But don't fret about the earnestness, continue to be happy and carefree. I can't always laugh and be funny, I think far too much…

Have you heard from Harry Schein? He's in Uppsala, and before his departure said that he'd write you from there. If he hasn't yet done so, it doesn't mean anything, he wasn't among your closest friends after all, and you'd get over it if he'd forgotten you.

When their days had been emptied of content, all that was left was how they spent their time. Seconds were fine, minutes, too. But the hours seemed to lack beginning and end. They flowed together, impossible to differentiate.

Lisl and Nuny signed up for a cooking course run by the Jewish Community Council. Lisl had lived her entire life with a housekeeper, and never had to cook a meal of any significance. But now, facing emigration and with a different and simpler future as an immigrant in sight, she needed to be prepared. Pepi did his part by studying English under Paul's instruction. For a few set strokes of the clock each week, they were given a break from idleness.

It's six o'clock, and Mom still hasn't returned from the cooking course. Presumably the strudel was no great success . . .

There is a ruckus—speak of the devil!—I'd barely finished writing that when the door opened and Mom came in with the strudel. So I take it all back. Tomorrow I'll tell you if the food was worth it.

As far as Mom's poppyseed-and-nut cookies, strudel, and so on go, the results are not bad, but I think it's the teacher who has done everything. Mom does indeed feel slighted, but between us, the cookies are good and because she seems to have a talent for cooking, hopefully you will soon partake in her cuisine. We can only hope!

Sheet after sheet of paper was filled with ink and longing and soon Pepi had written more than one hundred letters. The typewriter's keys for the letters of the word "patience" had begun to show wear, so often had he repeated that word.

The weather is splendidly gorgeous today, very hot. In fact, it's the year's first day of swimming weather, and so the trams heading toward Prater are full. We aren't doing much. Mom and Nuny are at the cooking course, I have a spare hour and will visit a colleague at his home. In general we don't have much to do. Even when the weather is this beautiful, we do nothing—there are too many people everywhere and one can never be sure.

III

The world around looked just as it always had, but nothing was the same. The butcher's shop was still on the corner, and he and his family offered warm greetings—but was their tone warmer when there weren't any other customers around?

Plans to emigrate to Pepi's brother in Montevideo had to be laid to rest when Uruguay put a stop to all immigration. But Pepi kept writing, determined to leave the place that wanted nothing more than for him to go away.

> *At lunchtime the sun came out and the weather became good enough for the big festival on Jesuitenswiese that the SA had planned. But then, around five, it turned bad, with one storm after another, cloudbursts as well. The people running from the Prater couldn't find shelter quickly enough and became soaking wet. This of course didn't apply to us. We stayed indoors. We wouldn't have gone out even if the weather was fine. It is not pleasant to be driven away even from a chair in the Prater.*

The flowering summer didn't make anything easier. Their faces grew pale. They could see the difference between those who were allowed to move about freely in the sun and those for whom it was restricted.

Neither were there moments of gold, white marble, and

shared joy left, the kind that had filled several nights each week, when everything was as usual. They'd dressed in their finery, had smelled good, and had expectantly given themselves to abandon. Pepi's brother Egon was a well-known journalist and editor in chief who once had his own loge at the opera where Pepi, Lisl, and Otto always sat, a bird's nest of red velvet, a second home. If the performances were Wagner-long, they'd take chicken with them to eat during the intermission.

Now the retired Egon and his wife were without their opera loge, apartment, and pension, penniless and living by the grace of acquaintances. Now they were spending their evenings at home. Lisl and Pepi went to bed at nine o'clock.

> *Now we can no longer visit Prater. And because that was decreed today, we are doubly happy that you aren't here and do not have to heed these restrictions. In any case we don't go out very much, I used to take the occasional walk through Rustenschacherallee, but now that's over too. It doesn't infringe upon or touch me, because I didn't do it that often.*

Otto wrote back, trying to cheer them up with anecdotes and calming news. But the fact is, he was getting used to it. Not just the oatmeal, the sweet bread with margarine instead of his evening chocolate, the homesickness that overcame him in sleep when he couldn't fend it off. He was also getting used to the shadow of guilt, as if it were sewn to him. So as not to take too much pleasure in the bicycle journey to and from the market garden, the gravel road that clouded with dust, the butterflies flitting alongside.

When they lacked almost everything, and he had it all.

III

Five hundred letters.

They lay in piles, meticulously sorted by year and date. The first typewritten page on thin paper—letters in long, straight lines—like a monologue without pause. Then, much shorter greetings, handwritten attempts to keep hope alive. Different hands had guided the pen, so different tones can be distinguished, differences in temperament. Sometimes the lines change direction, and the words wind up the edge.

The authors' hand with certain letters, the slant of the penmanship, or how an empty space was left between the words perhaps say something about their age, personality, and style: mother Elise seems dutiful, her older sister Grete's writing is large and even, as in a penmanship workbook, whereas the younger sister Nuny's quick, lively hand makes an impulsive impression.

In flashes it's clear that Pepi is writing under great pressure or is in a rush. He writes by hand, the text is hard to decipher and unlike itself. On the final cards, the words seem to have been arduously inscribed, slowly and without joy.

The names that conclude the letters, filled to the margins with greetings and longing, create a pattern of friendship, irritation, and warmth. Dad. Mutti. Aunt Nuny. Her Paul. Aunt Grete.

Those who were writing are dead. But the material itself, paper and ink, remains. If I were to shine the right light on them, I'd surely find fingerprints, some from seventy years ago.

Stamps are still glued to the envelopes. Sometimes Hitler is brown, sometimes dark blue. First he cost ten pfennig, but as the years passed his price increased a bit.

How many of those who came before us do we remember? Who can expect to be remembered? And who can remember everything?

In reply, these five hundred letters lie before me on the table and sing in chorus, harmonizing with themselves; a fugue that ends in murder.

11

On September 1, *Kristiansbladet* filled page three with Germany's declaration of war against Poland—"Hitler Appeals With Arms."

The next day the news was forcibly confirmed.

"Polish-German War in Full Swing" and "French-German Ultimatum in Berlin: Troops to Return from Poland or Face All-Out War."

All-out war.

Eventide led to a blackout in vision. Vienna in darkness. But it didn't really matter. Nuny, Paul, Grete, Elise, and Pepi were, according to a new ordinance, not allowed to be outdoors after eight in the evening.

On September 23, possessing a radio was forbidden. The Ullmanns turned in their device, but of course they bought another one, as everyone else did. Orders arrived that Jews were only allowed to buy food from "trusted" Aryans, but some didn't dare serve Jewish customers for fear of misunderstandings and reprisals. In certain cities Jews were only allowed to shop during certain hours. They were ordered to build their own bunkers. After a few weeks the rules about radios were tightened, and only those who provided their names and addresses were allowed to make a purchase, so the degree of Jewishness could be monitored. Confiscated devices were sent to the army.

> *Dearest Otti! I'm taking the opportunity to write a bit in Dad's letter. I hope everything will calm down, and that we won't face any problems. Otherwise, I don't have much to write about. I simply hope that all the feelings settle and that peace will return. You know how I like it when people get along with each other, I've preached that to you as well.*
>
> *My darling, take care of yourself. A thousand kisses,*
>
> *mom*

A number of the Swedish missionaries in Vienna kept a diary or wrote letters home. In their positions—neither the hunted nor the hunter, neither the hated nor the hater—they developed a particular view of the everyday. Pastor Johannes Ivarsson was one of those observing and taking notes. Such as when he accompanied hopeful would-be émigrés to the authorities responsible for issuing passports and other necessary documents.

"The Jew was given in each possible context encouragement to disappear, and one might have expected the authorities to have opened the doors and smoothed the way for his flight. Such was not the case. We, who also were helping these people with matters of emigration, were often under the impression that at the very last moment opinions shifted and they wished to retain the Jew at any cost!"

And he cited officials who had asked why the Jews were making such a fuss with all of these papers, when they had a gas line at home.

Pastor Johannes Ivarsson described Vienna in the fall of 1939 as a cellar with its entrances bricked shut: "I can attest to the fact that the walls were dripping with anxiety."

He hadn't known that men could cry such tears. Women, he wrote, often cry over nothing, but now he was witnessing grown men, old veterans of the front lines with many medals of valor, sitting in his room in the Swedish mission's building on Seegasse, wringing their hands, compulsive and hysteric, unable to control themselves. Most had nothing to survive on, since their savings had been seized and they were unemployed.

On Sundays, when he stood at the pulpit, before him were a couple of hundred dismissed government officials. They were former professors, doctors, lawyers, actors, engineers, and businessmen. Idleness was driving them mad, and that's why it was perhaps unsurprising that most received the notice of forced labor with a kind of relief. Initially.

The pastor himself needed neither to enter into forced labor nor to refrain from visiting the cinema in the evenings. So he, in the company of other Austrians, was among those who saw the chipper film about "the Jews' first-ever workday" and watched the professors, doctors, lawyers, actors, engineers, and businessmen handling a pickaxe and spade for the very first time.

"The Jew behaved awkwardly and looked helpless and ridiculous," the Swede commented, and added that the people in the cinema were choked with laughter.

And so he came to the conclusion that employers found Jews lacking as workers.

"The enterprise was a loss, and soon the lawyer returned home. The Jew had been given the opportunity to work and 'to become an honorable person,' but he had shown that he could not. In a way, this was true." So wrote Pastor Johannes Ivarsson in the Swedish Israel Mission's publication.

The mission's director Pastor Pernow also made notes about those first war years in Vienna: "Ever since that day in March

1938 when the decree was made that Jews were, within four years, to be gone from Germany, the road has constantly led downhill. It soon became clear to them that they had to disappear, either by awaiting death—through further violence, suicide, or starvation and privation, since all means of subsistence have been robbed of them—or through emigration."

But in spite of this, the many and thoroughly annotated observations about the grim surroundings, in spite of the insights into the ominous future—the privation of the Jews carried with it a certain joy. Yes, the fact was that Swedish missionaries were experiencing bliss and blessing in the darkest of nights. Pastor Pernow described it all in the mission's magazine—and can one not hear the quiet jubilation between the lines, as though from a person witnessing a miracle?: "The aforesaid decree, that the Jewish population disappear, was immediately followed by a remarkable spiritual breakthrough. The Jews began to flood the mission in ways we'd never dreamed. At every service and Bible study the venues—chapel, hall, and stairs—were filled to the brim with listeners, learned men, professors, doctors, jurists, managers, as well as simple folk. All equally destitute and helpless, but hungering for words of hope and comfort, that they listened to eagerly and of which they never seemed to hear their fill."

Indeed. Because of Europe's hatred of Jews, the Swedish Israel Mission, there to convert them to the righteous path, found a way to reach the lost: "At the outbreak of war in fall 1939 the influx was so strong we had to introduce double services every Sunday, at 9 a.m. and 11 a.m., and even though the first service began so early, people were arriving one or two hours in advance to secure a seat. When a comfortable big-city populace rises at 6 a.m. or 7 a.m. on Sundays to pay a visit to God's house, a miracle has occurred . . . It was a remarkable harvest time, during which hundreds of Jews were drawn out of the shadow of hopelessness and folded into Christ's merciful kingdom."

What left the strongest impression on Pastor Pernow—an "unforgettable experience," he said—was Holy Communion. The sacrament was attended regularly by at least two hundred communicants during the first year of the war. Seeing these multitudes of Jews streaming forth to the Lord's table to meet their Savior, whom their people have repudiated for 1,900 years, in order to be strengthened and repaired by him, so that they could withstand the test and not dishonor his name—what an uplifting sight.

The school in the village had said that Otto was welcome, but he didn't want to go. He was older than the oldest students, considered himself almost grown up and already more educated. Every morning he waited for Sister Wallengren to finish with the *Kristianstadsbladet* newspaper so that he could follow global events with his own eyes. He wrote home as diligently as his dear parents desired.

Otto realized that his long, uneventful days in Tollarp were the height of luxury, the most enviable state of affairs. He'd left Vienna a capricious boy, used to doing his best, but also to getting his own way. The lonely nights, the children's days at the orphanage, the feeling of not being in charge of his own life had made him grow. Pepi and Lisl had confidence in him. And as though they were resting their heavy heads on his fourteen-year-old shoulders, he understood that he was obliged to share for other reasons than merely his own pleasure. They needed him so they could weather the unease, the days thickening into night and fog.

If it hadn't already been formulated as a rule, Pepi now set parameters for their correspondence: give us the quotidian, give us progress, give us simple everyday facts about friends, food, weather, skiing conditions, and the bathwater's temperature.

Don't write about the region's Nazi meetings, about what's in the newspaper, about politics or developments in the recently outbroken war. Give us the view from your window so that we can see it, too, conversations about oatmeal so that we can sit with you and pour the white milk over applesauce each morning, give us your days in the fields so that they can be our days, our muddy shoes, and our aching muscles.

Otto received the message; no more would he ask for support and strength. Instead he would give to them who had none and thereby create an alloy, a gilded combination of benevolence and debt repayment.

> *Dearest Otti. Today a letter arrived from the second, and naturally we were very happy. We were moved to read about how well you embolden us with courage, and we assure you that we are looking to the future with courage and temperance. We trust in God, that he will change everything for the better and will hopefully reunite us soon.*

Otto and his friend Gerhart were now the only ones left in ramshackle Hemhult. Mrs. Eklundh decided that they'd become temporary workers for regional farmers in the fall, and so they moved to Tallåsen, a farm just outside the village.

The muddy fall dragged on. He spent October standing for nine hours a day in the potato fields, pitchfork in hand. But he was being paid. Bought rubber boots. Was his own man. Didn't have the energy to write home.

III

It shouldn't have come as a surprise, yet no one was prepared. Not Pepi. Not Lisl. Not Otto. Orders arrived in the post, and now they knew that nothing could be trusted anymore and uncertainty was the only certainty in this existence.

Vienna, October 18, 1939

Dearest Otti. We were very disappointed today, because we'd counted on receiving a letter from you. But not even a postcard came, which saddened us greatly. We hope there has simply been a delay in the mail, and that something might come in the afternoon or tomorrow. In your last card you wrote that you have much to do and we'd really like to know what you're working on and what's keeping you occupied. Unfortunately you haven't written a single detailed letter in the past few weeks, and neither have you answered all of our questions as I'd hoped you would. We have no idea what you're doing—aside from what you wrote about digging up potatoes—or how you're doing, what's keeping you busy, what you're doing this winter and what you'll be doing later, if your future has been addressed, that is if you all are to stay in Tollarp or if you're to go elsewhere, we don't know the status of your correspondence with Egon and Grete, if you've had news from them, if you've received all of my letters, including the ones about them...

Yesterday there was cause for great worry, because I was meant to be conscripted into construction work in Poland effective immediately, but during my medical examination I was temporarily excused because of the shrapnel injury in my back. For how long I cannot say, of course. In any case, most of us, as long as we are in decent health, must go, and I may yet follow behind soon.

The words were clear: Everyone was leaving. They'd no longer be in Austria, and would have to move to the new state being planned for people like them. The formulations about their future were grandiose and full of promise. But first, the men had to lay the groundwork, create order, and build. Then the women would follow.

Pepi had proven his loyalty to Austria, defended the monarchy, fought the opposition. But the Great War's shrapnel only granted him a week's respite. No more.

October 21, 1939

Dearest Otto...I'm afraid I must tell you something unpleasant. Early next week, I am apparently going to be forced to travel to Poland for construction work. Of course I won't be going alone, everyone must go, and so I won't be able to write you for a while. This last part saddens me, but Mom will be staying in Vienna and will continue to keep you informed. I know you're a clever boy who won't get up to anything that would make me sad. God willing, we will be reunited, and I hope that you, my good boy, won't cause me any shame now that I can't write to you daily. Just keep being the person you've always been, be courageous, honest, and decent, so that I may travel in peace.

Pepi hoped that Lisl would join him in Poland, but he also wished she wouldn't have to. He wished the work wouldn't be too hard or the time too long. What else could he wish for?

When the time for deportation came, he was noticeably affected. For some reason he didn't write on the typewriter, as usual. He knew this might be his last letter. Soon he'd get on a train with other able-bodied men who'd all travel together, and one by one, disembark at an unknown destiny. His handwriting is almost indecipherable.

October 25, 1939

Dearest Otti. Today I'm only writing a card. Tomorrow you'll receive a longer letter from me, the last for a long while. But Mom, God willing, will continue to keep you informed. We are healthy, which is the most important thing, and we hope you are, too. Always keep your family near and let's hope we never experience anything like this again. I would like you to be happy and forward-looking, so that we can be happy for you. As I wrote yesterday, continue to better yourself and study so that we don't have to be ashamed of you. Always make sure to find time for physical activity. Most important of all is to take care of yourself so you can keep in good health. Dearest boy. A thousand greetings and kisses.

your dad

The 912 men who left Vienna on October 10 didn't know this departure was the second step in Adolf Eichmann's plan for establishing a temporary Jewish state in Poland, close to the Soviet border. Another 672 men were forced to leave on October 26. Among them was Pepi.

> *October 27, 1939*
>
> *Dearest boy. Yesterday your father went away and I wish him well. I don't yet know when I'm to travel . . . My treasure. I kiss you a thousand times and hope to receive a letter from you soon. Maybe even tomorrow.*
>
> *Your mom*

Adolf Eichmann. Blackshirt, *Hauptsturmführer*, director of the Final Solution. It fell to him to rid Nazi Germany of people with Jewish heritage, and deepest Poland seemed a sufficient provisional solution to the problem. Close to the Soviet border. Waterlogged. A marsh. Backwoods. A treeless moor.

The district was called Radom, the river San, and the place Nisko. First the Poles moved out, then the Jews moved in. Adolf Eichmann oversaw it all personally. He wrote: "I said: Give me a sufficient subsistence area; then it will be possible to set up an autonomous Jewish pre-state [*Judenvorstaat*] from which gradual emigration could be carried out." And "We said to ourselves . . . this can be a solution for some time, at least for some time, so that meanwhile there will be no fire under our fingernails."

It was the Führer's express wish that those classed as Jews be sent away from German-controlled territory, so Eichmann created an assembly point: a Jewish pre-state. It's possible that this concentration of Jews near the demarcation line was planned as an initial step for their deportation across the Soviet border.

It all began with a transport leaving the city of Ostrava. Surviving witnesses have given accounts of how the group was taken to a hill with a panoramic view. There an SS officer informed them of the following: "About seven or eight kilometers from here, across the San, the Führer has promised the Jews a new homeland. There are no houses there and no accommodation. You will have a roof over your heads if you build one yourselves. There is no water. The wells are all contaminated—cholera, dysentery, typhus. If you bore for water and find water, you will have water." It is believed that this SS officer was Adolf Eichmann himself.

The next day a quarter of the men were driven out. They were forced to go eastward without a plan and warned that they'd be shot if they returned. The rest had to make do as best they could, making their way to the place that gave the whole experiment its name: Nisko.

After the prison camp was set up, further transports of men arrived from Ostrava. A few prisoners were never allowed into the camp, but were expelled directly without their baggage. During the autumn, another transport arrived with one thousand elderly Jews. Followed by two transports from Vienna. Among them was Pepi.

Lisl knew it would soon be her turn to leave. In Tollarp Otto was preparing himself to be even more lonely, very lonely, completely alone.

Pepi had disappeared but had left behind his inheritance: the appeal that his nearest and dearest not lose their courage. This appeal echoed through Lisl and reached the fourteen-year-old at the children's home.

October 31, 1939

Dearest Otti. I'm taking a little extra time to write to you today. I haven't heard anything from Dad yet, but I assume it will be a while because no post has yet arrived from those who traveled with that first transport. We must all be patient.

I've been given a fourteen-day deferment, so I can stay in touch for now. If I'm forced to leave, I will inform you.

These are difficult times and we must not give up. These were also Dad's words to me when he left, and I will live by them. After all we want to be reunited and make each other happy.

I'm curious about your next letter because I very much want to know what you're working with, and what it will be like for you going forward. Dad would very much like you to not only work, but also have a chance to continue your studies at school. Education is a necessity.

Nothing new here. We are, thank God, healthy and hope you are, too. Is Gerhardt still with you?

In Tallåsen, in the house in the grove at the end of the gravel road just outside of Tollarp, most of the rooms were empty. Otto spent a few hours working in the market garden during the week, where he helped the developmentally challenged, who were sorting apples into various baskets and putting the tools in order. He helped with the November plowing.

Pepi was unreachable out there in Poland, and Lisl lived with a suitcase packed in the hall. Otto's spirit sunk from him having to keep it up. His days were long because he wished for their end.

November 7, 1939

Dearest child. I received your card yesterday and I'm happy you're healthy. That's the main thing. I haven't heard from Dad yet. Unfortunately the mail is very slow. I also don't know how long I'll be able to stay here, if I have to move our correspondence might suffer, to begin with at least. Hopefully Paul and the others will be able to stay.

What have you heard from Egon and Aunt Grete? Is Gerhardt still with you, or are you on your own out there? I hope you're not catching cold and that you're taking care of yourself. One thousand kisses.

your mom

Pastor Birger Pernow had not only made sure that sixty-five children could come to Sweden, but he'd also saved some twenty adolescents and men who'd been involved with the mission's youth organization in Vienna. He'd asked his old friend and fellow believer Axel Andersson to set up a camp for them on his land in Tostarp. There was a youth house that could be expanded, and that's where the young men could live, be given a Christian life, and moreover be of use by doing health-giving physical labor while they waited to emigrate to another country. It was a transitional camp for Jewish-Christian youths.

Otto moved there two days before Christmas. From Tollarp to Tostarp, one Skånish village name to the next, from the category "child" to "refugee." When the tree had been decorated, a camera and tripod were fetched. The Christmas tree's sparse branches bent under the weight of burning candles. Before the tree are the twenty-five refugees, dressed in clothing as dark as their gazes. On the floor is the youngest, Otto.

Perhaps Christmas 1939 was distinguished by its particular lack of light. Perhaps the photographer was an impatient soul. The only thing in focus in the photograph is the tree. The people seem on the verge of dissolving. They're looking in different directions, moving their worried hands, and because they are turning their heads to the right as the picture is being taken, they look less like individuals and more like clouds, about to burst.

Otto was given bed number twenty-four.

A new order, a more somber mood, the hierarchy more defined, the very passage of time different: waking at seven and then exercise. Morning prayer in Swedish. Four hours of practical work during which the trees in the forest were felled and sawed into wood that Axel Andersson, the landowner, could sell at a profit. Those in charge of the camp noted in their documentation that a number of the refugees were weak of nerve and mind. When there was no snow, they might work on the sugar beet fields next door or in the adjacent gardens. Three and a half hours a day were to be spent on lessons, it was said, and so it probably was. At least during the winter when the fields weren't calling for a human hand to sow, weed, harvest, bring in, or be turned. At least if no rebuilding was needed, or repairs. Supper at seven in the evening. And thereafter prayers in German.

The Mission Covenant of Sweden ran the camp. The Swedish authorities had approved it. They were allowed to be there: Jewish-Christian and well-behaved. As long as they didn't stay.

In one of the first protocols from the refugee committee's meeting, it was determined that the authorities and general public should be informed that "the camp is intended for refugees in general and not for Jewish refugees alone, as well as being a transitional camp, and so will not contribute to the placement of exiles in Sweden." That is to say, the people in the region should have no reason to worry.

On the registration card from the camp, each and every one's profession is thoroughly noted. After Otto's name it read "profession: schoolboy." No schooling however had been arranged, and there was no school for him to attend.

In the group photo from Christmas, December 24, 1939, he looks very small, in spite of his fourteen years. Like a child.

Lines of relief: finally Elise received her first greeting from that somewhere in Poland where Pepi had been sent. He'd managed the trip, was healthy, and found himself in a place that barely had a name, but you could write to the post office in Rudwitze/San, via Kraków.

Otto didn't want to worry Pepi. However, his discomfort and unease seeped into his letters to Vienna, even though he knew he should hold his tongue. But when the replies from Mutti and Aunt Grete came, he realized his mistake. They could not help him.

January 4, 1940

Dearest boy, I read your letter from Dec 28 with great happiness. I can see you've begun to feel at home. The people taking care of you are truly good people indeed. You probably needed that letter from your dad.

There is nothing wrong with being the smallest, you'll grow into yourself soon. And you'll be able to study at the home, surely there are books. Perhaps Goethe and others, and you can read them until you get a real education.

Goethe. Otto could've laughed, but instead Elise's words opened the heavy door to his loneliness, and there was nowhere else to go.

In the refugee camp at Tostarp was the psalm book from 1937 as well as the Old and New Testaments. No German literature. No poetry. No Goethe. It was clear that Otto could only turn to himself, to his own abilities, his will to prevail and not despair. It was as simple as that.

Vienna, January 10, 1940

Dearest boy. Yet again, I've not received any post from you today.

Vienna, January 12, 1940

Dearest boy. Unfortunately I haven't received any post from you today either.

Vienna, January 14, 1940

Dearest boy. Finally I received your lovely letter today. You haven't written to me since December 28. I don't want to have to wait so long, for it makes me far too nervous. You also haven't answered all of my questions.

Vienna, January 15, 1940

Dearest boy. You know you still haven't answered my questions. A mere description of the home would be very interesting. Dearest, write soon.

Vienna, January 16, 1940

Dearest boy. My child, you have more than enough to which to respond. Sit down and write me a detailed letter.

If only he'd been able to speak with his father. But Pepi was in Poland, somewhat close to the Ukrainian and White Russian border, that is to say, not close to anything but the ground, the forest, and the river San. Only the small village of Ulanow had buildings. Waterlogged territories. Simple barns. Daily toil to strengthen the fortifications against the Soviet border. A white armband with a blue Star of David.

INSPECTED BY THE ARMED FORCES

Ulanow, January 17, 1940

My dearest best boy. Your letter from January 6 made me so very happy. It was the first letter from you that came directly to me. The other letter was of course sent via your mother, and it made me very happy, too, and I have also replied. But the letter that arrived now delights me, because, thank God, I can see that you are safe and all is well, and there's no need to worry about your future.

Mom wrote that you've left Tollarp. Saying goodbye to your friend Gerhardt must have been difficult, but you're not that far away from each other. Or was he placed elsewhere? Moreover you now have an opportunity to make new friends. You are, as I can tell from your letters, mature and . . . [unreadable].

Even if life hasn't turned out as we'd hoped, and the separation from us means that your childhood is turning out different from how I wished it would be, I'm still proud to see that I have a boy in possession of sense, intelligence, and determination. And who has also learned much besides, and so, if needed, can stand on his own two feet.

Dearest Otti, your words about the camp where you are now were very interesting. It doesn't surprise me that your friends are pious, that's how they are up there in Sweden, by conviction. And in this context I'd like to remind you of the words I wrote a few months ago, before I went to Poland: in these hard times trust in God and in our faith is a boundless help. You know I've always said that everyone prays to one and the same God in heaven, and it doesn't matter in which house of God this occurs. The point is that one prays.

I don't know if they're trying to influence you or convince you otherwise. But if so it's not a problem. I'll leave this matter up to you entirely, for if you choose to take such a step, it must come from conviction. I know you far too well and know that you have despised "sham piety" and therefore have a strong character. You've followed in my footsteps. I will most likely be hearing more on this from you, and will gladly advise you if I can. In any case it pleases me to hear that you have such sensible views.

Even your mother and I trust in God and that he'll help us soon. And that soon he'll bring us together. We must have patience, and wait until we may partake in his grace. Our very trust in God is what bolsters us these days...

Let me know if you need anything, and always be diligent. Maybe I can advise you. Take care of yourself and may God protect you. This is my only wish. Many thousand greetings and kisses.

your loyal dad

Otto may have been a refugee, but the camp in Tostarp was not suited to him at all. Not only was he the youngest at fourteen, but he was also the smallest. The only male there who didn't need to shave every morning. But his name was up on the work schedule along with everyone else's. During the second week of February he had kitchen duty. The young men took turns washing, trimming bushes, laying linoleum, ironing, and fetching water. And they thanked Jesus Christ every day. A new schedule each week, written in German and Swedish.

In Vienna Lisl did her best to live up to Pepi's ideal of a letter a day. She wrote little but often. Sometimes you couldn't tell one letter from the next, so similar were they. The question is whether a few days of silence would have been better than receiving a card a day with the same sentences, same questions, same longing for his next letter.

But that was Mom.

If he traced her pen strokes with his finger he could move with her movements, follow her tracks.

January 18 . . . I keep busy in just about the same way: I wait for mail from you and Dad. He writes diligently, because it is very important for him to keep in contact with me . . .

January 19 . . . No letter from you arrived today. Maybe one will come tomorrow. Dad wrote today. He is healthy and hopes to receive a letter from you soon. Have you written to him?

January 27 . . . What do you do all day? Do you have any chores? Or are you just playing ping-pong? . . .

Snuckiputzi—sending greetings and kisses.

Aunt Nuny

Paul sends warm regards.

Otto was following his heart and letting it be. Lisl received shorter, dutiful letters, but he wrote more and with hope to Pepi. He conducted the important conversations with his father, then as now. This exchange was also about strengthening family ties—Pepi was the one who needed strength so that he could pass it on to Lisl.

Ulanow, January 29, 1940

My dearest best boy. Today I received your letter from January 19, and I thank you very much for it. You've made me very happy.

I'm happy you're now pleased with your new home. I can really imagine that it was less agreeable to begin with, but that you've gotten used to it by now and all of your friends are nice . . .

As for the rest I was very much put at ease to hear that you don't have too much work. In gardening and agriculture, you are certainly experienced. I imagine that when we have the chance to see each other again, you'll have become a strong and handsome young man. Write and tell me how tall you are, and how much you weigh.

How is your Swedish coming, by the way? Tomorrow it will be a full year since we accompanied you to the station. You must be fluent by now.

It is sometimes with a heavy heart that I think back on accompanying you to the station, how we bade you farewell and how you waved in the window until the train had rolled out of the station. But in this year you've experienced so much. You went to good people, have become big and strong, and thankfully continue to be healthy. So I'm happy about that, because here at home you wouldn't have been able to have any of it. I thank God because he has protected you thus far, and I pray to him daily that he will continue to keep you healthy and kind.

I assume it's cold where you are. Here it was between –17 and –36 degrees Celsius. Thankfully I have weathered it well and hope that up there in the North you are also in good health. Take care of yourself, boy. [Unreadable] we will see each other again.

I'm including a group photo [unreadable]. You will have to tell me if I've changed. May God protect you. Many greetings.

your dad

Hope radiated from Dad's letter. In the envelope was also a photograph, untouched by the censor.

The whole picture is difficult to parse: seven city dwellers from Vienna, without armbands for the time being, looking calmly into the camera.

The men must have stuck together, formed friendship groups, they must've found a well with fresh water, a roof over their heads, a photography studio. Pepi wasn't the only veteran, they'd all been to war. And they must've been lucky. They were not among those who were driven from the camp without food, threatened with being shot if they returned. They were not forced to walk across the Soviet border or swim across the River San.

So there stood Pepi, facing a photographer, in a village named Ulanow, as though he were in a normal world. As though he and the other men were colleagues, any old colleagues.

Did Otto understand the picture was staged, a residual ritual from a life they'd once lived, known, and appreciated? The kind of thing one used to do, dressing in a sweater and tie, standing next to a friend, steadily gazing into the natural light until the photographer signaled that it was done.

One friend is wearing a black shirt under his blazer instead of a shirt and tie, another has two ballpoint pens stuck in his pocket. They are writers and readers, intellectual men. Only if you take a closer look can you see the worry. Pepi is thinner and dark around the eyes. He's not the only one trying to smile. The prisoners knew this photograph might be their last and wanted to put on a happy face for the sake of their families. But they are unintentionally revealing their shadow sides, and for this no one can criticize them.

On the back of the card those seven men signed their names in black ink: seven signatures, the slant distinguishing one from the next, a loop or the pressure of the pen. Seven individuals who wrote their names seven times on seven copies of the group photo, so that each and every one had their own copy.

One can see the picture as evidence in a criminal investigation, as a cry for help in a desperate situation or a way for a few prisoners to feel like free people for a moment that lasted as long as it took the camera's shutter to open and close. And maybe this damp-damaged, black-and-white photograph is all of these things. But above all it is a protest document. A quiet riot of normality and civilization amid barbarous violence.

Otto might not have understood the extent of the prisoners' misery in Nisko, but he understood he had an obligation to provide hope and good cheer. So he wrote nothing about his dissatisfaction or the desire to flee. Nothing about how almost anything else would have been better than the Christian camp in Tostarp, better than this drear and prayer.

One lone letter from Otto, fourteen years old, remains. For some reason it was sent back from Poland:

> *February 1, 1940*
>
> *Dearest Dad! I received your dear letter and don't suppose I need to say how happy it made me. I've already written about how I'm doing, in general. I like the work here very much, at the moment we're felling trees and bushes in the forest. Then you don't get cold because you're in motion.*
>
> *I've now had a chance to get accustomed to the new environment, as well. The camp is in a lovely location,*

because we have a view of the lake. Lake Finja. So on the whole it is rather lovely here . . . It has been snowing a lot recently, but it's not especially cold.

February 5, 1940

Dearest Dad. Unfortunately I had to interrupt my writing because they called us to table, and afterward I had no time to write.

A few days ago I was given ten kronor by the Lund Committee. For the second time.

A few days ago Pastor Hedenquist and his wife visited, and I spoke with him about my future. He promised to see if there isn't a possibility for me to continue my studies after all. But in any case, work is no bad influence—I've even put on weight and now weigh fifty-one kilos. The work in general causes me no harm, on the contrary. My muscles have grown, and I would gladly take on further physical labor later, if I can't study. And so, dear Dad, you can feel at ease and truly need not worry about me. For with God's help I shall pass these difficult tests and clear the largest hurdles. And so I send you my regards and kisses.

your loyal son Otto

Stuck to the envelope from Nisko was a strip with the following text: "Inspected by the armed forces." Pepi could write about freezing temperatures, about having friends, and that hope was alive—that is to say, he was living on hope—but not much more.

Oh, and that he prayed.

Otto's friends at the Tostarp refugee camp also prayed. The pastor in charge of the work and the operation wanted to see Otto doing the same. Jesus Christ, he repeated. Jesus Christ who died on the cross for our sins.

In the labor camp's raw chill, Dad's daily prayers to a general God on high who had not yet decided who his true and false prophets were didn't particularly bother Otto. He understood that these prayers were Pepi's lifeline when the temperatures sank to –32C, when he and the other men pressed against each other at night to stay warm. This too shall pass, the tundra will thaw. Patience.

It was harder to respond to the pastor in Tostarp, standing there with the New Testament in hand.

Then there were the letters home. Otto knew that Lisl and Aunt Grete were alone in the apartment. Not easy to find the words, the right brave tone that would keep his greetings from resounding with the emptiness around him, and enliven their home instead of filling it with worry.

February 8, 1940

Dearest boy. I heard from Dad that you've written to him, and how happy it made him, as you can imagine. How are you, my child? I could do with a permit entry for Dad, then he'd be able to return. Perhaps an affidavit will come in time. We're supposed to be getting out of here... What are you doing, my child? Do you have work? Do you have the opportunity to study anything? Be good and write again. I embrace you.

your mom

Elise's handwriting is rushed and sloppy. Some sort of belief in the future must have been ignited. Finally someone in America had promised Pepi an affidavit, someone who would act as a guarantor for him upon arrival, so he wouldn't be a burden on the country. The chink, the ray of light. Now they just needed an entry permit, she wrote.

Just.

Truth be told, they still "just" needed five copies of the visa application for the United States, two copies of the applicant's birth certificate, a quota number to establish the applicant's place in the arrivals line, and two sponsors who could promise the necessary affidavit. As well as their most recent tax returns, bank statements, assurances from another authority regarding the applicant's other assets, certificates from the German police regarding the applicant's good conduct, which meant two copies of documents from the police's files, the prison register, the military register, as well as all the other public details about the applicant. Then proof of the ability to leave Germany was required, as well as proof that the applicant had booked the journey out.

Josef prayed. Elise hoped. Otto tried to get used to things. He really did.

> *My dearest Otti. It has been a long time since you've sent me a long letter to read. I'd very much like to know about your new surroundings. You are bad at writing, this admonishment is something you will just have to take. Think about that now and write to me in detail, my dearest Otti. With whom else are you corresponding? Ernstl is your most loyal friend, is he not?*
>
> *Today is the first time in five weeks or so that the thermometer has risen above zero. How have you spent the beautiful winter days? Have you gone ice-skating and so forth? Have you made new friends? You see—I'm still your curious aunt. I hope you'll answer all of my questions. Write soon. A thousand kisses.*
>
> *Aunt Grete*

Hard to tell what plagued him the most—being the only boy amongst men or living with a shade of Christianity that colored the day earnest and long.

They wouldn't give up. But the more faithful they wanted Otto to be, the more estranged he felt. If he really were considered Christian—would he even be in a refugee camp? Wasn't it the prefix "Jew" that had sent him there, and the category "Mosaic" on the register card that had ensured he was alone, an orphan for now? He noted the attitudes of his fellow refugees.

Some took classes so they could convert to the evangelical faith and studied the New Testament as though they were going to become priests. Otto couldn't understand it.

But it was what it was. The camp in Tostarp was his home and he reminded himself of the positives: the location's natural beauty, a summer by Lake Finja, swimming after the workday. Not bad. Before, in Hemhult, the cries of small children had always managed to reach through the home's walls, finding him even though he had lain on his side and muffled the sound with his pillow. Here there were no young ones calling for mama. One simply didn't cry here. And that included him. At least that was a change for the better, was it not?

But Otto pondered his fellow refugees and their devotional prayers to Jesus. It was impossible for him to differentiate between what had happened—the Ostbahnhof, the dead leaves flying around the station in Trelleborg, Miss Sommer's voice as she tried to comfort the smallest—and the lot he and the others had been given. *J* as in Jew and M as in Mosaic. After this lot, this punishment, to devote himself to the man hanging on the cross for his sins seemed impossible.

The grown men in the camp were nice to him, especially Herr Lamper, who knew one of Pepi's friends in the camp and wished him well. And laying linoleum, building chicken coops, chopping wood—doable. But the rest? Impossible.

Did Otto escape? Was he transferred?

Maybe it doesn't matter, and no one can say anymore. He returned to Tallåsen, where Sister Cecilia Wallengren received him. Back to the oatmeal, but in a children's home where there were hardly any children left. He knew this wasn't a long-term solution, and yet it felt better.

Somewhere on the road between Tostarp and Tollarp, the two Skånish villages that had offered him shelter on the basis of baptism, he'd arrived at a decision. From having hardly understood the meaning of the term "Jew" to having to flee his country because of it, he'd made a decision. If that's how they wanted it, then they'd get what they were asking for. His time as a Christian was over.

Message to Pastor B. Pernow in Stockholm from Tollarp on February 29, 1940:

> After conferring with [unreadable] Lindblom I've taken on a guest—"until further notice"—Otto Ullmann. But now in possession of his passport, I see it's missing a residency permit from the Swedish authorities.
>
> The boy arrived with the other children from Vienna, but says he is "Mosaic." But still I pray you will kindly set this matter right.
>
> Reverently,
> Sister Cecilia Wallengren

Vienna, March 20, 1940

Dearest boy. Another few days have passed without a letter from you and of course I await one with great longing. I hope you're healthy and maybe you've already found work.

Have you asked Mrs. Eklundh if you can't go to school? Your Swedish must be perfect by now. If not, perhaps you could have private tuition?

I'm convinced that you will choose, and do, the right thing. After all, you've written that you will never stray from the straight and narrow path. Darling, I wish you a happy Easter and may all our wishes be fulfilled. I've also received a letter from Dad. Dear child. I hug and kiss you.

your mom

Mrs. Carola Eklundh in Lund's refugee committee noted that this teenager had not roused the farmers' goodwill. He was always left behind. Too skinny? She listened, she spoke warmly. Quick-witted, dark-eyed, and—what was it that was written on the registry card held by his saviors?—adaptable.

Otto was fourteen years old but understood he needed work and vocational training. The farmer's lot didn't speak to him. But the butcher at home on Löwengasse had always been a good friend. Otto simply took the matter into his own hands. He cycled to Butcher Larsson in Tollarp village and asked if they wanted to have him. The Larsson family said yes, and so he went there to learn.

The spring of 1940 might well have marked the start of a good spell. Back home in Vienna, Elise and Pepi experienced a sudden miracle, crying tears of gratitude instead of farewell, embracing each other in greeting rather than in parting.

Pepi was lucky to have survived six months in the Polish swampland of Nisko—he'd neither been banished, frozen to death, nor shot, he'd starved but survived, evading typhus and dysentery—and now he'd been sent back. Hitler's Jewish reservation had suddenly been shut down, Eichmann's plans had changed. For the first and only time during the course of the deportations, prisoners were being sent back home.

On April 13 Pepi arrived unexpectedly in Vienna. The worst was probably over.

Meanwhile Otto moved in with the Larsson family in Tollarp. The April weather flying by, he lay down by the stream and rinsed out cow stomachs. He wrote home to say everything was good, the family was wonderful. Pepi's homecoming made him happy, but he didn't want to think about Mom and Dad being together again while he was still on his own. He was doing his best, as always. But he hadn't anticipated five cow stomachs in a wheelbarrow.

We've written masses of cards and letters to the Larssons in Tollarp, and I hope you've received them all. I hope you're already there and that it's going well for you. What you're doing there will hardly be a waste of time, quite the opposite. Even if a career as a butcher—as you write—is not a particularly fine trade, it's good to learn. Incidentally the son of the butcher around here has said that he works in the butcher's shop even though he has a high school certificate. In other words, this trade is nothing to be ashamed of.

As far as your studies go, you know our opinion. I'm convinced that you, in spite of your work in agriculture or with the Larssons, will not forget to continue your education. One does not have to study at a college, the most important thing is to learn something, to acquire knowledge, to have a practical trade and to be decent.

Nothing was comfortable, nothing was really as he wished. It wasn't just the work as a butcher's shop assistant that chafed, it was all of him. The clothes from Vienna that he'd outgrown had to be left behind, clothes that Elise had marked and packed before his departure. One year and fifteen centimeters ago.

Otto really didn't want to cause any trouble. And he was only acquainted with one way of changing things, the one his father had taught him. So he sat down at a table, put paper in front of him, picked up a pen, and wrote. A few days later a reply from Pastor Pernow arrived.

April 25, 1940

The Israel Mission, Idungatan 4, Stockholm.

Dear Otto. I received your letter from the 21st. I'm sorry to hear you aren't getting on well in the new place. The question is why. Do they not treat you well, or what is it that you're missing? The circumstance of not being able to be with your friends doesn't come to bear. You're a big boy who in these difficult times surely has given thought to your future.

The important thing is for you to be where you can get a real education, and where you can learn something that will allow you to stand on your own two feet later. Because I cannot assess the situation from here, I can't take a position on your letter at present. I'm sorry you do not feel at ease. But a change can only be made if it is for your best. And so I've turned to Mrs. Eklundh, who wants the best for you, and I've asked her to investigate your situation, if possible personally, and then take the measures she deems fit. Namely to satisfy you, while creating favorable conditions for your continued progress. Have a little patience. We all have your best interest in mind, and you'll surely hear from Mrs. Eklundh soon.

It is especially important that you, where you are now, try to do your best, be diligent, and most of all polite and friendly toward every family member, so that there can be no just cause for complaint.

Warm regards,
Pastor Birger Pernow

Why did Otto quit the butcher's in Tollarp? The family had been good to him, so good that he hadn't dared tell it like it was—the whole endeavor was a mistake, butchery was not for him. Maybe he let them think the move was the Israel Mission's decision. In any case, Mrs. Hilda Larsson had no reason to think otherwise.

> Tollarp, May 2, 1940
>
> Esteemed Pastor Pernow
> Regarding the wishes of the boy Otto Ullmann to remain in Tollarp and reside here, I'm writing a few lines to the pastor, requesting that he be allowed to return. We need him, should he be granted a permit to work. We liked him very much, he was willing to do everything, he spent such a short time with us, no longer than eight days...
>
> If it's possible for the kind pastor to arrange for this, we would be very grateful. We very much wish for a reply in return.
>
> Reverently,
> Mrs. Hilda Larsson

III

In letter after letter Otto is beyond reach. A boy-shadow.

He comes to me from another direction, filtered through time, through the failing memories of others, through his parents' voluble replies to letters that no longer exist. If they write that he shouldn't be homesick, then I know that he was homesick, but he himself was elsewhere. His voice echoes. His silence echoes. His letters echo, as his missing letters do. This echo becomes my material.

The sound of his steps, the swing of his ax in the woods on a winter's day, the happy torrent of words when his dark-brown foreign gaze and stories about the outside world charmed the girls—I sense it, but I can only be where he's just passed by.

The letters spill across the table. They've only now been translated from German, so far I am their only reader. When I meet one of Otto's grandchildren, it's dizzying. I can tell her about how her father's father grew up, she can see him as a child, hear his parents berate him and long for him. And so for an evening, I am a medium, voices from the dead ringing inside me. Elusive yet.

Much later, when Otto was married, a father and adult himself, a relative told him that it was a shame he was an only child. If he'd had siblings who could have gone with him to Sweden, then he wouldn't have been so alone. Otto's reply was immediate. He was glad, very glad, that no one else had to go through what he'd gone through. Thankfully it had only been him.

They probably conferred, kind Pastor Pernow and friendly Mrs. Eklundh. What to do with Otto Ullmann? His parents hadn't made it out of the country, so it would probably be a while yet before they picked him up.

Mrs. Eklundh had taken a shine to Otto and probably consulted with her husband at home in Lund. A solution was proposed.

Otto would be a gardener at Mr. Ombudsman Albert Eklundh's. In addition to their home in Lund, the Eklundhs owned a farm with a house, land, and animals at the edge of Pjätteryd village in Småland. Gardening work. Yes, Otto had done that before. That was a good fit. So from Skåne to Kronoberg County he went. One hundred kilometers deeper into the country.

A little over a year before, Pepi had again and again written that Sweden was a country with sensible people where Otto could live a free and peaceful life. And the language would be easy for Otto to master, wrote Grete, it was so like German.

Peaceful, free, and like Germany. That's how it was.

It was right at this time that the county police superintendent was mapping the spread of Nazism in Kronoberg County. This wasn't covered in the *Smålandsposten* newspaper, so fourteen-year-old Otto was unaware. But the county police superintendent followed the developments and calculated, assessed, judged, and could summarize the activity around the SSS, the Nazi party headed by Sven Olov Lindholm, for the Swedish Security Service. Even if the Nazis' operations were quite small, Kronoberg County had a "not insignificant number of persons who can be understood to harbor National Socialist or similar opinions."

Otto was picked up from Ljungby station by horse and carriage. Taking the big road toward Agunnaryd, one turned right onto a long narrow road that continued one monotonous kilometer through the forest before arriving at a crossroads. If one then turned right again, the forest stretched into darkness. But to the left, land for agriculture and livestock spread out before one. A sturdy stone wall marked the border between a domicile and the rest of the land. The lake was at the foot of a grassy knoll, the marsh that had lent the place its name.

Kärrnäs may have had a Pjätteryd address, but it was as far as you could get from the village itself without leaving it. Småland's periphery, the edge of the edge: the Eklundhs' summer home, the Anderssons' leasing.

Otto would later describe the journey from big-city Vienna to rural life in Småland like going back a century in time. The outhouse. No libraries. The pitted fields where they played soccer.

The first thing you saw was Ombudsman Albert and Carola Eklundh's house, with its gently curving, raked gravel path leading to a veranda, adorned in summer by climbing plants. The house sat high, had good light, a view of the land and lake's edge. At this time in April the branches were still bare, the wood anemones grew in clusters, and yellow star-of-Bethlehems shot up from the ground.

Farther away, toward the forest, was the Andersson family's home, a smaller red cottage without the gingerbread work. There lived widow Agnes, who leased the land together with her brother-in-law Oskar.

The ombudsman lived on the farm periodically, even though each round trip from Lund cost him six kronor. His wife Carola Eklundh came out with her daughters Ingrid and Carin for the major public holidays.

Otto was given a room in the big house.

The land was ready to be worked, and this was Otto's first task: to put the family's kitchen garden in order so they could grow potatoes, carrots, and strawberries. He had plenty to do, and everything should have been good. He had a home for a while and work he enjoyed. He really didn't want to complain. For the most part he kept quiet and got along with the maids and the others. But still.

One person suggests that the ombudsman was not always kind and Otto was given grunt work on his plot. Another says that Albert Eklundh was the nicest person on earth. And perhaps it was something unrelated that led to Otto having to move—this time thirty meters away, down to the leasehold on the crofter's holding, where young Henrik and Astrid lived together with their mother Agnes. It was smaller, poorer, and simpler there. It was warmer. He was welcome.

A year and a half had passed since he'd been separated from his father, Mutti, aunts Grete and Nuny, and Paul. Between him and familial warmth lay the journey on the night train, a year at an orphanage, a refugee camp, and an escape, and all of those moments when a Smålandish farmer had crossed the home's threshold, inspected the children's faces, and then chose a little girl or the boy with the fairest hair. It had been one and a half years since he'd lived with a mother who liked to hug her child.

Agnes Andersson opened her home and her family to him. Otto opened his heart in return. And there was plenty of work.

May 7

Even if you have much to do, write anyway. We're counting on you. You know how we await your news.

May 10

I'm truly disappointed that you write so seldom, and I beg of you: write twice a week, as you did before. You can perhaps imagine that if we must wait for mail in these difficult times, we get extremely worried when none arrives.

May 18

Dearest boy! Since your card from April 22 we haven't received a single line from you, and you can imagine, my darling, how worried we are. And even more so when we see how Mrs. Edlauer keeps getting mail from Kurt... Dad is very sad that you aren't writing. Do you really have so much work to do? Surely you have time for a card? I can hardly comprehend that you haven't written since April 22.

June 4, 1940

My dearest boy. Yet again fourteen days have passed since we received your last letter. You can imagine our unease. Perhaps the word "unease" is not fitting. We are far more worried than that to have not received so much as a card from you—not even one with the absolute minimum of content. You know how much I'm waiting.

A long time ago, you wrote that you were going to return to Tollarp and take up a position with Larsson, something about which you harbored hope. Since then we've been writing to you without reply. We do expect one or two cards a week, and you should be able to manage that, however much work you have. I hope you are healthy and that you are well. Take care of yourself. A thousand kisses and regards.

dad

June 17

We've been waiting for post from you for more than ten days. Now it must be time for a letter. We've always expected to hear from you one or two times a week. But in this respect you've disappointed us lately.

June 18

Now we haven't heard from you since May 22. Mrs. Edlauer says that her boy writes punctually each week. We are very hurt that you write us so seldom. Think about how we are waiting and longing to hear from you and that it is our only great joy.

But Otto didn't have the time or the energy, at least not now. Summer was in full swing. He'd unexpectedly found a brother in Henrik, and Astrid was nice and sweet to him. While the two siblings worked the fields, he toiled in Eklundh's kitchen garden and plantings, and in the afternoons they all threw themselves into the cool lake.

Otto laughed in Kärrnäs. He wrestled with Henrik, and even though he was thin and small in stature he sometimes won. He took bicycle outings. Uncle Oskar taught him how to care for horses and how to do the crawl. Together they rowed out on Lake Möckeln in the evening and set their nets. Then they rowed out in the early morning and pulled them up. Mother Agnes cooked their catch. At night a suntanned Otto fell into bed and slept as though unconscious until it was time to help with the milking, load the jugs onto the bicycle cart, and watch Oskar transport them that long kilometer out to the big road where the pallets were.

Suddenly the days stopped hurting. Liking it in Sweden, after one and a half years, was a gift he hadn't thought he'd receive. No, he didn't have time to write, well . . . maybe. But not right now.

July 2

We're very worried because we haven't heard from you in four weeks. What's going on? Letters are arriving from all the other children in Sweden... We are in utter despair. We cannot imagine what's behind this. If you're healthy, write immediately.

More and more often, the letter just sat in his hand. "Herr Otto Ullmann" was written in blue ink on the envelope.

It was the same each time. He forced himself to start reading, even though initially he didn't want to. Outside the window, summer was buzzing, and the Andersson family's voices could be heard in the next room. But then he was drawn in. In Elise's curves, lines, and dots was his true home, the sepia apartment on Löwengasse. When he followed her ink across the paper, they could be together. Not because she was saying anything special, but because his gaze was where her gaze had been, and in this way they could look each other in the eye, through the paper.

He was helplessly pulled into the old world, into rooms where his previous life was ongoing, clear but unreachable.

Two worlds wall to wall. One was the calm greenery, Smålandish, cinnamon buns. The other: the rumble of city streets, baked goods with vanilla cream and excited commands from the soccer coach. As soon as Pepi and Lisl's lines were over, the words written, the last period made, Otto was flung out and the present hit him with full force. Kärrnäs, Pjätteryd, Sweden. He couldn't get his worlds to cohere, no matter how hard he tried. And yet he bore them both. And they both had to be accommodated.

His memory was reshaping, leaving some spaces empty, as if it was dissolving from within. There was the stairwell where his and his father's voices had intertwined in a song where the words always were the same: *einz zwei drei vier fünf sechs sieben*. . . That's how he'd learned to count as a child, and the sound could still return—an echo for two voices.

Or the chestnut tree in the yard with the bird's nest that had fallen from it and the three naked chirping hatchlings that had lain there like a three-leaf clover. Dad had put the nest back in its fork, and a few weeks later the young ones dared venture along a branch, dressed in ruffled feathers. But all that was part of the Vienna wreck now, that rotting ship, and had begun to sink.

Like the ravine in the forest. You had to watch out, said Henrik. Because even the strongest man had fallen down it, and once you were at the bottom, there was no way out.

The roaring city. Lamps lit at dinner time. The memory of shop-window displays on Kärtnerstrasse, the warm huts with *Glühwein* and sweet treats at Christmas, the greengrocer muttering that Jews should be hanged from the nearest tree, Professor Klein's cane, the chemistry teacher's swastika pin hidden under his lapel, how Otto had crept through the corridor during recess with Verner and Utas and had gingerly lifted up the collar for a peek—everything sank, was sinking, was sunken, sunk down to the bottom. With his parents still inside.

If the light fell in through the window in a particular morning hazy way, if he woke up because he was freezing at dawn, if he wasn't prepared and wasn't vigilant, the wreck might move unexpectedly and shimmer. Then he would catch a whiff of Dad's shaving soap. Like now. With the as-yet unopened letter in his hand, Vienna would suddenly stir in his dark memory, as if it were preparing to rise to the surface.

Mein lieber Junge. Be diligent, economical, punctual, decent, spry in all you do.

What did Lisl and Pepi know? About the horses' snorting breath, their hot muscles contracting and relaxing under his hands as he groomed them? Diligent student? He knew how to put a halter and bridle on and take them off, how softly he needed to slap the reins against the horse's flank to get it to pull. Yes, Mutti, yes, Dad. He was diligent. A quick study in the muddy fields of Småland.

His teacher and friend was Henrik, who walked ahead of him on the forest paths. He was getting the best grades now, Dad. In the art of sawing wood.

When were they going to kick their way up to the surface, leave that murky wreck behind, and come pick him up?

Without even seeing the words in the letter, it felt as though his father's hand was resting heavily on his shoulder. His father used to do that, and Otto liked it. But he'd never really been sure of why. Had Dad wanted to transmit his strength, or was it the other way around?

The letter demanded a reply. Like all the others he received. But not now. Soon. Later. Maybe tonight. Vienna's shipwreck glimmered. If he shut his eyes and held his breath, it would disappear into his memory's dark depths. If only everything could go quiet. Sunken. Engulfed. Finally.

July 2, 1940

To the Israel Mission:

If I may, I'm turning to you with a wish I hope you can fulfill.

Because of the provisions you've made, my son Otto has been in Sweden since February 2, 1939. He was initially housed in Hemhult, Tollarp, but later moved to one Mrs. Wallengren, and then to a Mrs. Eklundh in Pjätteryd—all according to information I've received in letters from the boy himself.

But now that some time has passed without a sign of life from my son, I've begun to worry, not least because I hear how regularly other children write home. I don't know the cause of my boy's silence. Previously he would write each week. I'm worried he has fallen ill or is unwell in some other way, and that this might be the cause. Respectfully, I beg of you for this reason to inquire about my son, and that you kindly inform me of the result.

With reverence,
Lisl Ullmann

Josef and Elise Ullmann, Otto's parents.

Back row: Margarete Kollman/Aunt Grete (Elise's sister), Josef Ullmann, Aunt Grete (Josef's sister, who managed to escape to England), Paul Kalmar (Uncle Paul), and Adolfine Kalmar (Aunt Nuny). Front row: Elise Ullmann, Otto Ullmann.

Otto Ullmann in Vienna with his parents, Josef and Elise Ullmann, Josef's sister Grete, and Elise's sister Nuny.

Otto Ullmann in the center, with his mother behind him to the left and his grandmother behind his mother.

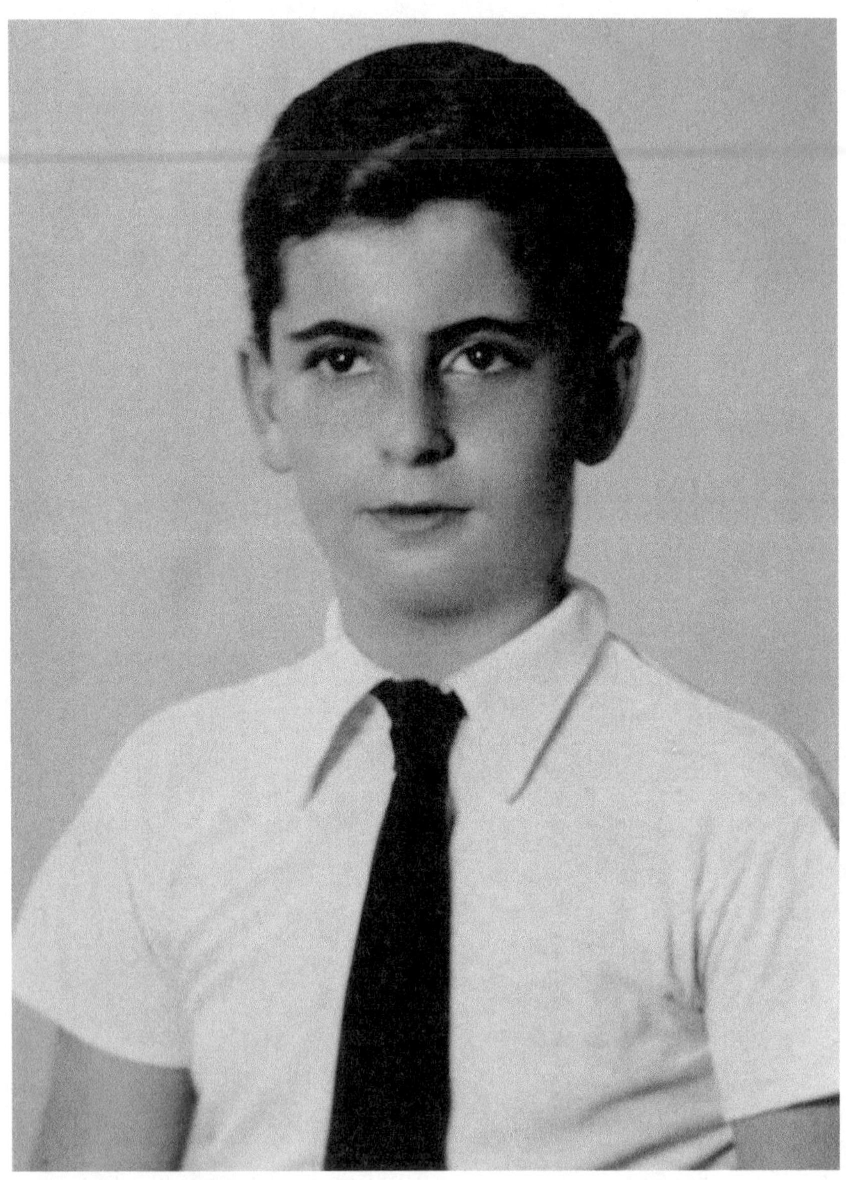

Otto Ullmann, Vienna.

A letter to Otto from his mother in Theresienstadt.

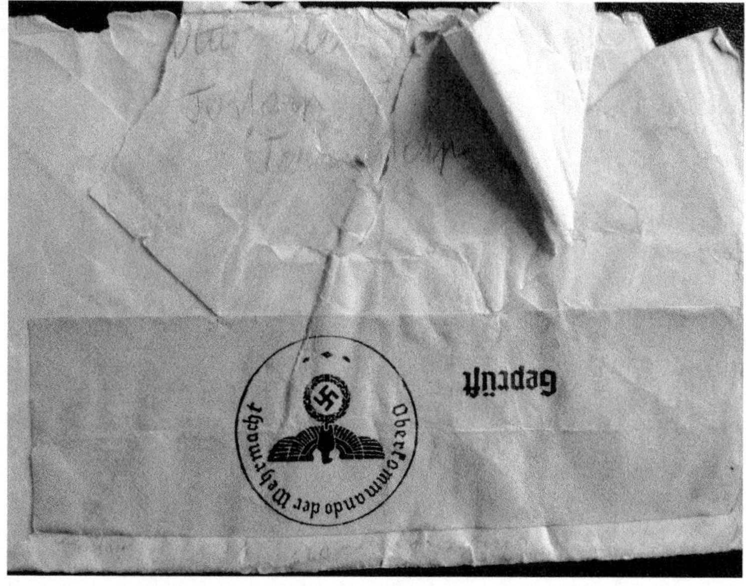

A letter (or envelope) from Otto returned to sender.

Otto Ullmann at the orphanage in Sweden, 1939.

Otto in Sweden.

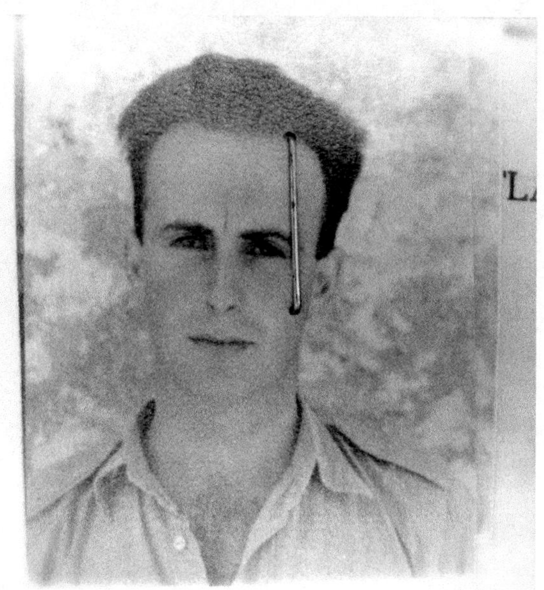

Identification document. Otto, 1948.

House of the Andersson family in Pjätteryd, where Otto lived for some years after the orphanage, and who became like a second family to him.

Otto Ullmann with unidentified Swedish woman.

The brown streak cut right through Kronoberg County. Meetings were held with speeches and song, with hatred directed toward those who were considered Jewish and contempt for what was called democracy.

On the farm in Elmtaryd, Agunnaryd, they liked to play bridge. The landowner Feodor Kamprad and his wife Berta had regular card nights with Rudolph Malmqvist, their hunting companion and an elementary school teacher, and his wife Ellen. Germany, Jews, and Chancellor H were recurring themes of conversation. The boy Ingvar was allowed to stay up and listen on the condition that he kept quiet.

In 1940 the Nazis in Jönköping were the most active in the county. They celebrated their seven-year anniversary and preferred to have their meetings in Master Gudmund's restaurant, where speeches were held that viciously attacked democracy; friendship evenings about Karl XII were hosted; and diatribes were launched against what they called "moral decay" and the Jewish press. Many turned up even though the majority of the party members had been conscripted for military service. During the birthday celebration itself Ensign Stål's tales were read aloud:

"Well now, my noble men, to strife away! Full well I've seen that fear no help can render; —Our war is great, —today is Dobeln's day! Sir adjutant, our grain is ripe; bear order O'er hill and plain, through groves to farthest borders, That all should boldly take the forward trade! Not here, but there, we prove our swords and lances; With such troops, the world-defiant one advances,—With them one ne'er awaits, but gives. Attack!"

And then they sang together and drank coffee.

III

Living with three people instead of thirty. Being listened to when you have something to say. Having your needs anticipated.

Otto was now fifteen. He worked with the ombudsman's flowerbeds, weeding the vegetable patches in the kitchen garden, and spent long shirtless days in the sun. Sometimes he helped in the barn or in the forest with Henrik under his Uncle Oskar's supervision. And when Oskar was enlisted, it was Otto and Henrik who drove the horses, felled the trees, sawed them and brought them home. Happier each day, and he gave thanks with his physical labor. Maybe that's why writing home had gotten harder. Wherever home was now.

He tried to answer Elise's questions and address Pepi's worry. They couldn't find Pjätteryd on the map, so he told them to look for Ljungby or maybe Älmhult. Did he have friends? He told them about Henrik. He gave an account of his fifteenth birthday, of the books he read and the newspaper's Sunday serial, of the unique traits of each of the two horses, that he was practicing the harmonica and was including a recent photo of himself. He poured out details describing the sunny waking hours, mother Agnes's smile, and the familial warmth. He studiously avoided the shadows at night, any feelings of hopelessness and anguish.

It seemed like this time in Sweden, in Småland's forests, was coming to an end. Pepi had been consigned to forced labor again, this time working just outside of Vienna, but he came home on weekends and—most importantly—the many letters he'd stubbornly sent off had finally yielded results. Someone in America promised to act as a guarantor for his subsistence. The most desirable thing had been arranged: an affidavit.

Vienna, August 25, 1940

My dearest, best boy. Mom sent your lovely letter directly to me, but only now that I'm home am I able to respond. Thank you so much for your lovely writing, yet another letter that moved me…

In your letter you answered many questions that I'd previously asked, rendering so much of what I wanted to know irrelevant. From the letter I can tell that you've made yourself at home and seem to have become a real Swede. Not just that, you're well acquainted with agricultural work and moreover are living together with good, fine people, you lack nothing, you have company, too, so I've read, and you can imagine that your descriptions made us very happy. Your being able to join in and hunt wild duck is interesting and you have surely, in spite of your youth, already had many valuable experiences that have given you insight into a whole new world.

I'm also happy that you could celebrate your birthday in a pleasant way—it is the second without us—and I hope with all my heart that you will continue to have it good in the future…

I, for at the moment it is only me, have received an affidavit, but cannot put it to use because I find it hard to leave and would like to wait for yours and Mom's. In any case it will be a little while yet, but most importantly, you are safe and well. Dearest boy, take care of yourself. A thousand greetings and kisses.

dad

Bitter herbs and honey, ambivalence and hesitation. An affidavit was without a doubt good news. But two were still missing.

Pepi's forced labor meant that he was away during the week, but that he could come home for the weekend. That was positive. On the other hand, he suffered greatly from the heavy, draining work. And Aunt Nuny was ordered to work at a factory, but not so far from Vienna that she couldn't come home in the evening. This meant they had a bit of coin to sustain them, which they shared equally.

On the other hand, they were now forbidden to have a telephone. The letters from Vienna brought no peace.

Otto knew Elise was plagued by worry. He should have been writing regularly, as he'd promised. But he too felt uncertain. The word at Kärrnäs was that he might have to move come winter. Otto didn't want to move. He was too old for the children's home, too un-Christian for the refugee camp in Tostarp. He would never go back there, and would rather become independent, find a job, any job, work hard. He knew he could make do. He was already alone.

Otto worried, but didn't want to send his worry to Vienna. They had enough of their own.

Anyway, there was no time to spare for letters when he and Henrik were to spend their days as oarsmen. Mr. and Mrs. Eklundh organized duck hunts in the reeds. The maids had their hands full carrying food out to the shooting party and carrying home the leftovers. People and bird hounds everywhere.

September 21, 1940

Dearest Otti, we have again become very worried, because we haven't heard anything from you since your last letter on August 21. I hope you are healthy. You did promise to write every week, after all. Please be so kind and remember that, because otherwise we'll be very worried. Thankfully we are in good health, and we hope the same is true for you. Hopefully we'll receive something from you today or tomorrow. One thousand regards and kisses.

your mom

Dearest Otti—many warm regards and kisses from me too.

Aunt Grete

"Thank God we are in good health." That phrase appeared ever more frequently in Elise's and Pepi's messages to Otto. Through those simple, almost meaningless words, they wanted to protect him from a reality that had long since burst the limit of what could be called a nightmare.

Pepi may have had an affidavit, a document of great value. So difficult to obtain, so crucial to have. But the affidavit—a term that no one had known only a few years before—had already been dulled by hopelessness. America's refugee quota for several years to come had already been met. Like Uruguay, almost every Latin American country had closed its borders to European Jews. German passport-holders could no longer flee to Great Britain, because officially they were enemies. And at home it was rule upon rule, barb upon barbed wire.

When bombs fell, Jewish people were not allowed to use the same air raid cellars as others. If their house only had one shelter, they had to stay in their apartments. Their coal ration was half as large. They were not given ration cards for clothing. They had permission to mend their shoes if they gave up soap.

October 9, 1940

Dearest boy. I've received your latest letter and was very happy to hear that you are well and can stay in Kärrnäs this winter, too. I'm happy you've found a place with such good people. I know you to be someone who is always nice and amicable toward everyone, which means that you are liked wherever you go.

That you have now also learned to ride is rather lovely. I only hope you are careful and make sure nothing happens to you. I would so love to see you on horseback.

One day you might also have your own little holding and then we can be together again. How nice that will be. But one must have patience. Don't forget to write soon, to keep me from worry.

Kisses and hugs.

mom

November 3, 1940

My dearest boy. No post arrived from you this week, but I assume we'll get something in the next days. As I've read in your last letter, you have much to do when the hunting party arrives. Then you probably don't have much time to write. But I still hope you will at least write a card so I know how you are. Thankfully we are doing well, and hope you are too. Write and tell us what you do during those long winter nights. Are you reading anything, perhaps in Swedish?... It would make me so happy to hear you are using your free time to educate yourself. I hope to hear from you soon. Dearest boy, take care of yourself. One thousand kisses and greetings.

your loyal dad

III

The days had a brand-new color. City brown and asphalt gray among the tall buildings and human masses had given way to verdant trees and black paths through the mire. Now Otto walked over moss, snapped twigs, and rested on rocks. Now he was the beater during the elk hunt, and nothing about those early mornings with the men, the smell of coffee and gunpowder, recalled the life he once lived.

Vienna.

Sometimes he told stories from home. About glittering Christmas displays on the Opernring, about cars and people getting in each other's way, about how a trip on the tram could be a journey through four, five, maybe six different languages. He was a good storyteller, and he noticed that this was impressive. If they hadn't been so warm and good to him, he would have laughed at their wide eyes. Mother Agnes may have read the newspaper thoroughly and followed world events, as did Henrik and Astrid, but only Otto had seen the world beyond Ljungby. He'd ridden the large Ferris wheel in Prater, and when he tried to describe everything you could see from up there, they could almost taste the salt on a pretzel, even though they were home in the kitchen in Kärrnäs.

Never did Otto speak about this longing. Never were the people in Kärrnäs allowed to sense the stranger who was just below the carefree surface, following Otto's gestures and listening to him talk, from the inside. Who replied with a quiet grimace.

Otherwise he spent the evenings studying Swedish grammar via a correspondence course. He'd come to the conclusion that he'd probably be in Sweden awhile.

III

The Nazi leadership in Vienna wanted to get their hands on the apartments.

On December 3, 1940, the chancellor gave his blessing for a request to begin the transportation of people classified as Jews out of Vienna. The official reason given was a "housing shortage."

Sixty thousand people were to be deported with increasing speed out to the General Government—that is to say East, to Poland. They were to be torn from house and home and to move in together in other houses, thereby freeing up apartments and creating so-called *Lebensraum.*

Pepi, Elise, and Aunt Grete were forced to leave Löwengasse.

They took the photographs with them. Small and large, glued into albums, framed and loose in envelopes; pictures of themselves during a snack break under the trees in the Vienna Woods, or satisfied after a good tennis match, on skis in Ischl. Photographs of Otto in his baby carriage, Otto with friends, in bathing trunks, on a soccer field. Otto in Sweden.

New address: Reisnerstrasse 3. The typewriter was small enough to carry, even though they were on foot. Auctions were held daily, during which entire furniture suites were sold to non-Jewish neighbors for no money at all.

Paul's schedule had once been full of English lessons with everyone who was going to emigrate and needed new language skills. Then he'd taught those who thought they were going to emigrate. In the end his hands were full with those who remained and were taking lessons in order to shatter their idleness. But they became fewer and fewer, and anyway, no one had anything with which to pay.

Did Paul and Nuny try to leave the country, did they, like Pepi, write letter after letter? Or did they figure that they were old and childless, that life had given them what was to be had. In any case, they didn't turn to the Jewish Community Council for emigration help.

Vienna's state governor publicly explained that the Viennese Jews' situation was hopeless, and those who happened to read the *Times* of London would have found out that no one could survive on the paltry food rations, if not for other people secretly giving them food.

The call came in February 1941.

Paul and Nuny had to report to an assembly point in Vienna, the one close to Aspang Station. This order came with the threat of harsh punishments for those who refused, and the departure was set for February 26. They were allowed to take with them at most fifty kilos of luggage.

On the specified date, they were forced to leave their apartment. Guards from the Jewish Community Council chaperoned them to make sure that they neither fled nor spoke to anyone.

Together with 979 other Viennese residents they stood there, with bags, baskets, children, and fears, at one and the same place. Waiting. Person by person, child by child, prayer by prayer, refusal to pray by refusal to pray.

Paul and Nuny, and all the rest. No longer Mr. and Mrs., no longer teacher, doctor, or cobbler, librarian, student, accountant, seamstress. Prisoners. Number 486 and number 487.

They were told that their train was the second in line. A previous transport had left for the same destination a few weeks prior. They had to give up their valuables and the money they brought with them. They were warned that if they were searched and valuables were found, an immediate death penalty that extended to all family members would be issued. They were given forty zloty. They knew their destination lay in Poland. They heard the place name "Opole" for the first time. Wasn't it near Lublin? They had to pay ten zloty in tax to Opole's municipality.

After a day of waiting the train departed.

That same day, February 27, 1941, the Nazis in Kalmar held a meeting at Röda Kvarn, and the hall, not including the gallery, was full. The leader Sven Olov Lindholm spoke standing on a podium alongside a color guard. The local newspaper *Barometern* had refused to run ads for the meeting, but the Nazis themselves were happy with the turnout.

Opole is almost impossible to locate on the map, and as soon as you find it, you discover another town of the same name. But it is the smaller, less significant Opole to which Paul and Nuny were deported, fifty kilometers from Lublin: Opole Lubelskie.

In the 1930s it was not a good place for a village: close to the border between the Nazis and the Soviets. Sometimes the village ended up outside of all frameworks. The Jewish population was then plundered. Such things happen. In 1939 the Nazis conquered Opole and turned the little town into an assembly ghetto. During the first year of Nazi rule, the number of residents of Jewish descent doubled. Unfortunately the number of houses and outhouses did not increase, nor did the access to food and water.

The trip took thirty-six hours. When Paul and Nuny arrived they were met with nothing but confusion. And people—all along the muddy streets. People from the previous Vienna transport, still unhoused. The villagers had already rented out their ramshackle barns and outbuildings. The synagogue was taken. On the floor, under each of the twelve windows, people slept on straw, using each other as pillows and coats as blankets.

The first night Nuny and Paul sat on their luggage. If there was space in a room or a box room, the elderly and women with children were given priority. The rest had to make do as best they could. Wooden bunks were cobbled together and stacked in already full barns, with hay laid on them. Walls were sealed and roofs were patched. Prisoners between sixteen and sixty had to be registered with the authorities for work. In solidarity all food that the travelers had brought with them from Vienna was pooled and given to a makeshift soup kitchen. Each person received a bowl of soup and a quarter loaf of bread per day. For as long as it lasted.

It must be said that at first the villagers helped with food. But then they started to charge. There were eggs, milk, butter, as well as meat. But a kilo of bread cost two zloty—four times as expensive as in Vienna. Without a way to earn a living, starvation was only thirty zloty away. So they sold their possessions for bread, sold everything that could be sold, everything the villagers wanted to have. But this ran out, too. It all ran out.

Security men from the SS, the local police, and the German army oversaw it all. Many prayed to God.

Paul and Nuny?

III

Otto's voice had deepened, his muscle mass had increased, and he'd outgrown his juvenile body. The language was not a problem. He was Swedish now. But he remained a foreigner.

The village of Pjätteryd lay where it lay, that is to say not far from Lönshult, Stenshult, Oshult, and Käxnäs—but at a distance from almost everything else. Gravel roads and spruce trees, ferns and wood anemones. No cafés with freshly powdered apple strudel and cakes with walnuts and apricot jam behind the glass counter. He heard the soughing leaves but no string quartets. They preserved lingonberries but they did not roast corn on the cob or chestnuts.

Here sweaty horses worked the fields, horses Otto had learned to ride bareback. Here the trees made up a dense forest, were marked, felled, sawed, and stacked as wood. Here he wasn't taught English word order, had no boxing ring or sparring partner, but he had learned how to smoke a pipe and tuck in snus. He tarred the dock, collected hens' eggs, and painted fences.

Sometimes Mrs. Eklundh would come out from Lund to her summerhouse together with the girls Ingrid and Carin. That was the closest to city folk that Otto came, but they kept themselves to a higher echelon, very friendly but a little older and out of reach. They spent time with their cousins on the farm next door but not with Astrid or Henrik or him. Otto knew that back home in Vienna they would have been his peers, but this was Pjätteryd and he was a refugee.

In Kärrnäs the days passed at a farmer's pace. Weather, crops, animals, hunger, temperature, and physical strength governed this existence. And it was good.

Vienna, May 11, 1941

My dearest boy, your latest card and letter calmed both your mother and me. We were also happy to see in the photograph you sent that you are doing well. At least you've grown substantially and the only shame is that we cannot get a proper look at your face in the picture, because you were photographed almost completely in profile. If you at some point get a picture where you can be seen from the front, do please send it to us. I really don't need to tell you how happy it would make us.

Paul received your letter and it made him very happy. He still misses you as a student. In your letter I can see your work does not leave you much free time. I have a certain insight into agricultural life and know there is much to do in springtime. Here everything is already fertilized and even the sowing of corn and turnips is done, and now we are planting potatoes, but even that will be finished soon. Unfortunately the weather is not ideal. It's cold and the chill impairs crop development, but fine weather will make up for it.

What are you growing? You're already handy behind a plow and have a deft hand with it. How are you faring with the horses? Do they obey you? They must be obedient if you're riding without a saddle.

It makes me happy to hear that you're so well taken care of. Please send the Andersson family my heartfelt regards and our thanks for being so kind to you. We'd write to them ourselves if they understood German. Please send our regards to Mrs. Eklundh as well, and thank her properly…

Dear boy. If we want to receive reports from you more often, then I don't need to list the reasons why, do I? Our longing is still as strong and grows with each day you are not with us. In a few months you'll already be sixteen years old. You might imagine that those two and a half years you've been away seem like an eternity. Meanwhile I know very well that your work is hard and strenuous and that you don't have a lot of time to write letters. Please heed my advice, and write at least one card each week, so that we know how you're doing and can be at ease. But a few lines are enough, for then our contact will remain unbroken. Beloved boy, I'm stopping here. Take care of yourself and may God protect you.

your loyal dad

On June 22, 1941, Germany began its invasion of the Soviet Union: Operation Barbarossa.

The headline of the German-sympathizing newspaper *Aftonbladet* read "Europe's Freedom War":

> Encircled by Western powers, Germany has broken its chains and is proceeding with free and increased strength to its European—its globally historic—mission to crush the red regime that has posed a constant threat to the very principle of freedom.
>
> Under the auspices of an artificial state, Moscow has terrorized our time. England made an incomprehensible and unforgivable mistake in not partaking in a European policy to create a united front against the Sovietized East from the start. Now Germany has been forced first to clean house in the servilely governed continent, and only then, with its back unburdened, to proceed to fight the most worthy battle. Under Germany's leadership, Europe is moving toward a people's war against the Red Empire. Finland and Romania are marching on the flanks. In the North, Finland had the great and honorable task of securing the springboard against Red Tsarism. Finland has already bled for this task and is now making new sacrifices for the North.
>
> There can be no doubt over the outcome of this war. Germany's own efforts and the organization of the allies means a victorious and invincible power. There is no doubt what the Swedish people are feeling at this moment. It is not an exaggeration to state that this day of global historic importance, when war broke out, will prove to be crucial to Sweden's future status.

Four German mobile killing units were unleashed in the Soviet Union with the mission to eliminate those classified as "subversive elements." A new phase had begun in solving the so-called Jewish problem, a phase of murdering civilian men, women, and children without forewarning.

From this day forward, the barriers were razed.

One can only guess what the Bolshevik-hating Feodor Kamprad, his mother Fanny, and the rest of the family in Agunnaryd thought about these developments. They were not alone in linking the Russian Bolsheviks with Jews, Jews with the Soviet Union, and the Soviet Union with threat.

The Nazi youth movement, Nordisk Ungdom, hosted summer camps, and young Ingvar attended at least one. He remembers the fire being lit in the evenings, songs being sung, and uniform buttons glinting in the light. The warmth of community.

Imagine youth's innocent pleasures, Ingvar Kamprad was but fifteen years old after all, a lone wolf seeking a pack. But the Lindholmers wanted to subject Jews to the Aliens Act. In each issue of their magazine they baited and collected names of those who were assumed to be of Jewish heritage. New members had to certify that they were of the Aryan race.

Meanwhile Otto was working on the farm in Pjätteryd. Though unaware of the other's existence, the two young men, Ingvar and Otto, were only a rowboat trip apart. Kärrnäs and Elmtaryd farms still flank the shores of Lake Möckeln.

In high summer Otto returned to work as a gardener. His temporary residency permit had to be regularly renewed, otherwise there could be difficulties with both the police and deportation. In July he wrote to his savior:

> Esteemed Mr. Pastor Pernow!
> Forgive me for bothering Mr. Pastor, but I was wondering if Mr. Pastor would be so kind as to arrange for my residency permit in Sweden to be extended. I am doing very well, I'm working again in Mrs. Eklundh's garden. It made me very happy to have been able to stay on the farm this winter and I thought it was fun to join in on hauling wood in the forest.
>
> Reverently,
> Otto Ullmann

On July 2, task forces running amok in the Soviet Union were issued new orders from their leader Reinhard Heydrich: execute all Jews in party and state functions.

Everything happened, every day. On July 5 alone, 2,514 Jews were shot in Kovno, Lithuania. And so on.

On July 18 Heinrich Himmler was made responsible for security in the East. A few weeks later he'd sent 11,000 troops to the swampy area called Pripet. On August 1 he issued an explicit order that "All Jews be shot. Drive the female Jews into the swamp."

And the Swedish government's policies toward those who were seeking asylum remained unchanged. In 1941 at least 3,674 people applied for protection and residency permits in Sweden. The Swedish government reviewed, judged, and classed 1,029 of them as Mosaic.

Of the non-Jews applying for entry permits over 86 percent were allowed to travel into Sweden. Of those who had an M placed after their name, just over 38 percent were allowed across the border. Sweden persisted in its refusal.

Ingvar was to attend Osby's coeducational school in the fall. In his luggage he had propaganda from the SSS and Nazi leader Sven Olov Lindholm. It was a boarding school, and the boys were normally housed in a building called Manhem, but because it was at full capacity, Ingvar had to share a room with another boy in the main building. There they had part of the top floor to themselves and used the fire escape as a private entrance.

Another Smålandish admirer of Führer Lindholm was Per Engdahl. He was seventeen years older than Ingvar Kamprad and an educated man who wrote poetry as well as political tracts.

He'd heard Lindholm make a speech in 1928, when the two of them were helping establish Uppsala's fascist paramilitary, and called Lindholm a firebrand and a brilliant speaker. Engdahl was an outspoken antidemocratic nationalist who wanted to formulate a "Swedish standpoint grounded in nationalism and socialism" based on Mussolini's Fascist Italy.

He was also a staunch anti-Communist, combating both the ideology and its adherents. And so it happened that in this year, 1941, he founded the movement Svensk Opposition (Swedish Opposition): "Communists often recruit the street's worst riffraff for their gangs. People who carry inferior genetic material easily become the bearers of an inferior movement. This is why Swedish Opposition wants racial sanitization that prevents such elements from procreating. We want a physically and spiritually sound population, who will therefore be unreceptive to Communist propaganda."

In his new movement, Per Engdahl had involved the entire Swedish-German National Association, in which Swedish upper-class doctors, lawyers, and professors were "[working] for fair judgment of the new Germany." The Lindholmers didn't like the competition, but Engdahl considered his movement to be complementary: "We are all fighting for the same end, if but with different means."

There are those who say the hatred of Jews was not part of Per Engdahl's political ideology. Ingvar Kamprad was among them. But in a number of writings, beginning in 1934, Engdahl expressed his view of Jews and others. The same year that Ingvar fell for Engdahl's charisma, one of his main messages was about how animals and plants are cultivated, whereas people are left to drift:

"In our country, in order to preserve and cultivate the race that makes it possible for Sweden's people to work to the standard we pride ourselves by, one must demand: sterilization of all inferior race elements; prohibition of marriage with extra-European races." And this addendum: "This does not only apply to negroes and Mongols, but also to Jews and other Oriental peoples."

Swedish Opposition's official line throughout the war doesn't leave much room for Ingvar Kamprad's description of reality:

> Sweden's Jewish dominion must be tirelessly crushed through the realization of the following five points: (1) A ban on all Jewish immigration. (2) A ban on Jews holding leading positions in the state, society, and corporations. (3) The right of the government to appoint a Swedish administrator in a Jewish company. (4) A prohibition of marriages between Swedes and Jews. (5) The assembly of all Jews living in Sweden in a specific colony, whose government-approved leadership will take responsibility for the conduct of Swedish Jews and Jews living in Sweden.

In the middle of the summer, July 29, several of the Nazi-sympathizing Swedish daily newspapers published three questions for Prime Minister Per Albin Hansson, written by Per Engdahl and undersigned by many prominent Swedes.

Why was a Communist party allowed in Sweden? was one question. Is not Finland still our concern? was another. The third questioned Swedish opinion and the Social Democrats' view of Germany and called for reflection, since Germany would defeat the "Anglo-Saxon powers."

It was designed like an ad, and readers of the *Aftonbladet* and *Stockholms-Tidningen* newspapers could answer the call using a special voucher. Swedish Opposition's Malmö division said they received over twenty thousand responses.

Osby sits just below the border between Skåne and Småland. A small place, but there were some thirty residents who aired their opinions. And why shouldn't they? Germany was a victorious power, nothing to be ashamed of. No wonder the kiosk near the school was well stocked.

During the school year, that's where Ingvar bought the Nazi party's newspaper *Den svenske folksocialisten* (*The Swedish People's Socialist*) and could follow the German war victories. It printed reports on successful anti-Jewish meetings held around Sweden and articles about, for example, the number of Jewish cobblers in the capital. In the same kiosk Per Engdahl's newspaper would soon also be for sale.

Maybe Ingvar was already recruiting friends to the Nazi party. He and three others were definitely having secret meetings in the Osby school's attic and creating a Nazi fraternity. They drew swastikas and broke their skin so they could be blood brothers. Perhaps—but not for certain—he cycled to Ryd on August 10 to hear the party's man in Kyrkhult, Karl-Erik Hindberger, speak on the square. Around seventy-five people listened, some audience members were in opposition, and after, words were exchanged.

Ingvar attended school and developed his political interests. He was reprimanded by the school's anti-Nazi leadership when he etched a swastika into a desk, and this taught the fifteen-year-old a lesson: be more discreet about your opinions.

III

Osby and Pjätteryd. Ingvar and Otto. They still hadn't met. Thirty-five miles by land wasn't all that separated them.

September arrived. In Vienna Pepi, Elise, and Aunt Grete were made to sew a yellow cloth patch—as large as the palm of a hand and shaped like a six-pointed star, inscribed with the word JUDE—on their left breast, just above the heart. But they write nothing of this in their letters.

On the Kärrnäs farm Otto's joy over being with a family was accompanied by calm. He hadn't felt this way since before that morning—8 a.m. on February 1 at the Ostbahnhof.

Agnes Andersson became the heart of Otto's new world. She had enough warmth to spare for him, too. The days began to trot along. The letters arrived each week from Vienna, anchor lines cast out. He worked. He studied for his correspondence course at night. He knew Nazis were holding regular local gatherings. What could he do but do his best?

That autumn Kalmar's Nazis were especially active. On October 9 they held a meeting at the new venue on Strömgatan 3. Forty-some interested people arrived to listen to a party member, a doctor besides, speak about the population question.

On October 15 the party wasn't allowed to rent the Röda Kvarn cinema, but gathered an audience of three hundred at the theater instead. The leader, Sven Olov Lindholm, spoke, this time about "Communism and other un-Swedish matters." A more intimate meeting was held with Lindholm afterward in the theater's club room.

One month later, on November 6, forty-some Nazis gathered to honor Gustav II Adolf's Day. The speakers were Allan Melin, Gösta Fridholm, and Erik Engström. The next meeting was held on November 20. Kalmar's son Erik Engström spoke on the subject of "Food shortages, job shortages, housing shortages." Ten days later the memory of Karl XII was celebrated.

The Swedish missionaries in Vienna saw the year that was coming to a close in a biblical light. Never before had such need been witnessed, they summarized, and the Jewish population was a people breaking apart, determined to emigrate.

"The greatest joy has been to be—an exile. And they have gone to the greatest lengths to reach this goal. Those who were able to secure an entry visa to another country have been viewed with the same envy as those who have won the lottery's jackpot."

Pepi and Elise must have agonized before doing what they'd promised themselves not to. Saving Otto had been contingent on a single immutable premise, formulated by the Swedish government and conveyed with the utmost clarity by the pastors at the Swedish Israel Mission: Otto had been allowed to go to Sweden on the condition that they would not follow him.

But now.

Neighborhood after neighborhood in Vienna was being declared *judenrein* as the apartments were emptied and the residents were crowded together with strangers elsewhere. They had to turn in bicycles, cameras, binoculars, and typewriters. They were forbidden to sell books.

Even though Pepi had found a financial guarantor overseas, he hadn't managed to arrange an affidavit for Elise and Otto.

So they broke their promise to the Swedes, the missionaries, the Board of Health and Welfare. They wrote to sixteen-year-old Otto. They asked for his help. Could they also come to Sweden?

Otto went straight across the courtyard to Mrs. Eklundh.

November 17, 1941

My boy. A few days ago we sent a letter that you must have already received and now we have received your letter from November 5, which made us so very happy, and that I would like to answer immediately.

First and foremost—thank you for reacting so quickly and for trying to fulfill our wishes. We never doubted that you would try to help us. In the meantime we have to wait and see how it goes with Mrs. Eklundh's inquiry.

I will contact Mr. Edling, but still would like to let a few days pass until you have more information, so that I won't cause unnecessary bother. Now we wait with anticipation to see if anything can be done. But for now this means waiting, as you so correctly write.

Thank you for the photograph, as well. As far as I can see you have become a big boy, it's only your hairstyle that does not please me—a veritable forest has sprouted on your head! But I assume that, since the picture was taken, it has fallen prey to scissors. A part suited you better, but you probably don't have time to style your hair. We like you whatever you look like, you know that.

I don't need to tell you how much we long to see you again, but because of all the hurdles, we can do nothing but trust that God will soon make a reunion possible.

I hope you're doing well and can find time to rest—I imagine you need it after the hard work. Now, with the snow-covered fields, I suppose the farmers don't have anything to do outdoors. I'm very well aware that there is plenty to do on the farm, but you must have more time now, the days are short, after all.

Mutti was so touched that you didn't forget her birthday. It was very good of you to remember Paul, as well. He too wrote about you in his last letter and wondered how it was going for you. If you could write to him, he would surely be very happy. The address is An den Judenrat für P.K. Opole über Pulawy, Distrikt Lublin General Gouvernement. He has a few students around your age, and is forever seeking you in each and every one. He can neither stop writing nor thinking about you, his favorite student, who was so good at languages.

What are your friends doing? Are you in contact with them? Most of them aren't far from you, are they, or is Hemhult far from Pjätteryd?

We are in good health, thankfully. We await and long for your continued reports. Hearty thanks for your love, take care of yourself and may God continue to protect you.

your loyal dad

I thank you kindly for the birthday wishes. Like you, I hope we can celebrate the next birthday together. You can perhaps imagine our longing. I want so much to wrap my arms around you as I did when you were a little boy. Now you are already an adult and a proper man. Take care of yourself.

your mom

Lisl waited and longed. She patched clothing, rarely went out. There wasn't enough food, but what to do? She was a poor cook, it tasted poor, she ate poorly. Items of value had long since been sold, and they themselves had gone from one home to the next and somewhere along the line a third awaited them, as did an end to their wandering. Her sister Grete and her husband irritated her. She didn't want to count how many people were no longer in the city, as if they had never been there. She waited for mail, for a positive reply, for lines from her son, for the mailman, for answers, for everything, for so very little, almost nothing at all.

When the days change shape, when they no longer are either recent or coming, but fall as the second hand must fall for every new second. When they become an aimless wandering in search of a door to rooms that had not yet been built—then a person also changes shape, becoming longing and losing themselves.

The child was gone, but Elise bore his memory like a pregnancy: how he'd lain next to her when she woke up, his eyes which had never been more than a glance away. Otto.

She clung to the idea of them being together again one day. It was ahead of them, waiting: a door with their name on it. They would find it, stop, grab the knob, open it, and step into the encounter. They would face each other, Otto and she, her son and his mother, and they would look into each other's eyes, searching for all the lost time. The day, the door, the encounter, the gaze—it all awaited her.

She knew it.

According to the description the Kronoberg County police gave to the Swedish authorities, his hair was black and his eyes brown. His nose was large and straight and his face shape oval. An additional description: small chin. He was 166 centimeters tall. Under the heading "distinctive features" it was noted that he was slight in stature. The reason for his stay in Sweden: Jewish ancestry.

And through a government order issued in November in the year 1941, stating that all German subjects of Jewish origin outside the borders of the German empire were to be stripped of their German citizenship, Otto Ullmann became stateless.

Tracks were laid, vents were sealed. The places being prepared for murder were called Chelmno, Belzec, and Oswiecim. And maybe it was now that the final strand of a series of decisions became clear.

The decision to empty Europe of people of Jewish origin had been made long ago. Now—in November 1941—it was a matter of method, the question was how. Instead of plundering, deportation, and starvation, the Nazis in the highest echelons decided to shorten the process to murder. As the invading forces had done in the Soviet Union.

On December 7, Japan bombed Pearl Harbor. A few days later Chancellor H spoke with his party leaders. "The world war is here. The annihilation of the Jews must be the necessary consequence."

Smålandsposten didn't report it, but Otto could read about the one hundred Jews who were to be executed by firing squad in Paris, about the penalty tax of a billion francs that Jews in France had to pay because German soldiers had been injured or killed in attacks carried out by the resistance movement, and that a large number of criminal Jewish-Bolshevik elements were to be moved east.

There is courage, and there is patience. Pepi and Lisl concentrated on the latter.

There are those who say that Jewish patience in Vienna in 1942 required great courage. Then there are those who say that patience only required blinders. Who knows. We are all equal before death.

Patience was Pepi and Elise's way through the days, patience was the railing the blind followed through darkness. Would the descent ever end?

When they risked losing their grip, they repeated the word again and again—to each other and themselves—they wrote it time and time again in their letters. They were waiting for everything to be different. To change for the better. For an opening.

Otto had turned to Mrs. Eklundh. He himself could not apply for Pepi's and Elise's admission to Sweden, but she knew more, had contacts, could maybe help.

The days passed. They waited for the results of Mrs. Eklundh's efforts. They waited through December, through January.

In February they were still waiting.

My beloved boy. On February 1 it will be three years since you left us. I would never have thought that we would be apart for so long. But destiny has made its choice and one can do nothing about destiny. We are happy you've ended up with good people, and we thank God you are healthy. We hope and pray to God that we will soon see each other again. All we hope is to see you again in good health. Kisses and regards.

mom

Dear boy—I hope to write in more detail in a few days.
dad

Pepi worked. Lisl wrote. They stretched their patience as far as they could, into an excruciating, discordant, drawn-out tone, and thus they had to be patient also with patience itself, and feed it with itself like a snake eating its own tail.

And Mrs. Eklundh, what was she doing? Was she writing letters to some official at the Aliens Office? If so, was she advised not even to try to help them enter the country? Did she discuss this with the good Pastor Pernow—and if such was the case, did he offer a fresh perspective, different from the one he'd so far held, namely that the children had been rescued on the condition that the parents would not be allowed to follow? Nonnegotiable.

Pepi and Elise cannot be found in any Swedish archive, neither with an inquiry nor an entry permit application. On the other hand this could be because their applications have been cleared out. It happens.

Or did Mrs. Eklundh know that there was no point in trying? Since October, Jews were forbidden to leave Nazi Germany.

In retrospect, certain circumstances and choices are difficult to understand.

As early as the summer of 1938, Josef Ullmann, the head of the family, had applied to the Jewish Community Council in Vienna for emigration help. Four years had passed since then. In his application were one incomprehensibility and two strategic mistakes.

To the question about whether he had contacts overseas, he'd left a blank space. Why did he not name his brother in Uruguay? To the question about his professional skills, he'd replied he was an editor, an office worker, and to a certain degree familiar with bookkeeping, when he should have written less about his ability to think and more about physical strength.

Finally, the application form had asked whether family members wished to emigrate together or one at a time. In June 1938, Pepi answered with two words: Together, preferably.

Reading other emigration applications from that time, one sees that most people also answered the question with two words, but different ones. They wrote: Children first. Though Pepi would send his son away only six months later, splitting up the family was unimaginable back on June 18, 1938.

Do these three points answer the question why he and Lisl still had not made it out of Nazi Germany? Can the consequences of a couple of words, hastily jotted down one June day long before war broke out, be judged fairly when read in the light of the present day? I don't know. Seventy years of long shadows obscure the view.

One other thing can be read in Pepi's application for emigration help from that June day, something he'd written down even though no one asked him to: the name of a person he knew in the Jewish Community Council. Perhaps it was this very person who was making arrangements for him now, four years later, in the raw cold of the first month of the year 1942. Maybe it was he who was making sure that Pepi had work.

The work was hard and intense and would not earn him a single pfennig. But Pepi's salary was paid in a currency more valuable than all the bills and coins in the Nazi nation. He and Elise were compensated in time. Lifetime.

Otto's daughter pushes her burden onto me. The white box from IKEA was driven over from her home, unloaded, and carried into mine. As I lifted off the lid, the smell of old paper rose up like a spirit from a jar, asking what I wanted.

Otto got sick at the end of his life and softened. He spoke with his daughter. She'd begun to ask questions about her temperamental father's childhood, where his rage came from, and she had understood that the answers were in what was left unsaid. And so he gave her the letters from Lisl and Pepi. A pile of 368 letters from the year 1939. And another with 117 letters from 1940. Only three letters from 1941, but thirty-five from the next year. And then all the ones from Aunt Grete, Nuny, and Uncle Paul.

The dust from the box, the brittle sheets of paper, the everyday phrases that filled them... The closer to the bottom I got, the more the letters seemed to be abandoning themselves. Ever emptier of messages, they became their own content. As if they were following a principle of fear: messages submerged in anxiety become as heavy as the total amount of words omitted.

In spite of this, the letters had linked parent and child just by being sent from one place to the next, passed from one hand to another. But now. Could they fulfill some of our wishes—Otto's daughter's, my own?

Could they be the first point in the prosecution, so that he, the boy, could be given redress?

Could they be the needle that pierced the silence his children had been born into? They'd gone along—an entire family—pretending Otto wasn't in pain and time could heal.

"I don't want to pass this on to my children," said Otto's daughter.

Perhaps these compactly stored letters—the deciphering of them—could dissolve the pain so that only the memory would be inherited, nothing more.

Each page carries its weight in ink. Each word bears layer upon layer of reproach and destitute longing; why are you not here so that we can take care of you, why are you not a child so that we can be your parents?

Each letter, every word is a stone to bend down and pick up. A stone to pocket. A stone to carry to the grave.

III

The city of Vienna pulses faintly like an old heart. The house on Löwengasse 49 is still there, and inside the front door is the same stairwell where once the voices of Otto, Pepi, Elise, and the others echoed. On the floor the same marble flower pattern and in the courtyard the chestnut tree still stands, four stories high.

Tram tracks, street signs, statues—most of it is still there. Pissoirs, the stench from the drains, and a particular Viennese surliness, seventy years on. You can stroll down the streets, but what played out on them cannot be read in the asphalt. You see elderly people and realize that they were here back then. But their faces reveal nothing about what they did, experienced, and with whom they'd identified.

Near to some of Vienna's prized gems—St. Stephen's Cathedral and the clock at Hoher Markt—is Judenplatz. A synagogue is hidden behind the buildings' facades and next door, the entrance to the Jewish Community Council's office, framed by guards, metal bars, and luggage x-ray machines.

That's not where I'm going.

Around the corner is a modest door, almost invisible, leading past a restaurant kitchen. The smell of reused grease fills the stairwell. The floor and walls are splattered with spillage and dirt. Here? A simple sign with an arrow pointing to a door one floor up. Here.

A historian at the Jewish Community Council's archive opens up and shows me the way in. Box upon box, carton upon carton of material stacked in a large apartment office. So many documents. So many people. So many dead.

In the heat of the microfilm projector we begin researching Josef Ullmann's activities during the war years, the man who tried to write his son every day. Which words did he leave out? What was unwritten?

A day or so before, another historian, at the Archives of the Austrian Resistance, had given me a pitying look when I told him about the letters from Pepi and Lisl, that so many were about the weather and health and not about what was actually happening. She said, "You have to read between the lines."

That's why I've come here, to the Jewish Community Council's archive, which is hidden behind an apartment door without a sign, in a stairwell that looks like a trash dump, behind a curtain of fumes from *Wienerschnitzel* frying. There, one floor up, the past is only partly unpacked in a locale as disoriented and decayed as a human memory; a storeroom for what is between the lines.

I have written down my questions, listed the notions that need to be upgraded to facts. Was Josef Ullmann a victim of Adolf Eichmann's Nisko project? Was he deported on October 26, 1939?

Yes, there's his name on the list. Original documentation. He and 656 other men were carried as transport number 2 to a Polish no-man's-land near the Soviet border to lay the foundations for a Jewish state. Minus forty degrees Celsius. There they had to make do the best they could, all the way until April, when Governor Frank complained that there were too many Jews in his protectorate, and the project was halted as quickly as it began. The men were sent back to where they came from. Some of them. The ones who survived. Pepi had been lucky.

Later, at the end of 1940, he was forced into more labor, but Lisl never wrote what work he did. Did Otto know more than the scant information she shared: Dad is gone but he comes home on the weekends? That mystery is still unanswered.

But then.

Pepi and Elise stayed in Vienna during 1942. By then he'd long since had to give up his typewriter. The letters to Sweden are shorter, more repetitive, and for the most part in Elise's handwriting. If Pepi wrote to Otto, it was in single sentences, such as "Dear boy—I hope to write in more detail in a few days," or "Dear boy. I now have a moment to spare. Most recently I couldn't write, and had to enlist Mutti as a proxy. I couldn't take more than a short break today either, but I want to hear how you're doing." And "Unfortunately my work doesn't allow me to respond in as much detail as your dear card deserves. I'm occupied day and night and write to you during short breaks."

Lisl wrote similarly: "Because Dad is busy at work at the moment, I'm writing you a card so our correspondence isn't interrupted."

In letter after letter, month after month, Pepi seemed to be so intensely occupied that he lacked the energy to write to his only child. But busy with what? Could a Jew be a street sweeper, a cleaner in these times? Which job assignments could there possibly have been?

When I arrive at the archive at Judenplatz, I'm only really counting on being allowed to ask these questions, not on getting any answers. But then the first clue appears, in a document about a different topic altogether.

To determine where Pepi and Lisl actually lived during the war years, I needed a historian's help. In Vienna there was no demarcated ghetto. People were forced to move in with each other all over the city. One address, Robertgasse, recurs in the letters, and the historian at the archive produces a register of the tenants. And there their names are, neatly noted: Josef, Elise, and Margarethe.

But there's more. After Josef Ullmann's name is a note in the "employer" column. It says Kultusgemeinde. The Jewish Community Council.

The archive's historian and I were glad to find the information, but not surprised. So Pepi was working at the Council. That seemed logical, who else would've hired a Jew in the midst of war and Nazi rule? But which tasks could have been taking up his time, day and night?

The historian explains that there were two options: either Pepi worked in the Jewish hospital as a carer, or he was a volunteer. Then he found more microfilm, and we each take one to scroll through. The hospital personnel on one, those who registered as volunteers on the other.

And we find Josef Ullmann's registry card among the volunteers—he was working in the research group.

Investigation. This seems logical, too. He was a journalist, after all. But what research did the Jewish Community Council need to carry out in Vienna in 1942?

On January 7, 1942, Josef Israel Ullmann was hired by the Jewish Community Council. The next day he reported to his supervisor in one of the Council's many research groups, and began his first workday.

It was a little calmer in the beginning. He was left with some spare time to write.

January 10, 1942

My beloved boy. Your precious lines from December 29 were a true joy to read. We haven't been that happy in a long time and your letter confirmed yet again what a treasure we have in you. You are still our kindhearted boy, and neither time nor distance can change that.

I'm happy to hear that pains are being taken to arrange another foster home for you. When we read about how good you have it and hear about the Christmas presents you've received, then Mom and I feel very happy. Even if we would so very much like to have you with us, we must admit that you have it much better out there. Above all you have the chance to be independent. You've had many experiences and are now "at home" in agriculture. By the time you finish your agricultural education, the future will be wide open for you.

We think it's a shame that you must move in spring, because you've had such a good time with the Andersson family. But you yourself write that you're going to a larger farm, and if you continue to be nice and decent anything is possible. Decent, nice, and loyal—that you have truly remained. And your letters and cards, which have thankfully been arriving with regularity, attest to the good spirit that has always distinguished you. You are still our good boy. Even if we couldn't be with you during these years when you have grown from a boy into a young man and have perhaps required advice and help from your parents, you can be sure that we were all with you in thought. We are happy our prayers for your well-being have so far been answered. We know you have to work hard and that the lot of the farmer is not an easy one—but it is not a thankless task. We hope that you with your diligence and intelligence will know success.

We, too, had a few bitterly cold days. It has gotten warmer now, but the thermometer still sits below zero. It certainly wasn't as cold as where you are. You are, to my best knowledge, protected by warm clothes, and then one can weather –30°.

I will send one of the photographs to Paul, it will make him so happy. In his latest letter he has again encouraged us to send his warmest regards to you. For this reason I am giving you his address once more: An den Judenrat für P.K. Opole über Pulawy, Distrikt Lublin General Gouvernement. Don't lose it again. He received your New Year's card and was very happy that you remembered him.

Dear son, another great thanks for the letter and the photographs. Take care of yourself and may God protect you. Warm greetings and kisses.

your dad

III

One autumn day in 1938 a triangle was created, and four years later its contours remained: Lisl and Pepi in Vienna. Pastor Pernow, the savior, in Stockholm. Otto in Pjätteryd.

Mrs. Eklundh's efforts to help Elise and Pepi come to Sweden had not yielded results. There weren't any other ways out, they knew no other counsel, and now they had a clearer idea of what awaited them.

They asked Otto for help again. And because he'd already tried with one of his benefactors, he now reached out to the other, using his newly acquired Swedish language.

January 20, 1942

Dear Mr. Pastor Pernow!
I am doing very well, I am hauling wood in the forest and we have much to do. The boy on the farm and I are hauling the wood, for the master has been enlisted.

Today I received a letter from my parents and understand that they are not doing well at all. They have again requested I ask if there isn't an opportunity for entry to Sweden, but as I know through my experience with Mrs. Eklundh there are no such opportunities for them at present.

I do wonder if Mr. Pastor couldn't perhaps help with this matter. Perhaps, with God's help, I will be able to see my parents once again.

Best regards to everyone at the Swedish Israel Mission.

your devoted Otto Ullmann

Meanwhile Pastor Pernow was in his office on Idungatan, writing a long text about his work with Jews and the christened.

III

John the Apostle bore witness to a remarkable sight, recorded in the Book of Revelation's seventh chapter:

> And I saw another angel ascending from the east, having the seal of the living God: and he cried with a loud voice to the four angels, to whom it was given to hurt the earth and the sea,
>
> Saying, Hurt not the earth, neither the sea, nor the trees, till we have sealed the servants of our God in their foreheads.

The chosen people.

How much time can it have taken for God's angel to mark 144,000 foreheads? That's how long the moment described by John the Apostle lasted. Countless moments have passed since then. Yet there are some who believe that this moment holds more weight than all the others that have since come to pass. Pastor Birger Pernow was one—and that's why he cited this very passage from the Bible when called upon to explain his view of the Jews.

The pastor believed John the Apostle's testimony. He was sure that the Jewish people had been singled out by God. And he was equally sure that they had betrayed him. This is why he offered the following five words in comment on that night of November 9–10, 1938, the November pogrom.

One can speak of the murders, the suicides, the abuse, torture, and vandalization in many ways. One can choose one's words when reacting to the imprisonment of tens of thousands of people accused of no crime but being born. Pastor Pernow chose these words: "Now God is at work."

When Otto's letter begging for help reached him, Birger Pernow was an experienced missionary, and, because of his fluency in German and solid knowledge of English, he was, as usual, well informed about the situation in Europe. Now a part of his work during the war years was to be documented and his thoughts were to be written down, and everything was to be collected into a book.

Pernow had seen the hatred. He had seen the consequences. And he'd often been asked why. Not just by his Christian friends, but also from the hated themselves. Why?

In spring 1942 he took some time to think and formulate a response to what he perceived to be a central question. He never questioned the truth in the assertion that Jews had always been hated. That's the way it was.

> One often encounters the question: "Why have the Jews always and in all places been hated?"
>
> There is no easy way to adequately answer this question, for it is connected to the Jewish distinguishing mark or rather with the Jewish character. To exhaustively

> describe this Jewish character, a specific Jewish essence, is not easy.
>
> It isn't only made of the familiar energy that unfortunately often finds its expression in an unsympathetic way of elbowing oneself ahead, nor in other flaws Jews are accused of having. It goes much deeper. The innermost core of this character seems instead to reside in the tension between the divine election and rejection. To have been called and chosen as God's covenant and servants, trusted with the entire divine salvation revelation and with the high holy task of communicating this to the rest of the population, but then to have divested themselves of the revelation's light and blessing—that must leave a deep impression.

The Jews had been chosen by God to spread his message, but when the Messiah appeared he went unrecognized and they'd repudiated him.

Birger Pernow was deeply moved by the enormity of this. In his eyes all of humanity's salvation had been delayed for several thousand years because of the Jewish betrayal. Unforgivable. And yet a good Christian must do just that. Forgive.

Inside the pastor's tall, slim body two equally strong forces met like two armies prepared for battle: the fact of the unforgivable against the need for forgiveness. And had he, if but for a Bible verse, given in to his rage and disappointment over the Jews, then evil would have won. He had to turn to goodness.

Hence the mission work, the preaching, the hundreds of letters back and forth across wartime Europe, the many long work hours, suffering from overexertion. Hence the campaign for children that saved Otto and ninety-nine other young people from the murderers. The pastor had to descend and reveal the right path, using words and actions.

And now he was gathering his thoughts at his desk, he who had been the Swedish archbishop's adviser on Jewish matters. That's when the letter from Otto praying to save Lisl and Pepi arrived.

Mr. Pastor. The good, tall, skinny Mr. Pastor and director of the Swedish Israel Mission. Did he speak with the Swedish Ministry of Foreign Affairs? Did he call up one of his old contacts at the Board of Health and Welfare? Perhaps.

Or did he remind himself of the conditions that the Swedish government had set precisely via the Board of Health and Welfare, allowing the children to enter the country, but forbidding their parents? He himself had reminded a friend and colleague of them, in a letter a few years prior:

> For this reason I would like to ask you and all of you to firmly decline such inquiries from parents, for they go against the very conditions of the children's stay here. The very purpose of the children's aid is to provide relief for the parents as they emigrate and create a new existence by receiving their children for a year or so here in Sweden. The parents should, then, be required to retrieve the children as soon as possible. With regard to the German children, those parents have committed to this in writing. And it is indeed because of this principle that the Board of Health and Welfare has granted us the right to take in the children. If now we were to try and help the parents come here, we ourselves will have gone against this fundamental principle and will find ourselves in a strange

> light with the Board of Health and Welfare. Unfortunately these requests show that the parents have not understood this point or at least have not taken it seriously. I will therefore consistently decline all such requests, and I'd be much obliged if you would do the same.

It's impossible to know what Pastor Birger Pernow thought or what actions he took when he read Otto's letter. We only know that he replied, probably that same day.

> January 22, 1942
>
> Dear Otto!
> Thank you for your letter from the 20th. Regarding your parents, I must unfortunately inform you that our authorities are not granting entry permits at the moment, therefore it is not possible to bring them here. Regrettably it is not in my power to help your parents. But never forget that God can help, if only we pray in the right way. Perhaps He is not helping in the way that we would wish, but by his own method.
>
> With regards
> Your BP
>
> PS. Kindly inform us of your master's name, and if you are receiving a salary, and if so, how much. The information is needed for the Board of Health and Welfare.

This is how a life-changing decision can be conveyed, a death blow dealt. In passing, in a friendly tone. Regrettably.

The possibility of emigrating from Nazi Germany had already been choked. For the previous few months, no people of Jewish origin had been allowed to leave the country. But that was not Pernow's reason for his refusal. And yet his explanation—the Swedish government wasn't allowing anyone in—was a bald-faced lie.

The truth was that at least 2,466 people applied for entry to Sweden that year. As in the previous year, the Swedish government divided the applicants into two groups: Jews and Other. Just like the year before, 86 percent of non-Jewish applicants were granted entry to the country, while the portion of successful applications for the Jewish group was notably less. The Swedish civil servants' notation was given to 158 people in need of protection. Of these 39.9 percent were allowed in. How many is that? Not many. The odd one. But Pastor Pernow didn't want to save more.

January 26, 1942

Dear Mr. Pastor!
Many thanks for your letter. The impossibility of my parents entering Sweden is very sad indeed, but I hope God will protect and preserve them, until such time as they can come to Sweden.

In reply to Mr. Pastor's question, I can inform you: My master is named Oskar Andersson. As for salary I have none, but I am occasionally given pocket money.

Warm regards
Otto Ullmann

Pepi and Lisl were living on borrowed time, on borrowed ground, and they knew it. Did Otto understand—or did he believe the pastor? Did he think that God would come to their aid, if only his prayers were strong enough and said in the right way?

A few years later Otto applied for Swedish citizenship. On the application form his answer to the question of his faith was "nondenominational." None. He had converted to rage.

III

Elise, Pepi, and Aunt Grete had been evicted again.

Now they were living in a small apartment on Robertgasse, in a so-called Jew house, together with old Mrs. Julie Böhm, whom they'd known for many years.

Traces of the original tenants remained. But Klara and Leopold Papanek had been forced to leave as prisoner 529 and prisoner 530 for the ghetto in Łódź on October 23, 1941, never to return.

No one can say if Elise, Grete, Mrs. Julie Böhm, and Pepi got along. Nor can one say if Pepi had somewhere to rest after his shift or where Elise sat and wrote the letters to Sweden. Grete worked in a factory six days a week, so there was a little income. They weren't allowed to buy milk, meat, or fruit, but Mitzi brought food when she was able, cautiously, because it was now a crime to help a Jew. If Pepi had the energy he and Lisl might lie together, whispering about their son Otto, imagining him skiing in the white winterland, enjoying his white milk or just standing there, smiling at them with his clear eyes.

It wasn't that Pepi didn't want to write, but his work consumed his time and whatever energy he had to spare. For a few hours now and then he shut down and slept, exhausted from keeping everything at arm's length. Then it took hold again. Only now and then could he find a spare minute and the strength to get himself, his thoughts, and his responsibility as a father together.

Vienna, February 8, 1942

Beloved boy. Today I have a little time and am making sure to write. To our great joy we received your letter today with photographs and I cannot describe how moved I was by your lines, and by being able to meet your loyal gaze in the photo. You cannot imagine what your letters mean to us in our existence here, and how we interpret your faithfulness and courage as proof of God's great mercy.

A week ago it was exactly three years since you, then still but a child, left us. Those three years have been filled with sorrow and difficulty for us, but the entire time our longing for you has overshadowed all else. And when we've had letters from you, we've been glad that you've been well received and are in good hands. But we've also felt that though you are far from home and far from those closest to you, you haven't changed. You've continued to be a good and decent person, and this has given us power and strength. The people you've lived with have been good to you, that is very calming…

We'd be very happy if you told us something about your friends. I would very much like to know with whom you spend your free days, what your friends are called, whether they are friends from here or new acquaintances?

You wrote once that a few people formed an orchestra that even plays at dances, and because you were always very musical you are surely involved—or do you only dance?

And what are your thoughts about the future? When will you attend agricultural school in order to perfect your craft? That would round off your education.

Do you still correspond with your friends? Write about that in more detail one day, if you have time. Here there isn't much news to report. Thankfully we are healthy and our only joy is in your letters. So write often and diligently to us . . . A thousand kisses and greetings.

your dad

Beloved boy, every line from you means so much and brings us so much joy. I'm happy to read that you are healthy and are doing well. Continue to take good care of yourself.

your mom

III

With icicles on the branches as well as birds singing, it's hard to say if it was winter's last day or spring's first. Pole marks in wet snow, once frozen and now melting again, Henrik's broad back, a ski's length ahead.

Otto liked competing and made an eager effort to catch up with and overtake him. Henrik, more good-natured, often let him. Sometimes he put up a fight for first place, but both of them knew that it was more important for Otto to win. After five kilometers they stopped. Then the pipes came out and they had a smoke.

They'd brought the camera with them. With his black winter cap atop his black hair and the black pipe in his mouth, Otto looked like the sliver of joy that he was, completely at home in the forest, breaking into a sweat, skiing or with forest ax in hand, whistling arias that echoed through the cathedral of ombudsman Eklundh's snowy coniferous forest.

His time in Pjätteryd was coming to an end. For almost two years he'd practically felt at home in the house by the lilac bower next to the forest behind the fields at the lake.

Maybe the reason was there wasn't enough work or food. Or maybe the idea was that he'd get a proper vocational education in agriculture, because Mrs. Eklundh had arranged a new position for him as an agricultural student. Soon he'd pull up those slender roots and move for the sixth time in four years, to the next farm, one with more animals, larger fields, and a greater variety of tasks. The new master at Sjögård, just outside of Ljungby, was called Lidén.

To stay, make ties, take root, find your way home—for someone like Otto this was impossible. Forbidden longing, useless words.

April 12, 1942

Beloved best boy. My most heartfelt thanks for your warm wishes on my birthday. I'm happy you remembered it. The card did only arrive yesterday, but the delay is not your fault. So once again, many thanks.

By the way . . . I wish to write about more than just the birthday. Namely that Herr Edling has visited me. He spoke well of you, so that we could be proud. He said that one could imagine you were born a Swede by the way you . . . write and formulate yourself. Herr Edling also told us about your enterprise, about you, and I must say that after his visit I was more calm as far as concerns you.

I will also write to Mrs. Eklundh—because Herr Edling has told us that she speaks German—and ask her about her plans for you, if you're going to stay there or attend an agricultural school.

What else are you doing, my boy? You probably have plenty to do, for surely work on the fields has begun. How are you? Thankfully, we're healthy and await your next letter. Are you in contact with the friends who arrived with you? Have you heard anything from Gerhardt, is he still in Tollarp? How is skiing? Did you compete in that ten-kilometer race? The time for snow is surely over.

Have you written to Uncle Karl in Stockholm? I'd very much like to hear how he's doing. Paul and Aunt Nuny have asked after you again and I have sent regards. This made them happy. Otherwise, they're not doing so well. Dear boy, I'll write soon again.

dad

Beloved boy. I too thank you for your letter, which has brought me much joy. I hope you'll remain our sweetie pie, our pride and our greatest joy.

your mom

Paul and Nuny are not doing so well. With words usually used to allude to colds, a sprained ankle, or a headache, Pepi described his closest friends' condition in Opole. It was April 12.

What did he know?

Had Nuny and Paul described the crowded living conditions? When one of them shook the lice from clothing, they dropped onto someone else. Or how the fever spread through their bites, muscles aching, one after the other falling ill, speckled skin, then death, how the winter nights had been marked by funerals, more than five hundred.

In March, another 2,800 prisoners arrived in Opole. Now there were more than ten thousand people in a town with three hundred buildings.

Joseph Goebbels, the Greater German Reich's propaganda minister, kept a diary. On March 27, 1942, he wrote: "From General Government, beginning with Lublin, the Jews are now being sent eastward. Quite a barbaric method is being used, which is not suitable for a more detailed description, and of the Jews, not many will remain. It can be said that on the whole sixty percent must be liquidated and forty percent can be used for work. The former Gauleiter of Vienna who is to carry this measure through in quite a circumspect manner and employing methods that do not seem too conspicuous."

The next phase of deportation began.

III

Vienna, May 14, 1942

We received your letter from the 30th and are happy that you are well and healthy. We are also healthy and as soon as Dad has time he'll write to you himself. It's been a while since we've had a letter from Paul and Aunt Nuny, but we're counting on receiving something within the week…

Now you have a lot of work on the fields. Aunt Grete and Mitzi send hearty greetings. If you have time, describe your home and your surroundings so that we can at least read about what life is like for you in the letter. Take care of yourself.

Otto had left Kärrnäs but the letters followed him to the next farm. He'd said goodbye to his best friend Henrik, to Astrid, who had been like a sister, and to Oskar and mother Agnes by saying that they'd been the closest thing to family he'd had in Sweden. Something in the way he said this made them remember his words for the rest of their lives.

Soon he would turn seventeen and need proper vocational training. He was on his way to being Farmer Lidén's agricultural student in Rataryd.

Otto had gotten used to being independent, to parental

love coming to him in the form of hastily jotted-down words on simple postcards. He'd gotten used to Pepi and Elise's constant longing, the shadow in his shadow. Sometimes he brushed up against hopelessness—they were supposed to have gotten out and picked him up long ago—but for the most part he tried to put it out of his mind. It wasn't hard. After a day behind horse and plow turning the earth, sleep arrived like a heavy blanket to be drawn over his thoughts.

Mrs. Eklundh had arranged the position for him, and he understood that Sjögård would be good for his education. He also knew he was cheap labor during the most demanding time, during spring sowing, summer harvest, and potato digging, but that he might not be able to stay longer than that.

What were the people like on the farm? Did they like Otto? Did some have German sympathies? A few years earlier the Lindholmers, the Nazis, had drawn a crowd of 150 to a meeting in little Ljungby.

June 30, 1942

Dearest boy. We received your card from June 22. It's very nice of you to write us regularly and hearing from you is our greatest joy. We still haven't heard from Paul. Dad has a lot to do now, but as soon as he can, he'll write to you in detail. Mitzi says that she'll reply to your letter. Surely you've received our latest letter. Thankfully we are healthy. If you have more time, don't forget to write how tall you are now and how much you weigh. I'd very much like to know. Might you have a new photograph? A thousand kisses.

mom

July 18, 1942

Dearest boy. Now we are waiting again, longing for news from you. Surely you've received our letter and card. In two days you'll be seventeen years old. Dear, once again I wish you all things good and beautiful. Let us pray that we'll soon be able to embrace you. Nearly four years have passed since we last saw you, and our longing only continues to grow. Dad will write to you in more detail. He has much to do. I hope we'll receive mail from you in the next days. Three weeks have already passed since your last letter... A thousand kisses.

mom

Nowhere in the letters does Pepi say what his work was. How could he? Was he having nightmares?

He'd been employed since January 8, 1942. Every morning he reported to his supervisor, then he and the others in the group received a list of names.

List, alphabetical order, death sentence.

There were those who wanted knowledge, and those who did everything they could to avoid it, and some who knew but wouldn't tell and others who insisted on hoping for the best. What category Pepi belonged to can no longer be known.

The lists contained name upon name, and he could only be sure of three things: The people listed had to go. As long as the list was in his hands, his name was not on it. As long as his name was not on it, someone else was being forced to go. There—three conclusions to cling to, like a fence, so as not to think further about it, beyond it.

The days became a constant, stressful meander, from door to door, address to address, to find the people listed. He and the rest of the group only had a few days to locate them. Hence, research.

The Gestapo decided who should be deported and provided a number, a train station, and a departure time. During the next step, the Jewish Community Council could sometimes negotiate the release of individuals or families, if substitutions were provided. The Council was made responsible for those selected to find their way to the train. If one was missing, another had to take their place. It wasn't personal. It was a quota system.

Around one thousand people were called to each deportation train. The calls—or rather the orders to report—were issued by the Jewish Community Council. As might be expected, not all of the people behind the names appeared at the station. Some had died. Others fled. And others were hiding, crouched behind fake walls or under loose floorboards. This is where Pepi entered the picture.

His task was to pinpoint them, to strike the dead from the list, to note the ones with proof of emigration, along with enabling the departure of the rest.

Sometimes no one was home. Then he had to talk to the doorman, neighbors, relatives, continue his search at another address. The wife might be alone at the home address. Maybe she'd say her wanted husband was working. This is how it could go: she'd say there must've been a mistake, she and her husband weren't supposed to be deported, it was impossible. Then Pepi had to reason with her.

He was tired. But they were on the list, he must have replied. The woman might have said they'd just received a certificate granting them an exemption, so Pepi had to call the responsible party at the Council, and if her story was correct, he'd make a note on the registry card, signed J. Ullmann, and keep going. Often there was a hurry. If those listed had already left the country, the Council had to be informed quickly so others could be deported instead.

The year was 1942. Pepi had his hands full at work.

III

Sjögård was a lonely place.

The ones nearby who sympathized with Germany would have liked to see Otto make mistakes, but he gave them no reason to comment, although his mood probably could have been better, the light in his eyes brighter, and the weight inside less heavy. Once again Otto had relocated, not because he wanted to but because the circumstances demanded it. He had bid farewell to Agnes, who had been like a mother to him, and to Henrik, Oskar, and Astrid. He had said goodbye to the dogs, the horses, to the farm that had been his home for two years, and now he was newly arrived at another. The Anderssons became yet another family he had to leave behind, and this new loss was added to the first one, a new ache was added to the old wound. Would it never end?

All he wanted was to be home again, together with Pepi and Elise, back in his usual good big-city life. Besides that, the people in Rataryd were nice and he was in good health. He was the goalkeeper on the village soccer team.

The letter is gone. Like all the others he sent to his parents, it has disappeared—during a move, on a train journey, in a mass cremation?—but Otto's feelings in the spring of 1942 echo faintly in his mother's reply.

My dearest. We've received your letter from May 28th. You cannot imagine how happy it made us. You are our greatest joy and we hope that one day we will wrap our arms around you again. Write more such letters . . . then everyone will hold you dear. We're happy to hear you are so well liked, and it is moving to know that everyone holds you dear. We love you over here, too . . . We still haven't received a message or letter from Paul. Aunt Grete and Mitzi are longing for letters from you. Dad will write you his own letter. Have you received my photo? Dearest boy, a thousand kisses.

your mom

The first train out of the teeming ghetto in Opole Lubelskie had departed on March 31, 1942, and was heading east. A total of 1,950 people had been roused from slumber and rounded up on the market square near the ghetto walls. From there they'd been forced to march to the train station in Naleczow where the cattle cars awaited. The terminus was the Belzec camp. In the ghetto, wooden barracks had been built. There the Jewish police collected people's possessions.

Paul and Aunt Nuny had evaded the winter's typhoid epidemic, tried to endure the famine, and had avoided deportation to Belzec. In June, Elise and Pepi finally received word from them and passed it on to Otto in Småland. They were healthy, but not doing well, Pepi wrote. What that meant, one can only guess. Just as unclear was when the letter from Opole had in fact been written, and how long it had taken for it to reach Vienna.

On May 25, another two thousand people marched from Opole to Naleczow station, where the train awaited them. After that: Sobibor.

Summer arrived.

Three camps constructed for murder and connected by railway had now been tested and cleared for what was called Operation Reinhard: Belzec, Sobibor, and Treblinka.

On July 19, the day before Otto's seventeenth birthday, Heinrich Himmler issued an order about Nazi-occupied Poland, the General Government. You could also call it a death sentence: "From December 31, 1942, no persons of Jewish origin may remain within the General Government, unless they are in collection camps in Warsaw, Cracow, Czestochowa, Radom, and Lublin. All other work on which Jewish labor is employed must be finished by that date, or, in the event that this is not possible, it must be transferred to one of the collection camps. These measures are required with a view to the necessary ethnic division of races and peoples for the New Order in Europe."

Those classified as Jews had six months left in Poland. Six months.

11

The gravel road is embedded in an avenue, so narrow that the tree branches reaching for each other meet and form a roof. The farm on the right side is red and large, but last year's shoots and brushwood conceal the farmhouse waiting at the road's end. The farm is called Elmtaryd, the village Agunnaryd, and now the two places' initials help make up one of the world's most recognizable company names.

With the avenue behind you, you can turn left—toward three buildings around a gravel square with a flagpole—or right, where a smaller red house without a veranda stands on its own.

From the red house, you see the estate from below. But to those who make their way toward the light-colored main building and turn around to gaze back out over the grounds, the red house is beneath you, farthest down the slope.

An estate for the estate owner, cottages for tenant farmers. The same gravel road, the same avenue, the same leafy crowns. The same ground being farmed, the same harvest being tended to, the same early morning sounds from the barnyard animals. Only the conditions for existence differed.

Here Otto was to become a farmhand, assist the groom with his daily tasks, clear the ditches, repair the wooden walls, rake the muck, spread hay, and do anything else that needed doing, as per estate owner Feodor Kamprad's wishes. Not yet, but soon.

Ingvar, the son of the owner, was sixteen years old. He sympathized strongly with the Nazi Sven Olov Lindholm and his movement. And in this he was not alone in the area. That year the Swedish Socialist Unity held meetings in Jönköping, Kalmar, Alvesta, and Moheda. In Växjö, the Nazis had drawn an audience of 1,500.

But Ingvar found their message far too aggressive and hateful, he recalls today. Another strong leader had caught his interest and awakened his admiration: the fascist Per Engdahl.

Later, Ingvar wouldn't often write letters by hand, and if he did, he'd capitalize everything in a clear and notably impersonal way. But in 1942, he was a young man and the time for capitalization had not yet come. It was with a scrolling, sloping, and unpracticed hand that Ingvar wrote his letter dated April 24 in Agunnaryd:

> The undersigned is interested in true-Swedish literature and therefore also in your newspaper *Vägen Framåt* [*The Way Forward*]. If you would be so kind as to send me several complimentary samples of the aforementioned, as well as information on how to subscribe, and so forth.
>
> In hopes of good relations and with Nordic greetings, I thank you.

And then his name, penned inside a striking arch.

In *The Way Forward*'s next issue, he could read article after article by the admired Per Engdahl about a people's community founded on ideas instead of material values. As the leader of Swedish Opposition, Engdahl linked hatred for Communists with hatred for Jews, stubbornly arguing that the one necessitated the other. The following was in one of the first issues Ingvar received: "The Jews are a foreign element in the Western ethnicity. And like everything foreign, they seek to explode and eat away at the organism in which they live... The causes of Communism should be eradicated, but Communism's progenitors, those who speculate in incongruities, shall also be crushed. An anti-Communist movement can therefore never reach its goal, if it is not also anti-Semitic."

And in a later issue, Engdahl continued on the same theme:

> The most radical solution to the Jewish question is a deportation of Jews to a specially designated place. Within these borders, they can build their own state as they see fit... But this does not stop us in our country, as we await this European development, from solving the Jewish question within our own borders in a manner satisfactory to Sweden. We must, then, implement the following demands: All further Jewish immigration must be stopped. Jews must be removed from leading positions in the state, society, and corporations. The State must be able to appoint a Swedish administrator in a Jewish company as and when they see fit.

As the charismatic Per Engdahl published this text, the consequences of his thoughts were being taken to the extreme across the German border. This was sixteen-year-old Ingvar Kamprad's reading material, and he would do whatever he could to be present when Engdahl was making public appearances in the area.

At the same time he subscribed to the hard-line young Nazi newspaper *Ungt Folk* [*Young People*], and in it he bought space to publish a midwinter greeting to the Swedish Führer Sven Olov Lindholm. In the December issue, printed in black ink on white paper: "I. Kamprad in Agunnaryd."

Only a few months later, he would get his own personal file at the Swedish secret police, the Swedish Civilian Security Service.

Under the heading "Nazi," it is recorded that he was member number 4014 in the SSS—the *Svensk Socialistisk Samling*—Sweden's Nazi party.

In the file, a letter from November 1942 is cited, wherein Ingvar recounts recruiting "a number of friends" to the SSS, and hopes to "submit a not-contemptible number of membership applications" in future. In the same letter he claims to have enlisted five subscribers to *Ungt Folk*, and says that he would not decline any opportunity to work for the movement.

Älmhult, 2010.

INGVAR: People saying I was a Nazi, it gave me a bad reputation. And I was, for a very short time. I was very engaged in something called Lindholm . . . well, not engaged but a member. Was I a member? . . . I don't think I was that either. I was a strong sympathizer [. . .]

Later when I went to Osby Coeducational School, I got to know a book printer called Hultberg, and he knew someone called Per Engdahl, and I was allowed to attend a meeting even though those of us living at the boarding school weren't allowed to go to any damn political meetings. It was said that Osby was a red-brick house built on religious grounds.

And I partook a few times, and I had—it must have been during my time at Osby—the opportunity to hear Per Engdahl talk to a small group of ten or fifteen people. And I must say that I continued to admire Per Engdahl [. . .] And he was absolutely no hater of Jews, either. If one were to describe him, it would be more as a fascist.

I fell for two things, and both were wrong. One was Mussolini's corporatism. He said that everyone working in the leather industry should band together, they're a group. Different factions shouldn't be fighting against each other, rather all farmers should band together and be a group, and so on. I thought it sounded mighty good. But as it turned out... it was an unforgivable sin of youth. But I believed in it.

And with regard to racism, Per Engdahl was against mixing people. He said: "Ingvar. Why is it called 'Malay'? Well, Indians and Chinese were marrying each other."

And I myself can happily attest that during my travels in the Far East, in every Malay factory, where we still buy our commodities today, there's a big difference. No one has to point out to you, if you walk through the factory, you can see for yourself where the Chinese are sitting and where the Malays are sitting. And according to Per Engdahl this is because... well, let the Jews grow amongst themselves and be their own people, let the Indians grow amongst themselves and grow in their own way. Don't mix them, because mixing isn't good. And he used the Malays as an example. And I believed that, too. But that is also goddamn wrong.

[...] What was the situation at IKEA last Christmas? I'll tell you: people from eighteen different nations who work at our central warehouse. Wonderful people. Once upon a time you used to say "Negro." Today you can't even say the word "negro-ball" [a Swedish chocolate confection]. And yet one of my very best friends, he is a super-Negro.

Hard to wait as keenly for the postman. Hard not to.

Elise often stood at the door, looking through the peephole, into the stairwell. Lines, sentences, signs of life might arrive, telling them how her Otto was doing, that he was healthy and doing well. But at the same time—when the postman passed their door without leaving any mail there was also an uncomfortable sense of relief. Nothing from Sweden, perhaps, but also no thick envelope from the Jewish Community Council.

The unmistakable thick envelope. Time was short for those who received one such envelope. You had twelve, sometimes twenty-four hours, to report to the assembly point with luggage weighing no more than fifty kilos and travel funds equivalent to forty zloty.

One day it arrived.

The letter the postman handed over with a particular inscrutable look was addressed to eighty-year-old Mrs. Julie Böhm. Otto had known her his entire life and called her "Grandmother" even though they weren't related. Recently, she, Pepi, Elise, and Aunt Grete had shared everything that could be shared: space in the small apartment on Robertgasse, the long drawn-out days, and the unending pang in their stomachs that could be mistaken for hunger but was in fact starvation.

The day Julie Böhm received the envelope, and they all realized what it meant. Lisl wrote to Otto.

August 19, 1942

My dearest, we have received your dear card from August 11 and are happy to hear you are healthy, which we are, too. Dad still has much to do and will write a letter as soon as he has time. We haven't heard from Aunt Nuny. Aunt Grete will write soon and Mitzi says hello. Have you heard from Kurt? Where is he now? Dearest, if you have more time, write. You know how much we are waiting for a message from you.

A thousand kisses.

Mutti

It says nothing about the day's event, what the postman had brought, about the trains that were running at all hours. Nothing about old Julie Böhm, who had her suitcase open and was gathering her things. She is omitted, a shadow between the lines, so Otto wouldn't have to know and Elise wouldn't have to write it. So that what was happening almost wasn't happening, as long as it was left unsaid.

The next day Mrs. Böhm had to make her way to the assembly point. Around her neck was a yellow paper sign bearing the number 33.

She and the others had to wait until all one thousand or so people were pressed together. They looked at each other and realized that most of the people now boarding the train were very old. A rumor about a special home for the aged spread. A few wanted to make clear then and there that they preferred a south-facing window.

Maybe the Jewish Community Council's people had deemed Pepi trustworthy and meticulous, because as 1942 advanced, his work took a new direction. No longer was he simply locating the missing people on the lists, there was more to it.

Everyone in the research group had been given a job description where every moment was thoroughly and precisely detailed. Or perhaps it was more like a register of possible crimes and their strict punishments. Nothing in his workday was voluntary, and he couldn't act independently without risking his and Elise's lives.

Three schools had been chosen, large and conveniently located near the train station and its platform: the assembly points. Once a group was assembled, there was only one way for them to go: to a train.

According to orders from the assembly authorities, it was now Pepi's job to seek out those who were to be deported, in their homes, on the day of departure. He was under no circumstance allowed to enter the apartment. Instead, he would position himself outside the door, so that those who had to depart could not slip away from their home and no one else could enter.

When they'd finished packing, his job was to make sure the baggage was correctly labeled. Did he also have to hang the signs around their necks?

It was also Pepi's responsibility to turn off the apartment's water and gas supply, and then to take possession of the key. As said: each moment on the job was detailed in the job description. Including a point about pets. If there were any, Pepi had to make sure they were fed.

Then he took the prisoners to the assembly point. On the way there, he was the one who made sure they didn't talk to anyone or hand over any letters or other items or communicate in any way with others. He wasn't allowed to be at the assembly point during his free time.

If someone fled, the prisoner was replaced with two of the Jewish Community Council's workers: a simple and practical way to eliminate the risk of empathy, compassion, or old friendship ties that might lead to aiding an escape.

Mrs. Böhm left nothing but space in the apartment on Robertgasse. Where she had sat was no one, where she had lain was empty, where she had spoken was silent. Just a few days later, the postman stopped by again.

Fräulein Margarethe Kollmann.

Did Pepi try to get Aunt Grete off the list—had he known? There is no answer to be found, because Grete was his sister-in-law, and she wasn't included in the circle of close family members who were offered protection in exchange for his daily work.

Ten days after Julie Böhm left Robertgasse, Aunt Grete walked to the assembly point. Around her neck was a sign, number 712.

Pepi wrote to Otto that same day. Several weeks had passed since his last letter.

August 30, 1942

Dearest boy. I've been very busy and am sorry I haven't been able to reply to your lovely letter before now. Today I will devote a few hours of my free time to writing letters, and naturally, you are the first person to whom I'm writing.

We were very happy to read that you celebrated your birthday in a lovely way. Life is easier for us when we can see that you are living with such devoted and thoughtful people. Our life may be full of trials, but to know that you have it good makes existence easier and helps us endure our separation from you. We are grateful to everyone who has prepared such a fine seventeenth birthday for you—with all of our hearts. Send them all our regards, and tell them that they've not only made you happy, but us, too. Having thought of you on your birthday is a given, and you can imagine we are also longing intensely to see you again soon. May heaven continue to protect you, and if a time comes when we no longer are able to communicate—never forget that we are with you in thought and our wishes will always follow you.

We still haven't heard anything from Paul and Aunt Nuny. Now Aunt Grete has left us, as well. She asked us to send you warm regards.

Soon it will be our turn.

On Monday, August 31, 1942, Aunt Grete was forced to board a train to White Russia, destination Maly Trostinec. The trip took four days. The train arrived on Friday, September 4.

Aunt Grete, along with another 1,004 prisoners, was taken to a place where she had to part with all of her possessions, valuables, and cash. She was forced to undress in front of the others and the armed soldiers. Naked, she was made to walk to a certain part of the woods. There she was shot.

III

Pepi had done what he could to buy him and Lisl time, but now the grace period was over. The deportation trains had been running all through spring and summer, and the number of people with Jewish heritage had diminished so drastically in Vienna that the Jewish Community Council no longer needed all the research groups and could no longer negotiate anyone's freedom. Council employees were put on the same lists that they themselves had administered. Pepi prepared his son for what was ahead, one letter at a time.

September 20, 1942

My best boy, finally I have time to reply to your letter of August 23. In that time you've surely received replies to previous letters and cards, in other words you shouldn't have been without mail from us. We've also received a card from September 9.

The letter, as you know, made us very happy, and we're grateful that you're healthy and in good spirits and the hard work speaks to you. As we see it, you must be the perfect farmer, and we like the fact that you've been given a raise. You're performing your tasks just as well and conscientiously as I've always thought you would. Knowing you are well cared for calms us greatly. We've been able to endure these years of separation only because we have known that you have it good. And when I receive a letter as fine as the last that came from you—then I thank fate.

We've had to endure difficult tests and God's hand rests heavily on us. But we take comfort in the fact that you are safe, and we regard the descriptions of your well-being as a blessing. May God also continue to protect you when we find ourselves at an even greater distance from each other and it might not be possible to keep in touch. I'm convinced that you will always choose the right path and live a decent life and we, with God's help, will be reunited.

Your words about the girl from Kärrnäs truly made us happy. Send us a picture of her, but above all, a picture of you. In any case, you must hurry if you want us to receive them. As you can imagine, we'd very much like to have your picture when we go away.

Hearty thanks for the greetings from Mrs. Eklundh and Mr. Lidén. Please send them our regards, too. And to Astrid. How is the dancing going? You've always had a talent for it. Do you play any instruments? It would be a shame not to put your great musicality to use.

There is nothing to tell about Paul and Aunt Nuny. And Aunt Grete is gone. Dearest boy. Take care of yourself, and may God continue to protect you. Many kisses.

your dad

September 26, 1942

Beloved boy. We have been waiting for a letter from you for a long time and hope that it will arrive soon and that it will contain the promised photographs. I know you have a lot to do and that it's not easy to write a letter after a day's work, but I hope that you've managed to find some spare minutes to send off a few lines.

You can't know how happy we'd be if your letter made it here in time. We have to move in a few days. If you don't hear from us, don't be too sad. Even though it will be difficult to be without your dear greetings and letters, we feel—in spite of the challenging trials that have been visited upon us—it is heaven's grace that you, our dear child and only treasure, are safe and well. And our prayers culminate in a heartfelt wish that God will continue to protect you, and that all of us shall know the grace of a joyous and felicitous reunion.

You left us as a child. The memory of you riding off in the train almost four years ago has been a recurring image that we have carried with us through the years. We think of you always, beloved boy, and that's how it will stay. In the same way, we see in your letters that you always think of us, too, and that we haven't been forgotten.

Now you're almost an adult. You've had to learn early on how to stand on your own two feet. You are diligent, hardworking, and thankfully not dim. But above all, my beloved boy, you are a decent person and I'm sure this means you'll be liked wherever you go. I'm convinced that you will continue to be nice and conduct yourself with decency. I also hope that you will stay this course, and never stray.

With this difficult path before us, we carry a feeling of ease about you, and our trust in God will help us along.

If you need advice, speak to Mrs. Eklundh, who has stood by your side so far and to whom I will also write. I will also write to Herr Edling. You might also contact Onkel Karl. You do have his address in Stockholm: Sandelsgatan 40.

Dearest boy, we are not sad. Neither should you be. We hope that one day we'll meet again and will be able to find joy in our reunion. Take care of yourself and may God continue to protect you. I hug and kiss you a thousand times.

your loyal dad

Dearest boy. I hope that we'll receive a letter from you in time, and that we'll be able to keep in touch. I hope and pray to God that we will remain in good health and see each other again. Dad and I are hopeful, as always, because we only have one wish: to be reunited with you. I know that you are a good and kind boy, and we think of you always. Take care of yourself, darling boy. I hug and kiss you a thousand times.

your loyal mother

Could Otto tell this was a farewell letter?

Tend to your musicality, Otto. Even if we can't write to you in future, we're with you in thought. Stay on the straight and narrow path and live a decent life. We aren't sad. Neither should you be.

On October 2, 1942, Josef and Elise Ullmann, prisoner numbers 1110 and 1111, were put on board transport IV/12 from Vienna, destination Theresienstadt, Czechoslovakia.

For months no news had arrived from Opole.

On October 24, 1942, four hundred policemen, supported by Ukrainian troops, went behind the walls of the ghetto. They forced out its residents and made a selection. A small group of young people as well as those with specialized trades were chosen and sent to the Poniatowa labor camp. The others had to march to Naleczow station where the cattle cars were waiting. We know the rest.

After this, around five hundred people remained in Opole.

Paul? Aunt Nuny?

All we can know for certain is that the prisoners who weren't forced on board the death trains had to gather the possessions left behind, they had to sort the clothing, toiletries, personal mementos—and make sure everything was sent to Lublin for safekeeping. Then they were shot.

A few names to weave into the story, a few people, their words, their actions, their silence: Bishop Dibelius of Berlin, SS Officer Kurt Gerstein, and the Swedish archbishop Erling Eidem.

In November 1942, Gerstein contacted Bishop Dibelius in Berlin. They'd known each other a long time; the bishop had officiated at Gerstein's marriage and had laid members of his family to rest. Now the SS officer needed to have a conversation with the man who cared for his soul.

Bishop Dibelius couldn't comprehend how a deeply faithful Christian could join the SS, but there was an explanation. Gerstein's sister-in-law had been committed to a mental institution and died under unclear circumstances. When Gerstein caught on to the Nazis' murder of the mentally ill, he decided to join the SS to find out what had actually happened. When he found out, he stayed. Because someone had to be on the inside to bear witness, as he told Berlin's bishop.

So they met that November.

Kurt Gerstein's job had been to improve the hygienic conditions in the concentration camps. He also built facilities where soldiers on the front could be deloused. When his technical knowledge became known, he was tasked with improving the efficiency of murder by gas. Then he was asked to procure an ingredient for the poison gas: hydrogen cyanide. And it was during a field trip to Belsec, Poland, in August 1942, that he experienced what he now had to tell.

Bishop Dibelius listened.

The place. The many flies. The train. The disrobing. The whips. The diesel engine. The aftermath. Searching for hidden gold in the corpses' cavities.

Gerstein had already recounted everything, his statements verified with documentation, for a Swedish diplomat he met by chance, because he wanted the Swedish government to do something. And he didn't stop. Gerstein would go on to tell this story again and again, to around one hundred people, before taking his own life in 1945. But now he was telling Bishop Dibelius, and he, in turn, understood that Gerstein's purpose was to spread information so as to prevent further murders.

Now the bishop of Berlin knew. But he himself could not go public with the information. Neither could he contact anyone who was considered an enemy of Nazi Germany. He needed to give the information to a neutral party, who in turn would spread it, someone trusted in the community, in a position that commanded respect.

Enter Archbishop Eidem. He visited Berlin to attend the installation of a new prelate in the Swedish church, and as usual he got together with his old friend Dibelius.

Erling Eidem seemed to be the right person. Hailing from a country that was not among the warring factions. Having the ear of the government. A deeply faithful Christian to whom people listened. Dibelius recounted everything he'd learned.

Archbishop Eidem was deeply moved, but he was more pious than Bishop Dibelius had understood.

In Eidem's world, politics, in direct contrast to the Christian faith, was equatable to dirt. He considered himself God's humble servant, and though he occupied the Swedish church's highest post, he couldn't consider himself a powerful person. He had nothing to gain from the public arena, the worldly existence was not for him. If asked to define himself in the world, he'd probably have said that God was everything, Erling Eidem nothing.

When both Kurt Gerstein and Bishop Dibelius put their hope in Eidem, that he would sound the alarm, they'd been mistaken.

Archbishop Eidem processed what he'd been told, and it colored his words in Berlin. First he held a speech during a German-Scandinavian Society luncheon and asserted the equal value of all people with such power that it drew tears from all who were present. A few days later he preached in Lützen with unusual intensity about how Swedes and Germans were no better than others and an empire based on power and might is doomed to go under. So powerful was the speech that the Swedish envoy Arvid Richert felt compelled to approach the Swedish journalists afterward and ask them to underplay the account so as not to get on the wrong side of the Nazis. Eidem, however, mentioned nothing of what he'd heard—neither about the mass murder nor the plundering of corpses.

Once back in Sweden, the archbishop contacted certain people with German ties, those he thought might hold sway over Nazis in powerful positions.

Someone else might have chosen a different course of action: seeking out government representatives for conversation or writing an op-ed, perhaps giving a radio address, stirring things up, agitating and inciting engagement. But not Erling Eidem. In his world, according to his view of himself and his faith, there was no alternative. Politics and faith were separate matters, and so they should remain.

Exit Archbishop Erling Eidem, the one who spearheaded the initiative that saved Otto.

Ingvar defied his school's ban on political meetings and went out into the Skånish November night to see Per Engdahl himself at Osby's Stora Hotell.

Enthusiastic: that's how he describes himself in retrospect, and he calls Engdahl born to seduce. Some fifty supporters had gathered, and when the meeting was over Ingvar was lucky enough to be sitting a coffee cup away. A conversation began, and pride swelled in the one being noticed. The political vision he was aligning himself with was about building a society where the individual was subordinate to "community" and nation. Society should be divided into strong interest groups, and their chosen leaders should make decisions on everyone's behalf. No universal suffrage, no state caring for everyone, no, the opposite of that: corporatism.

From this point forward, Ingvar Kamprad lived a double life, with double loyalties: to the rancorous Sven Olov Lindholm and to the fascist leader Per Engdahl, with his slightly more academic image.

No one can say there was a lack of information. Neither the farmers in Rataryd nor in Rottne were without a radio. Those who wanted to know knew a lot, but those who didn't still knew a bit. They knew enough. And yet it was only now that the pain crept in. Though not many wanted to write the word "Jew," everyone could spell "kindred."

On November 26, 1942, over five hundred Norwegians of Jewish heritage were arrested and forced on board the steamship *Donau*, berthed in Oslo's harbor. Soon thereafter their belongings were auctioned at a market in the city. Those listening to the news on Sweden's radio broadcast heard the Norwegian news agency's telegram about the event read aloud: "The Norwegian Jewish Problem has found its final solution. All Jews living in Norway, including women and children, have been put aboard a German 10,000-ton cruiser leaving for an unknown destination."

What wasn't reported was that the Norwegian women and children were gassed as soon as they arrived at Birkenau. More deportations followed. A total of 763 Norwegian Jews were arrested, twenty-four survived.

The Swedish population was told the truth, but not the whole truth, because the press was asked to keep quiet about the attempts to aid refugees. Over nine hundred Norwegian Jews had managed to come to Sweden, where they were detained or went into hiding. Sweden had a policy of silence, and the journalists obeyed.

But when the details of the deportations became known, it was enough to awaken the empathy that hadn't been roused by previous reports of persecution, suicide, or the large number of entry-permit applications. Now the leading journalists were waking up. Now the patriotic associations were holding meetings in support of the Norwegian Jews—now, when the murders were only a border away.

"A ship arrives full of people! This ship represents a small segment of the great anguish of our time. What is happening here is foreign to the Nordic spirit, the imagination is hardly strong enough to fathom the suffering contained in that ship, out there on the North Sea's furious autumn waves, driving toward its dark destination. Once again we are gripped with bitter sorrow for Norway's fate," wrote *Aftontidningen*.

And the *Svenska Morgonbladet*: "And now at the very end, like placing the tittle over the *i* in a message about a thousand Jews who were sent to Poland as prisoners. One is astonished. To take a mass of blameless people, first arrested, then ruined and sent like a lot of slaves to a foreign forced labor camp. Such traffic is so frightful one could not have imagined, not even in one's worst nightmares, that something like this could happen in a Nordic country, much less in a country as freedom-loving and humane as Norway."

Göteborgs-Tidningen: "These are people just like you and me who are being treated in this way. Torn from their homes, robbed of everything. Who are seeing themselves and their children stowed like cattle for export to the ghastly slave market, which the lords of the 'new order' established to satisfy their need to avenge and assert themselves."

Maybe Sweden was starting to wake up and individual minds were changing, like gusts of wind? Many reacted. Protest meetings were held. Several of the Swedish church's men used the Advent service on November 29, the first Sunday after the deportation, to preach against hatred and persecution. The dean in Gothenburg filled the cathedral to capacity and quoted from Luke: "If these should hold their peace, the stones would immediately cry out."

Beautiful words in the third year of war, the seventh since the Nuremburg Laws were declared.

On December 3, the Swedish prime minister ordered his envoy in Berlin to inform the German government that Sweden was prepared to receive all remaining Norwegian Jews. But to the Germans this was out of the question.

Dagens Nyheter wanted to find out which of the year's events had made the biggest impact on people, so the editors conducted a survey. The deportation of the Norwegians was the obvious answer, and the final edition of the year printed comments from the surveyed. A young man said, "Saw the Jewish deportation up close at the border, will never forget it." Another: "Though truly I am no friend of the Jews, I want no part in such horrors."

III

Otto toiled. September's grain harvest. Then the potatoes had to be dug up and the animals brought in. In November the fields had to be plowed and prepared for the next year's crops. No letters came.

He kept in touch with Mitzi, now that there wasn't anyone else. She found out that Pepi and Elise had been deported to Theresienstadt.

The German-sympathizers at Sjögård grew louder with each battle won and believed the setbacks to be temporary. There was no doubt that a final victory was imminent, nor was there any doubt about who on the farm believed themselves to be on the side of right. Not even the Soviet troops heading toward Stalingrad gave them pause.

Otto was a farmhand. Rage crawled under his skin, everything he wanted to say to their faces was formulated and ready to go, but he kept quiet. Storing. Collecting. Becoming a pressure chamber.

His friends were in Kärrnäs. Christmas, New Year's, winter activities—everything came and went. He had long, warm thoughts of Lisl and Pepi, but was also trying to avoid them.

Then the last day of January arrived, and the news broadcaster reported that Germany's Sixth Army had surrendered at Stalingrad. A few days later, on February 2, came the news of total capitulation. Masters and farmhands were gathered around the dining table, the radio on, when they heard the news. Otto, too.

Could the one be separated from the other—sorrow, punishment, revenge, tears?

It rose. The surface tension broke. Otto jumped up from his chair and shrieked, clapped his hands, could not keep quiet. He knew that some of the others were enraged and disappointed, but he was dancing. And the cheers rose in Sjögård, Rataryd, Småland. Inside Otto Ullmann.

III

A few weeks later the first sign of life in half a year arrived.

SENDER ELISE ULLMANN
THERESIENSTADT (PROTECTORATE),
Q 507 POST BARISCHOWITZ

February 23, 1943

Beloved boy. We haven't heard from you in a long time, but we pray to God that you are healthy. Thankfully we are healthy. I hope that you received the letter I wrote from here. Each day we wait, full of yearning, for a letter from you. How is Mitzi? Give her our address so she can write to us as well. Write even if you don't receive a reply. The post here is under much strain, but all mail arrives as it should. I hope this letter finds you well. Perhaps you can send a photo of yourself? A thousand kisses.

your mom

It had been said that Theresienstadt was a relatively good place, you could live there. Someone had even heard the word "paradise" mentioned. Outside the train window they'd been able to see the deep green Czech forests, small brown-washed villages, fruit still red in the trees.

Lisl and Pepi got off the train at Barischowitz together with everyone else. Their luggage was unloaded onto truck beds by youths with Stars of David on their white armbands. Those unable to walk were allowed to ride along, whereas the rest of the prisoners carried their hand luggage as part of a long train of people moving through orderly neighborhoods, toward the old fortress. It was beautiful, too. But they weren't allowed to stop; they marched on, down what seemed to be an endless road, to barracks where uniformed men were waiting. Then: inspection. Every pocket, every seam was investigated, all bags, all baggage. Medicine, scissors, razor blades, chocolate, cookies, thermoses full of cognac—everything was stolen. Some prisoners were given back their luggage, others not. Then onward, to rooms where they were to sleep on the floor.

When Pepi and Lisl arrived at Theresienstadt around 55,000 people were living there as prisoners. There were 219 buildings in addition to the barracks. People slept everywhere, the men amongst themselves, the women and children amongst themselves. Pregnancy was forbidden.

The prison camp was run by SS men, mostly Austrians, and under them was the Council of Jewish Elders. Intermittently letters and packages were forbidden, and the punishment for prisoners communicating with the world outside was severe.

The Jewish Council made various arrangements. Women cared for the aged. Men could join the Jewish police. Smoking was forbidden, but smuggling was constant, or cigarettes would be rolled from dried chestnut leaves or tea. There was a sick ward.

No documents remain that could tell us what Elise and Pepi did there, or how they survived. But the facts speak for themselves. The plumbing system was old and insufficient, and kept freezing and breaking. Over one hundred people per toilet. Lice. Shrinking food rations. All it took was for a simple children's illness to break out, and several hundred people died. On an average day nine men might be hanged because they insulted German honor.

Mail for the residents of Theresienstadt is permitted under the following conditions:

1. At most three postcards a month. These shall be written in the German language in clear handwriting if possible, using capital letters or typed.
2. The postcard shall be furnished with the recipient's exact address in Theresienstadt and then be placed unstamped in an envelope with the address: The Reich Deputation of the German Jews, Berlin—Charlottenburg 2, Kanstrasse 158. The deputation will attend to the further transport of the mail.
3. It is furthermore allowed once a month to send a gift in the form of a postal package, weighing at most one kilo without a written supplement. This shall be sent directly to the recipient in Theresienstadt.
4. Postcards and packages can only be sent to residents in Theresienstadt who have personally confirmed their addresses.
5. Directions must be carefully followed to avoid risk of infringement, thereby impacting the postal traffic.

July 1943

The Reich Deputation of the German Jews

The rules were constantly changing. Sometimes you weren't allowed to receive packages. Sometimes you were allowed to write four postcards per six-month period. First cursive was forbidden and only block capitals were allowed, then cursive was allowed and then forbidden again. Each letter was examined.

Pepi and Elise shared their right to correspond between their loyal Mitzi and Otto in Sweden. Mitzi also kept in touch with Otto via simple, everyday letters, and she did what she could to send food packages to the prisoners.

SENDER ELISE ULLMANN
THERESIENSTADT L. 215 PROTECTORATE

July 3, 1943

Dearest, best boy. First and foremost, our best wishes for your birthday. May all of your wishes come true. May God continue to protect you and preserve your health. This is our daily prayer. We've received both your cards, and they filled us with joy. Thankfully all is well with you. Thank you for your loving birthday wishes to me and Dad. We are healthy, think of you daily and long for you endlessly. Write to us even if our replies come with some delay. Mail of all kinds arrives as it should. We have received greetings from Mrs. Eklundh and from the Andersson family. Send them our regards.

To you, my dear boy, we wish you all good things. Take care of yourself. Warm greetings and kisses from Dad and your mother

Elise Ullmann

The Central Bureau was the division inside the Swedish Secret Police that inspected and censored mail. Letters were steamed open, transcribed, and glued shut.

As part of the surveillance of extreme organizations, mailboxes belonging to Swedish Nazis were regularly searched. Incoming and outgoing mail of the party office in Stockholm was inspected—both to and from the mother party, the SSS, and their hard-core youth organization Nazistisk Ungdom (Nazi Youth).

In spring the police had a look at a number of circulars. They included the newspaper *Rätt* (*Right*), published by Nazi Youth. One recipient was Ingvar Kamprad, Elmtaryd. In a memo in Ingvar's personal file at the Security Service, it is made clear that *Rätt* was only sent to those in the movement who had "some sort of functionary post."

In May Ingvar was to take his junior secondary school certificate at Osby. The same month the police discovered that he'd conscripted a friend to the Nazi youth organization. On the membership application Ingvar himself had written: "I am currently at a school, where it is necessary to keep this secret. Can report that we, in spite of difficulties, have spoken with the owner of the printer to reproduce your circulated propaganda flyer 'How would the Bolsheviks kill in Sweden?' in a somewhat altered form."

In the fall Ingvar began his studies at the Gothenburg School of Economics and Business Administration. Perhaps he considered giving up the Lindholmers' more hard-line Nazism for the Swedish Opposition and the esteemed Per Engdahl. Ties were not cut yet, but new ones were being made.

When Per Engdahl began his speaking tour in Gothenburg in September, Ingvar was there to aid and support him. Because the fascist leader suffered from poor eyesight, he needed assistance, and Ingvar was the one who usually escorted him there and back, between the train station and the event venues. Sometimes they stopped at Bräutigam's bakery, where Ingvar read the newspapers aloud for his idol, who committed them to memory and commented.

If the deportation of Norwegian Jews had awakened Swedish opinion, it was only now, one year later, that Swedish refugee policies changed in practice.

In Denmark the Nazis planned to deport all Danes of Jewish heritage to Theresienstadt, but one or more responsible parties chose to leak the information about the planned raid in advance. The Danish resistance movement acted quickly in conference with Sweden, and over seven thousand people were transported at night on fishing boats across the sound.

Ingvar's father wore jodhpurs, wide around the thighs, the excess fabric forming a point, buttoned or laced around the shin so that the polished boots could easily be pulled on. Ingvar wore them, too, I'm told, though I didn't ask.

"He strutted about the farm in those jodhpurs. Like his father before him."

In the area they say everyone was aware that the Kamprads were Nazis. They also say they were fine people, estate owners, Germans, and that their word was law. But all that is said, is it true?

Those who wore jodhpurs considered themselves to be somewhat elevated. Barons, foremen, inspectors, officers, forest guards, pilots, chauffeurs, motorcyclists, and horsemen.

Ingvar spent most of his time strolling the streets around the school of economics in Gothenburg, and so it took a while before he found out that the farm had taken on a young man by the name of Otto as a farmhand, or "agricultural student," as he would be called on paper.

But Ingvar's little sister, Kerstin, remembers.

III

The morning is mild, a haze hovers above the grass and the molehills.

Kerstin's freshly painted house sits just outside the village, and she's waiting in the kitchen doorway. A chair has already been pulled up to the dining table where we are to sit. No coffee, no glass of water, only generous conversation.

The photo album comes out, and the eighty-year-old woman with the high forehead and clear eyes across from me also meets my gaze from the black-and-white childhood pictures. Chalk-white hair bleached in the 1940s sun. Side part, wooden cart, lilac arbor.

Her older brother Ingvar is standing there, too. He's looking into the camera, frozen in time and preserved, the boy who would grow old and become Sweden's richest man.

And father Feodor, mother Berta, and grandmother Fanny. There they stand on the gravel. Outside the stone house. On the steps. Together. Each on their own.

KERSTIN: I remember it clearly, as if it were yesterday.

ELISABETH: How old were you then?

KERSTIN: I must've been thirteen years old. You understand, Otto was a farmhand at Kärrnäs. He lived with the tenant farmers there, now I can't remember what they were called. And Kärrnäs was too small, there wasn't enough work. Then someone said to Otto, I don't know who, but they said: look up the Kamprads, they speak German. So he came here looking for work. They sat there in the kitchen.

ELISABETH: Were you there, too?

KERSTIN: Of course. He came here and told us about himself, about his family, about Vienna, about who he was. And Dad, he looked uneasy. He looked at mother and said, "Naah..."

[Kerstin pauses as though thinking back, and imitates her father's hesitancy.] "Naah..." That's what he said. And looked at my mother Berta. And then mother looked back. She could look strict, I remember that look—and then she said: "But Feodor. He's only a child." And that was the end of that.

ELISABETH: Do you think she understood what your father had wanted to say? What he was thinking?

KERSTIN: Yes.

ELISABETH: ...That he had objections because...

KERSTIN: Otto was Jewish.

ELISABETH: Did you also understand that that's what Feodor was thinking?

KERSTIN: Oh yes. But mother said "Feodor," and gave him that look. "He's only a child." And that's how it went. I'll never forget it.

You understand. My father didn't like Jews. He didn't, you see. And that's a long story. It has to do with his family in Germany having a lot of property, but then they had a lawyer and he was a Jew, and then everything was lost. And it was that Jew's fault. It left its mark, and my grandmother Fanny passed that on to him.

ELISABETH: What did you think about Otto?

KERSTIN: I remember Otto being so small, so thin. And that he had a big nose.

I didn't know what a Jew was. My mother's cousin married a Jewess, and one day they came for a visit. Mother asked me to run and fetch Father. And I ran as fast as I could and shouted to Father: "Come, come quick! There's a Gypsy hag here!"

I'd never seen anyone who was that dark before, and all I knew was that Gypsies weren't to be trusted.

That's how it happened. Otto Ullmann was taken on as a farmhand at Elmtaryd. He was to live in the farmhand's room one floor up at the tenant farmer's, with a view of his workplace, the hundred-meter-long barn.

And there was plenty to do. The Kamprad family's groom had a relative with tuberculosis and needed time off, so Otto was allowed to step in and take his place. The monthly salary was 125 kronor plus free room and board.

Milking every morning, so the milk car could pick up the jugs at 7:15. Times of war, times of blackout. When Otto went down to the barn in the mornings he had to point his flashlight at the ground so the light wouldn't leak. Then fetch water and wood. After that, breakfast with the family. And thus the day progressed until fatigue took over in the evening.

He was eighteen years old. Only a child, Berta had said. Maybe it was his weedy frame, maybe it was the story about his solitary journey that moved her. Or was it her will to do good that reigned? Berta Kamprad was active in the Red Cross, had cared for war children from Finland. Now it was Otto who'd found the warm path leading to her heart. He was always ready to serve, and quick, prepared to do as she asked.

Feodor, the landowner who didn't like Jews, noted her tenderness. Kerstin, the little girl, noted it, and when Ingvar came home for summer vacation, he noticed it too.

"Too nice," that's what locals still say about Berta. I don't ask about that either, and yet they tell me. An angel, they say of Berta Kamprad. And her son Ingvar agrees. The nicest imaginable. She embraced Otto. Why? I wonder, when we talk about it. Because that's who she was, my mother, Ingvar replies. She was a preacher of kindness.

There was something about her that made Otto feel like he could confide in her. She listened for a long time, carefully and without her eyes flitting. And Otto talked. About Pepi, intelligent and respected by all, with tons of friends and contacts around the world. About Lisl, always prepared to put others first, and her loving and winning way. In Berta's kitchen on Elmtaryd farm his loss came to life, and Josef and Elise were visible, as shimmering and good-hearted as one only becomes in the light of years of forlorn longing.

In the evening there was milking to be done again. The pails were carried up to Grandmother Fanny, who divided them amongst the household. Did she ever meet Otto, did they ever speak German together? As Ingvar's sister Kerstin recalls, they never had anything to do with each other.

On the Kamprads' farm, one didn't need to scrimp with food, even though it was a time of rationing. They had milk, and from it Berta churned butter and made cheese. They had chickens and other animals in the barnyard, so they had eggs and meat. From the lake they had as much wall-eye and perch as they could ask for.

Otto had arrived at his seventh home. What had they

written on the registry card at the Swedish Israel Mission on Seegasse that autumn in 1938? Adaptable. There is indeed something about children from a children's home. It is said that they smile more than others.

III

Nothing was orderly anymore. The letters came pell-mell, if they came at all. Who knows which got stuck along the way, were stolen, were thrown away, or quite simply were lost.

All mail from Theresienstadt passed though the censor in Berlin, and now Otto was receiving a letter that had been on its way for several months. Even though it was written in January 1944, the stamp shows that it only reached Berlin in April. Then it took more time for it to reach Kärrnäs farm in Pjätteryd, where it was sent on to Otto in Elmtaryd.

SENDER ELISE ULLMANN
BAHNHOFSTRASSE 15, THERESIENSTADT
POST BARISCHOWITZ PROTECTORATE

January 3, 1944

Beloved boy. Now two months have passed since we last heard from you. We've already replied to your most recent card from September. We hope you're doing well and are healthy, and we count on hearing from you soon again. Of course being surrounded by your friends in Kärrnäs means you have it good. And thankfully we too are healthy. Mitzi wrote that she received a letter from you and your people, noting Mrs. Eklundh and the Andersson family in particular. We wish you all good and happy holidays. Beloved boy—take care of yourself, write soon. All mail is arriving as it should. May God continue to protect you. Kisses and greetings from your dad and Mutti.

Elise Ullmann

Time was out of step. The mail rounds, the censor, the high-speed machinery of murder—nothing could be measured anymore. It all depended on the hunger, the cold, the degree of hope or hopelessness. Any prayers only applied to the next half hour.

"All mail is arriving as it should," Elise wrote to Otto. Those words formed a sentence that would be repeated in several of the handwritten cards that found their way out of camp. A riddle.

"All mail is arriving as it should." This could have meant that packages of food would reach them in days of famine or medicine in times of sickness. Or that clothing was needed in order to survive that raw, unheated place.

Pepi and Elise knew that the letters were preinspected, and they had to obscure their words so the message would not go amiss. They trusted in their son's cunning. It's unclear if Otto understood, but he corresponded with his dear Mitzi, who made sure to send packets to Lisl and Pepi as often as the authorities allowed.

One might wish that the SS men and the prisoners handling the packages did not steal. One might wish that Theresienstadt had in fact been inspected by the Red Cross when they visited the camp in 1943. But instead it was a pretend inspection, and in the Red Cross report, life in the prison was hailed as exemplary.

One might wish that Elise and Pepi had asked for weapons to organize an armed uprising. But one can neither know nor judge. One can only keep in mind that they were peaceful, loved soccer, the opera, and each other, and most likely carried with them the ancient knowledge that people with a heritage of vulnerability have told themselves in all times of persecution and hate: The wind does not break a reed that bends.

Well, don't misunderstand me here, but I fell in love," Ingvar Kamprad says sixty-five years later.

When the term ended for the students at Gothenburg's School of Economics, Ingvar traveled home, as landowners' children did during the holidays. The farm always needed manpower, for the animals and in the fields. That's when he heard about the new farmhand. They met.

One could imagine the scenes that might have taken place. Ingvar was eighteen years old, and the doubly engaged Nazi—son of a Jew hater and the grandson of a Hitler lover—came home and found the one-year-his-senior Otto there.

But Ingvar fell in love. Friend love. Otto and Ingvar. Ingvar and Otto.

It was always easier to be a farmhand in the summertime, nice to be outside, lovely to swim, but now it became fun, too. Ingvar's friendship with Otto opened up the days to spontaneity and rule breaking, for shared dreams of girls and love.

Ingvar's three cousins Stina, Margareta, and Inga-Britt came for a summer visit and stayed on a nearby farm. When Ingvar and Otto were done with their toil, the girls were there. Otto didn't know which one made his knees weaker, Stina or Margareta. They had horses and the young people went riding together.

They took swimming excursions equipped with a picnic. They played with each other, summer games, youth's games.

Otto and Ingvar worked together. They took care of the barn, milked the eleven cows, and kept everything tidy. They took turns crawling up the loft to pull down the hay, one of them up there pulling it down, the other spreading out the hay for the animals. They cleared Feodor's ditches. They rowed out on the lake at night and fished for eel.

There were enticing outdoor dance pavillions in both Oshult and Bråna Backar—but before heading out on their bikes, they wanted to get their blood going. Ingvar took out a few demijohns and together they concocted a recipe for a drink dubbed "brew." The ingredients were what was on hand: crushed potatoes, wheat, and sugar. They stole honey from mother Berta's beehives and poured that in, too. Then they let everything sit in a sunny spot behind the barn, fermenting until the pressure caused the cork to fly off. Then little bugs flew in. It didn't taste good, but it had an effect. The summer of 1944 tasted of dry cigarettes and vile moonshine. And why not?

Otto and Ingvar biked from one dance to the next. They tallied kisses. Fights broke out. Sometimes they put an arm around the same girl, but the most important thing was to stick together. Otto and Ingvar shared both their daily toil and festivities. Girls liked Otto because he wasn't like anyone else, and Ingvar because he was tall and handsome. Sometimes they were out all night and because the cows had to be milked, they simply didn't sleep. They met up at the barn, each on his own bicycle.

It was a youthful time that laid the foundation for a friendship that would last nearly a decade.

No longer alone. It was a glorious summer.

Every Saturday Ingvar received the publication *The Way Forward*. Even his father Feodor read the newspaper's opinion pages, news articles, and unattributed anecdotes: "It is clear that individual attacks on Jews took place in Germany both before and after Hitler's rise to power, but these 'persecutions' were but child's play compared with the persecutions Germans have been subjected to in their own country for decades. It is the Jew and no one else since the dawn of time and with the most studious and refined means any mind could ever concoct, who in practice turned the word 'persecution' against all those who were suspected of standing or would come to stand in the way of the Jewish bid for power!"

But politics weren't discussed at the dining table at Elmtaryd. The kitchen was Berta's domain and she demanded that they eat in peace. Otto knew Feodor was a German-sympathizer, and Feodor knew Otto wanted nothing more than the downfall of the Nazis. They brushed up against it, they commented on the news reports on the radio. But besides that, the everyday and the summer took over.

Ingvar's little sister Kerstin was never allowed to join her older brother and Otto in their games. She and her closest friend spied on them from behind the house, and sulked when Ingvar and Otto went on their way without a word. Sometimes she tied their shoelaces together when they were asleep as revenge. Once she heard them having a swearing competition, the one worse than the other. She'd never heard anything like it, but they just laughed and kept working. Yes, everything was lovely. If you don't take the letters into account. On the other hand they didn't come that often.

The next greeting reached Otto at the end of July. Hitler glaring to the right, in a medium-brown tone, cost fifteen pfennig. The card was dated April 3, 1944. Pepi had written a few lines on his fifty-first, and last, birthday.

SENDER JOSEF ULLMANN

PARKSTRASSE 6/6, THERESIENSTADT PROTECTORATE

April 3, 1944

My beloved boy. It has been a long time since we've heard from you. I hope you are healthy, thankfully we are. How are you, do you have a lot to do? We're waiting and longing for a sign of life from you. Does Uncle Egon write sometimes? Give him our address and send him our regards. Also do ask Mitzi to write to us. Write soon. Take care of yourself and may God be with you. Greetings to all, a thousand kisses from

your mom and dad

III

As I said, no order. When Otto received that letter, it was already three months old. Pepi and Lisl had addressed it to Kärrnäs, but Otto hadn't been there for six months. So they couldn't have received any mail from him since he'd moved.

But a week later, he received two letters on the same day. One had been en route for nine months. Which conclusions could he draw? Life might need nine months to come into being, but death needed no time at all.

SENDER ELISE ULLMANN

BAHNHOFSTRASSE 15, THERESIENSTADT PROTECTORATE

November 2, 1943

Beloved boy. Once again you've made us very happy with your card. Most important of all is that you're healthy and happy. We too can report that we are well and all is good. Your move to Ljungby surely corresponds with your wishes. Don't forget to send our regards to the Andersson family from there, as well. We'd very much like to have a photograph of you, can't you send one? We think of you daily and pray for your well-being. Write soon again, beloved child. Be healthy and may God protect you. Many thousand kisses from

your dad and mom

The second letter was just over two months old. No guarantee of life, but still.

SENDER JOSEF ULLMANN

PARKSTRASSE 6/6, THERESIENSTADT PROTECTORATE

May 20, 1944

Beloved best boy, we've been missing you and your letters for a long time, but we hope that you are healthy, as we are healthy. Here all mail is arriving as it should. Mutti and I hope to soon receive a sign of life from you. Say hello to Mitzi for us, she writes us often. Say hello to the families Eklund and Andersson, too. Write soon, stay healthy and may God protect you. A thousand kisses from

Mutti and your loyal dad

Otto answered. But even if he wrote, it was as though the letters were never detailed enough or sent with enough regularity. Even if he wrote, he knew that Lisl and Pepi could neither come for him nor could he go get them. Even if he wrote and even if he prayed, he knew the letters might not be reaching them. And whether or not he wrote, it would torment him for the rest of his life: the knowledge of the joy these lines gave to his parents, and the fact that he was rationing it.

He lived his life as a Smålandish farmhand and had decided to make the best of his time, of his salvation, of Sweden. The girls could be divine. He planned to continue his correspondence courses in the fall. As he saw it, studying was the only path leading out of the barn, and he was going to take it.

August came and went like a heat wave through the body. His father wrote again, but when the letter reached Otto in September, several weeks had already passed since it had been dropped off at the post office in Theresienstadt.

SENDER JOSEF ULLMANN

PARKSTRASSE 6/6, THERESIENSTADT PROTECTORATE

June 30, 1944

Beloved boy. I want most of all to congratulate you on your upcoming birthday. Our wishes and prayers for your well-being will be especially strong that day. Beloved boy, May God continue to protect you and may all your wishes come true. And above all take care of yourself. We're doing well. We've heard from Mitzi that you haven't received a letter for a long time. We hope our cards have reached you. Write to us soon, and again: Mail of all kinds is arriving as it should. Send the Eklundh and Andersson families our regards. A thousand kisses from

your mom and dad

On September 28, a transport left Theresienstadt. Among the thousand-some prisoners on board was Josef Ullmann, called Pepi by those closest to him.

Prisoner number 992.

The train stopped at the station in Oswiecim, a village east of Kraków that the Germans called Auschwitz.

Elise was alone for five days. For five days and five nights. Then she too boarded a train, transport Ek.

Prisoner 975.

The train traveled the five hundred kilometers between Theresienstadt and Auschwitz. It was October 4. Elise Ullmann was fifty-three years old.

Otto knew nothing of this. Instead he received yet another letter. He saw that it was dated in August but couldn't possibly know that it was already old, very old.

August 19, 1944

Dear boy. Since my last letter to you, another two months have passed without us having had a reply from you. But I hope that you've written to us and that your card will soon arrive. Thankfully we are healthy and hope that you are, too. Have you heard from Mitzi? Send her our heartfelt greetings. And send our greetings to your people, above all the families Eklundh and Andersson. Write soon. We long for your lines, especially because the post from Sweden arrives as it should. Take care of yourself. May God protect you, a thousand kisses from

Mutti and your loyal dad

III

Seven months later, on May 8, the war ended. Only then did Sweden open its borders. Around twenty thousand people came to Sweden through the campaign named for the white buses that transported people out of the camps and ruins. Among them were perhaps seven thousand Jewish former camp prisoners. Committees were created around the country, refugees were cared for and tended to in more than 250 boardinghouses, missions, schools, and several hospitals. Many Swedes got involved. As though that were the obvious choice. As if the realization about what had happened had not come too late. And it was possible to say and print in a book that caring for these human wrecks from a historic global catastrophe became Sweden's task, Sweden's blessed part in the world war.

This was done and this was said and the words were published. It was good.

Those saved were also interviewed and testimonies were published in books and articles. Pepi and Lisl were not among them.

The peacetime spring warmed the country and became postwar summer. Per Albin Hansson created a new government. In Agunnaryd Ingvar and Otto continued their conquest of nights and the local girls.

But no letters.

Otto wrote to relatives and friends in England. Mitzi looked through the names on the lists from various German authorities, and Pepi's older brother Egon, who'd managed to get to America, made inquiries in all imaginable newspapers in countries of exile, in refugee camps, with the Red Cross. Nothing.

Without Otto knowing it, Ingvar kept in constant contact with his other life.

And there they walked side by side, Otto and Ingvar. Two young men with suppressed feelings and double agendas. Otto, who carried his childhood and family in a room tightly sealed with loss, while being a poor farmhand in an involuntary reality.

Ingvar had no other friend who was as close to him, and yet he was a fixture in Per Engdahl's innermost circle. So much a fixture that though he was known for never being wasteful, he gladly gave his kronor, time, and skills to stoke enthusiasm.

He initiated close and warm contact with the organization's secretary Bengt Olov Ljungberg, and in their correspondence they discussed everything from town-square meetings to Ingvar's plans for his company.

Only three weeks after peace had been declared, Ingvar was asked to recruit local members and encourage them to make economic contributions. In a letter from May 31 he was tasked with making "sure Gothenburg pays its share of this month's fee properly."

Swedish Opposition changed its name to the Nysvenska Rörelsen (New Swedish Movement). Ingvar sold *The Postwar Agenda* and the proceeds went right back into the organization.

After that summer Ingvar enlisted his old teacher and Feodor's opponent in bridge—Rudolf Malmquist—to the New Swedes and also paid his twenty-kronor fee. In Malmquist's welcome letter dated September 19, 1945, the movement is described as being small, having big economic problems, but strong "idealistic values."

Can one speak of hope? Could Otto have harbored any? How could he not have?

How many lists were left, which had the Gestapo burned? Could Lisl and Pepi have been traced amid the war's disarray of trains carrying people to their deaths? Where in the wasteland could they be found, where were her hairpins, was someone else wearing his carefully polished shoes?

Otto found out in July of 1946.

As if Messrs. Hitler, Lindholm, and Engdahl had come up with it all themselves.

At the Edict of Milan in the year 313, it was decided that Jews were no longer allowed to live in Jerusalem. Marriage between Jews and Christians was forbidden and sexual relations were punished with banishment. Neither were Jews and Christians allowed to break bread together.

At the Council of Clermont in the year 535, Jews were stripped of their right to hold official office. Three years later they were forbidden to hire Christian servants or to keep Christian slaves, and so could not pursue agriculture.

They were given a curfew during the last week of Easter, as per a decision at the Third Council of Orléans.

At the Council of Toledo in 563, they were forbidden to celebrate Easter, follow Jewish dietary laws, or marry according to Jewish custom. Breaches were punishable by being burned at the stake or stoned to death.

Thirty years later it was decided in Toledo that Jewish literature be burned and that Jewish children were to be taken from their parents and put in monasteries to be raised as Christians.

In 692 all Jews were ordered into slavery and their property was confiscated.

Nothing new under the sun of the Holy Trinity.

In 722 Pope Leo III forbade Judaism across the empire, burned down the synagogues, worshippers still inside, and ordered forced baptisms.

The French archbishop declared in 829 that Jews were stealing Christian children and selling them to the Arabs.

During the Easter sermons in 855, the people in the areas around Bézier were encouraged to take revenge on the Jews for nailing Jesus to the cross.

In 1012 Jews were driven from Mainz after refusing to convert to Christianity.

Ten years later Rome suffered an earthquake and a hurricane. The Jews were accused of having incurred God's wrath and were burned at the stake.

In 1078 Pope Gregory VII determined that Jews were not allowed to hold appointments that put them in positions superior to Christians.

In 1081 Jews were forced to pay extra tax to the church.

In 1096 Crusaders throughout Europe committed mass murder of the Jews who would not convert to Christianity.

At a church meeting in Rome in 1179, it was declared that Christian testimonies in trials would always precede those of Jews.

In 1215 it was determined that Jews should wear special clothing so they could be distinguished from Christians.

At a church meeting in Oxford in 1222 building synagogues was forbidden.

Ten years later Pope Gregory IX forbade friendly relations between Jews and Christians.

In 1236 Jews in France who would not become Christian were murdered.

In Vienna in 1267 all Jews were asked to wear special clothing. That same year Thomas Aquinas declared that Jews must live in eternal submission, and the French king declared that all the Jews in the empire had to wear a purple symbol on their clothing.

At a church meeting in Hungary in 1279 Christians were forbidden to sell or rent property to Jews.

One year later, the church in Poland demanded that the Jews there be isolated from the rest of the population.

In 1306, French Jews were expelled and their property confiscated. Two years later, Jews in Suttzmatt and Rufach were accused by a bishop of having desecrated the Holy Communion, and they were burned alive.

In 1320 over one hundred Jewish communities were annihilated in northern Spain and southern France by Christians demanding they convert.

Jews were murdered across Europe at the end of the 1300s because of sermons in which they were accused of causing the plague and the Black Death.

In 1434 the church council in Basel forbade Jews an academic education, and they had to attend conversion sermons and live in designated parts of the city.

Eighteen years later, in 1451, Pope Nicholas V forbade Christians to have social contact with Jews.

In 1492 all Jews had to leave Spain within three months or be baptized. A few thousand were burned at the stake. One hundred thousand fled. The same year thirty thousand Jews were expelled from Sicily.

In 1509 Holy Roman Emperor Maximilian I ordered that all texts opposing Christianity be destroyed. Jewish homes and synagogues were searched, literature was confiscated.

In Venice, the Jewish ghetto was established by Pope Paul IV in 1516.

In 1539 Martin Luther wrote his diatribe "Against the Antinomians." Four years later he published "On the Jews and Their Lies."

In 1555 Paul IV was reelected as pope. His first measure was to have a wall built around the Jewish neighborhood in Rome.

In 1685 Judaism was banned in France. Catholicism became the only sanctioned religion.

The Russian empress Catherine II declared in 1794 that Jews were to pay twice as much tax as Christians in the same social class.

It could happen. It already has.

III

A few months later, Otto applied for Swedish citizenship. For this reason the chief constable in the Ljungby police precinct paid a visit to Elmtaryd and the estate's owner Feodor Kamprad, to find out about Otto's character and diligence, as mandated by the Ministry of Justice itself. Feodor certified that Otto had been honest, sober, and proper. He further confirmed that Otto had held a position on the farm as an agricultural worker since 1944, partaking in all manner of tasks, and had performed his duties without complaint. All that he could allege with regard to Otto's political views was that in his years of service, Otto had been unable to suppress his hatred for Hitlerism.

At the end of 1946, longing for the big city won out over security and friendship, and Otto left the farm.

He found jobs in Stockholm, worked at several places that were eager to keep him on, but each time he quit of his own volition. He spent the evenings studying through correspondence courses. He was never a burden on society. His employers gave him good recommendations, but Otto was restless. His application for Swedish citizenship was denied.

There was rage. A sense of nothing being right—not him, not where he was, not his surroundings; Swedes who'd never had to flee, lose a home, whose biggest problem during the war was a lack of coffee during rationing. All those years he'd spent crouching down, proud of his ability to adapt. All the days he'd spent mucking out the stalls, plowing the fields in the clay soil. All the letters he hadn't answered. He'd decided to move on, but anger lived its own life just below his words, behind his thoughts, and it became impossible to settle down.

Lisl. Pepi. They'd been inextricable parts of each other. Now that they were no longer, the phantom pain lived its own nonlife, transformed into rage. And whenever he tried not to think about it, it ached and burned.

In November 1948, Otto traveled to Palestine to fight for Israel for nine months.

No words or documents remain from that time in the desert and his assignment as a sniper. Only a few photographs of dusty houses and young men sharing their soldier life and soldier death. But instead of cleansing and redress, he left the war with a new pain added to the old one. Wherever home was, it wasn't there. What had been hurting had not healed, instead it had sunk in deeper.

But this was nothing to speak of. Life went on. In Jerusalem he bought souvenirs for his friends in Småland.

III

Ingvar's little sister Kerstin, his cousin Inga-Britt, Lisa who cleaned and helped out at Berta and Feodor's—all of them were drawn into Ingvar's first team of workmen, building the foundation for what would become the IKEA empire. It was only possible with financial support from Ingvar's parents.

Ingvar had founded the business back in 1943, and at that time it was fountain pens, watch bands, and file folders that he was buying and selling. But he had come to think of the local furniture makers and their small businesses situated around Lake Möcklen; it might be a good idea to go into the furniture business. He added his initials to those of the village name and got going. Ingvar Kamprad Elmtaryd Agunnaryd.

And he invited his comrades from the New Swedish Movement over to Elmtaryd, and ahead of a Midsummer celebration the New Swedes joked that they'd refrain from wearing uniforms so Ingvar wouldn't have a heart attack.

He was seen as their colleague and benefactor. In all the remaining letters, the leadership of the New Swedes was trying to get him to donate more money or was thanking him for his latest contribution. He also acted as the publisher for one of Per Engdahl's books, *A Comprehensive General Education in Politics*, distributed under the pseudonym Sten Jonsson.

Right after the war, in 1945, Per Engdahl organized the escape of both Danes and Swedes who had been in the Waffen-SS and who'd been put in a camp to await the administration of justice. In his memoirs he writes: "We got them out of the camps and hid them in various places. There were several farms in the Skånish countryside that were at our disposal."

Engdahl helped a group of Nazi prisoners in the General Hospital in Malmö by bribing a nurse to put them in a particular room. At a specified time, they jumped out of a window and down to waiting cars. Then they were moved around from farm to farm in Skåne.

"From the harbors in Malmö and Gothenburg, boats for Spain and Latin America were departing," he writes. "Yet the majority of them were transported to West Germany, which was considered relatively safe."

Now Engdahl was adjusting what he'd said and written about Jews, claiming that he had been influenced by certain "then-reigning racial biological doctrines."

Already in 1947, he and his New Swedish Movement took the initiative to organize a Nordic meeting in Copenhagen for right-wing extremists. Among the participants was the Belgian Nazi leader Johan van Byck, representing the newly created Vlaams Bloc.

Per Engdahl and Ingvar Kamprad had now become close friends, and naturally their letters began with "B B." Best brother.

What made them seek each other out—the young businessman building his company and the soon-forty-year-old learned fascist with his unending flood of words? The two men both hailed from Småland, but that is hardly a sufficient link. Maybe the fact that Engdahl's New Swedish Movement suffered from a constant lack of funds could have been one reason to cultivate a relationship with the young Kamprad.

Ingvar offers his German relatives as explanation, the Nazi ideas and the admiration for "Uncle Hitler" he'd inherited from the large house on the farm. But even after the war, when the consequences of these thoughts were clear to everyone, he stayed with the fascist movement.

Surely he understood he was important to it, with his growing business and income. And maybe he inspired the fascist leader to formulate ways to govern nations that were reminiscent of how one helms a successful business. No one but Ingvar himself can answer this question, and he's declined the request to answer more questions for the time being.

Surely young Ingvar noted that the fascist leader surrounded himself with fine folk—people Ingvar very much wanted to know. Learned professors, court of appeal judges, and doctors attended the meetings and parties, and some of Sweden's biggest and most successful entrepreneurs and businessmen were in Engdahl's inner circle. For Ingvar there were contacts to be made and networks to build. So the two were drawn to each other, did each other favors, and exchanged letters.

With his friend Engdahl, Ingvar discussed everything from his fiancée's melancholy to odd problems regarding the launch of a furniture line. During Whitsuntide 1950 Ingvar participated in the New Swedish Movement's national assembly, and just over a month later he was to be a bridegroom in Stockholm.

Agunnaryd, June 30, 1950

Dear Per!

First I would like to offer warm thanks to you for so kindly wanting to witness me become a husband. It will be, as I mentioned, in Solna Church on Saturday, July 8 at 15:30. After which there will be a simple party at Hasselbacken.

In addition to my parents and my sister, from my side you and my best schoolmate from my time in Gbg will attend... It will be a simple affair, but it will be particularly festive for me in that you so kindly wish to come...

Furthermore I would like you to know that I'm proud of the opportunity to belong to the New Swedish circle and make no secret of it among my relations and friends, with whom I do not do business... In haste and with best regards

Ingvar

Per Engdahl came to the wedding and made a beautiful speech.

When Ingvar's wife came to the Kamprads' farm in Agunnaryd, jodhpurs and riding boots were ordered for her, though she did not like to ride.

Ingvar continued to contribute company money to Engdahl's political activities, even though he'd complained in the letters about the cost of printing the IKEA catalog and of having a furniture showroom in Stockholm. In some letters, his wife added a short handwritten greeting.

And Ingvar gladly sent New Swedish greetings to the organization's secretary Bengt Olov Ljungberg, and to the editor of the newspaper *Vägen Framåt* (*The Way Forward*), Yngve

Nordberg. He was a friend and brother of the entire New Swedish Movement's leadership.

The same year that Per Engdahl took the time to attend Ingvar's wedding at the Solna Church, he was also a central figure in binding together and strengthening several of Europe's right-extremist movements. In Rome an international Nazi conference was held with participants from Italy, Spain, Portugal, France, West Germany, Austria, Switzerland, the Netherlands, and Belgium. The British fascist leader Oswald Mosley also attended the meeting, and Per Engdahl wrote an agenda for Europe's future, which the conference accepted.

Six months later he organized a large meeting in Malmö with some of the most important far-right leaders in Europe present; there representatives from France and Switzerland wanted to set out an active racial policy. Together with Bengt Olov Ljungberg and Yngve Nordberg, Engdahl represented the host country Sweden. It was decided to launch a monthly publication whose editor in chief was to be a German ex–SS officer. His collaborator was—who else?—Per Engdahl.

What could Ingvar Kamprad have known, what did he support, what has he since forgotten?

In the late fall of 1951, the year that Per Engdahl helped start the international European Social Movement in Malmö, Ingvar wrote to thank him for his latest book, *The Renewal of the West*: "First, hearty thanks for the book. It will be really rather pleasant to encounter something sensible—since this is something I can't count on with the eternal nagging about armchair this or table that."

Now and then Engdahl visited Elmtaryd. He ordered a sofa from Ingvar, but it's unclear if he was given a discount.

And meanwhile, Ingvar's friendship with Otto was strained but endured. Ingvar had started to build his life's work. When Otto had taken a look around the world, he returned to Elmtaryd, to Ingvar, to IKEA.

III

I was supposed to be a pearl diver," said Otto.

That's how his future wife Ingrid remembers it beginning. They both worked for Ingvar in the large house on the farm. Otto was different with his big curly hair, his stories about diving in the Red Sea, about Jerusalem and the world. They'd met before, when Otto was Feodor Kamprad's farmhand and she was a child of one of the Kamprads' tenant farmers. Now she was to turn seventeen, and he was funny and interesting, though a decade older than she, so rather old. From his desk, he would gaze at her with such intensity she ended up switching places with someone else to avoid it. A friendship began.

It could be compared to a collective, those early days of IKEA. Ingvar, Otto, and another three colleagues all lived in the large house where they worked.

Ingvar recalls:

> When Otto arrived and we began in earnest, it was in the big house. My grandmother had died and I was allowed to take over on the condition that I make some repairs... It was a rather large old farm with a rather large house and it had enough room for Otto and that girl who was called Samuelsson, and a girl called Eivor Ros, and then there was a boy called Ernst Ekström. So there were five of us in fact. Then my cousin Inga-Britt came into the picture, but

she lived with relatives. So we were a little troop, Otto and I were salespeople responsible for small brochures and ads in newspapers and everything.

Ingrid still lived with her parents in the red tenant farmer's house but crossed the yard every day to go to work in the gray wooden house. There she took care of mail orders, fabric samples, and card index registers.

Ingvar was now twenty-six and newly married. Otto was his right-hand man. But even if the two of them could still have a good time, it wasn't like the old days. Anyone there could see how Ingvar's wife felt sidelined by the old dance pavillion stories Otto and Ingvar shared, that she felt left out by their happy nights with drink and cigarettes and nothing again ever being as simple as it was before. Not only was Ingvar working almost around-the-clock, Otto was in spite of everything just an employee and should really have kept more of a distance.

And so the business grew. The outbuilding that they used as a warehouse was not big enough, the milk churn stand they used as a loading bay for mail-order packages was constantly being enlarged, and the postal service had its hands full. After a few years Ingvar wanted to expand. He decided to move the business to Älmhult.

And Otto? Did he want to be independent, had he had enough of house masters and superiors? He wanted to leave the countryside, create an existence far away from dairy cows and stone fields. There was the familiar echo of another life with opera houses and trams, cafés and city traffic. There were paved streets with rivers of people. He decided to move from Småland for good and go to Stockholm.

Ingvar was very disappointed, he says today, but Otto left anyway. There was a break in their friendship, but not an end.

Ingvar's friendship with Per Engdahl ran parallel.

A double life. Separate realities. Ingvar's best friends were the fascist Engdahl and the Jewish refugee Otto. Was he split in two? Did he tell himself that no person is a monolith, thankfully, no one is die-cast? Is this the explanation for his parallel worlds, with two real-life opposites so close by? Was there space for contradiction inside Ingvar? Or did he quite simply shut it out and pretend it didn't exist?

There is no answer, not even when Ingvar today takes his seat in the chair named "Jules" and thinks about it. No. Why would that be problematic? A friend is a friend. End of story.

And according to this logic it was only natural that he'd keep in touch with Otto. They would work together one last time, in Stockholm. Ingvar exhibited his wares at conferences and needed help, and Otto would work alongside Ingvar's father-in-law selling beds and mattresses in a space on Drottninggatan. But that didn't last longer than a year, and left among Otto's papers is the testimonial of his friend, employer, and boss. Otto had been trustworthy and performed his work to his complete satisfaction, Ingvar Kamprad certified. The year was 1952.

Ingvar and Otto parted as friends, but they parted.

In 1958 Per Engdahl was made the head of the international European movement. Ingvar's old idol experienced his biggest successes during the fifties and watched his dream become reality when Europe's far right movements connected and grew.

When the West German government led an investigation into neo-Nazism in the country in 1962, it turned out that Sweden was the primary source of printed propaganda for German Nazis and Per Engdahl was identified as a key person in the Nazis' international network.

Later he spread the idea that the right-wing extremists in Europe had to stop using the sullied term "race" when they wanted to fight immigration and minorities. Instead they were to speak of culture: "An immigration that creates significant minorities with its own patterns always constitutes a threat to a people's existence and therefore against the culture it represents."

His rhetorical revolution still provides the groundwork for anti-immigrant movements around the world today.

III

As soon as Ingrid was old enough, she left Elmtaryd too, and she and Otto went to the opera house in Stockholm to see *Swan Lake*.

They married and eventually had three children. Otto again applied for Swedish citizenship, but he was only granted it in 1955, on his third attempt. By that time he was thirty years old and had been living in Sweden for seventeen years.

For a time he worked as a journalist for various Swedish newspapers. Later he ran his own business, first in advertising and then in restaurants.

For several years following his departure from the farm at Agunnaryd, Otto occasionally returned to spend a few days in the big house with Berta and Feodor. They were old now. Mutual appreciation, perhaps friendship, had arisen.

Of Feodor's anti-Semitism one can only say that the young man who came to the farm in 1944 as cheap labor wasn't hated. After the war, when Otto had almost nothing to do on the farm, he and Feodor hunted woodcocks. They mixed their own snus and hid it in the barn so Berta wouldn't find out. In the daytime, they went for walks with the dogs in Feodor's woods, and in the evenings Otto took one Hermods educational course after the next. Master Kamprad went around in his boots and jodhpurs. *Mein Kampf* was in his bookcase and had been both browsed and read, but this hatred did not apply to Otto Ullmann.

Älmhult, 2010.

Soon we'll have spoken for more than two hours. Many of the people who have been named are dead, but their names linger in the simply furnished workroom on Ikeagatan in Älmhult. We think about them. We remember. They're used as building blocks in a post-facto construction. Is that right? Has history been recounted correctly?

The machine-made coffee in the plastic cups has gone cold. Across from me sits Ingvar Kamprad. A picture of him is reflected in the tabletop's glossy veneer. A blurry reflection, an image of an image. The surface is hardly scratched, the edges hardly chipped. And Ingvar himself has become a symbol of the determined Smålander, the world-famous entrepreneur, the good crisis manager, the clever trend follower, the strong and enthusiastic leader. The one who gives the consumer masses what they want.

A model image. A mirror image. A sensory image. As if refracted through a prism, he becomes what the viewer wants to see.

It worked well on a national level, too. IKEA markets Sweden, which markets IKEA, so the nation and the company become images of each other, as their respective self images grow.

Ingvar has become an icon, but just as split in three as the country of Sweden.

First so close to the German culture that the border between the two countries could hardly be distinguished. Language, thoughts, and ideas flowed back and forth as if they were communicating capillaries.

Then there was regular friendly humanity. Although Sweden didn't want to let in "contingents," a trickle of individuals could find their way into Swedish society, one at a time. That could work, then friendship could arise. You could have a good time together, toil together, take care of forests, animals, and fields together. As if there were no connections between ideas and their consequences. Or what was it that one person answering the *Dagens Nyheter*'s survey had said about deportation: he was no friend of the Jews but wanted no part in such horrors.

Finally, the nation of Sweden and Ingvar the person share one more quality—perhaps they even cultivate it. Forgetfulness.

INGVAR: I lived with my grandmother up in the big house at least for as long as I lived at home. And when that father of mine hit me, and he did that quite often, so... if I could only make it up to Grandmother's, that was the end of that.

JOHANNES STENBERG, INGVAR'S ASSISTANT: She saved you.

INGVAR: Yes, goddamn it, she often did. And when I started out as a businessman, I went to Grandmother first. So when she died, they were packing... and there were things that she'd bought and had no bloody use for, but it was little Olle, as I was called, who'd sold them to her. Then my courage grew, and I dared approach the neighbor.

ELISABETH: Yes, that was something that caught my attention. When you describe to Bertil [Torekull] how you talk about Uncle Hitler as though he were a member of the family or…

INGVAR: No. It can't be in the book that I've said "Uncle Hitler."

ELISABETH: Well, that's what it says in Bertil Torekull's book.

INGVAR: Then it's wrong.

ELISABETH: Okay.

INGVAR: I've never said "Uncle Hitler." Maybe Dad…

ELISABETH: But…doesn't this sound at all familiar?

INGVAR: No. Have I said "Uncle Hitler"?

JOHANNES STENBERG: I think that seems strange, too.

ELISABETH: You describe how it was your grandmother's happiest day when Hitler entered…

INGVAR: Sudet…That's correct.

JOHANNES STENBERG: That stands.

INGVAR: That's one hundred percent correct.

ELISABETH: And then, in connection with that, there's a sentence or two around it. If you have the book here, then…

JOHANNES STENBERG (retrieves the book from a shelf, sits back down, and reads aloud): "Page thirty-eight: The happiest day of her life, celebrated with a coffee party for everyone around, was and remained the day that Hitler invaded the Sudetenland in 1938 and…"

INGVAR: Yes.

ELISABETH: You're on page thirty-eight?

INGVAR: I can tell you, I've never said "Uncle Hitler."

ELISABETH: Here it is.

JOHANNES STENBERG (continues reading): "My childish reaction was of course it was nice that 'Uncle Hitler' did so much for grandmother's relatives and [. . .]"

INGVAR: Eh, well, I don't recognize that. Me saying "Uncle Hitler." That would have been when I was sitting with Grandmother. But then I must have been damn young. When was that? That was...

JOHANNES STENBERG: ... 1938.

ELISABETH: So you're eleven... Twelve.

INGVAR: I admired my grandmother. She was everything to me. Everything she said was law to me [. . .]

I ended up in the wrong hands from the start. During the war the Germans had a propaganda newspaper called *Signal*. And Grandmother got that. And when I was twelve, I could read and do a little arithmetic, and then I was allowed to read it. And there was some ad... Could it have been for the Lindholmers, or how the hell did I get involved with them? How did I get a hold of it, I can't account for it, but it could have been an ad in *Signal* that I answered. And then I received a ton of material and that's what brought me to Sven Olov Lindholm. But I understood quite quickly that that was cockamamie. Because it was pure racism! Beating Jews to death and all that.

ELISABETH: So you cut off contact with...

INGVAR: Yes, yes. So when I came to Osby, how old can I

have been then? When are you done with elementary school? Fourteen, fifteen. When I went there I crossed paths with that Engdahl movement [. . .]

ELISABETH: But what about Otto being Jewish, and yet you were drawn to these movements, was that ever conflicting for you?

INGVAR: We talked about it from time to time but it wasn't a disturbing relationship at all.

ELISABETH: But you had thoughts about it? There was no opposition in you?

INGVAR: Not one damn bit.

ELISABETH: How does that work?

INGVAR: It wasn't too darn hard. Because when I realized that I was wrong, I realized I was wrong [. . .]

JOHANNES STENBERG: But when I hear you talk about Per Engdahl, there isn't any anti-Semitism in those relationships at all . . . There were other things . . .

INGVAR: I don't know how history works. But the loser always gets plenty of undeserved blows. Then the question is what the centuries will do to set it straight [. . .] So the question is, can research after the fact come closer to the truth or will it remain a lie? Will Hitler and Stalin stay black, or is there some white as well? [. . .]

ELISABETH: I've read Bertil Torekull's book and in it he says that your dad, he didn't like Jews.

INGVAR: Dad—first and foremost he was anti-Bolshevik. And you could say he was a Nazi. That he was deep down, but he didn't convey it to me that way. But he was anti-Bolshevik and he often spoke of the yellow threat, that the yellows will eventually take over the world. And the devil knows if there isn't something to what the old man said, if you look at our situation today. It's a question of wanting to work, people who want to, enthusiasm, and so on. And there's plenty of that in the Far East.

ELISABETH: But he associated anti-Bolshevik . . . I mean, Bolsheviks were also Jews?

INGVAR: No.

ELISABETH: It's a pretty common association.

INGVAR: That's right, most oligarchs are Jews. You can't get around that.

ELISABETH: But taking in this Jewish refugee, didn't that pose a conflict?

INGVAR: Not at all [. . .] You can probably say that Father was a Nazi in his soul and heart. But in a different way. There's no chance in hell that he'd hit a person or want to murder a person or any of that.

Maybe he was one of those who didn't believe in concentration camps, there were lots of people who asserted that theory. Per Engdahl, for example, he told me that after all of these terrible incidents in the concentration camps, one can't imagine this to be true in modern times, and so on . . .

ELISABETH: But do you remember what you were thinking, and what you knew? Did you reflect on Otto's background? And what happened in Germany?

INGVAR: What the hell am I supposed to say? We were friends, and who gives a damn if he was Indian or

Jewish or Sami. I've been very involved with the Sami in Norrland, so I suppose I can say that.

ELISABETH: But you knew about his parents' fate?

INGVAR: Yes, Otto told me about it!

ELISABETH: What did he say then, do you recall?

INGVAR: Yes, he said, "My father was murdered," if that was in Auschwitz or Theresienstadt, I can't say, but in one of those camps [. . .]

ELISABETH: What I'm curious about—as you can tell—is how it all fit together. A person thinking Engdahl's ideas were important and right and still being close friends with someone who'd experienced the consequences of some of those ideas. What were your thoughts about that?

INGVAR: There was no conflict for me. Per Engdahl was a great man, that I will maintain for as long as I live.

III

So what actually happened? Did Ingvar call Otto?

No, says Ingvar. Or it's not impossible but it's not something I remember.

"Of course," says Otto's wife Ingrid. "I was the one who picked up the phone. It was when that book about Nazism was about to come out."

So he must have made the call in 1998.

"Ingvar asked me a strange question, as I was almost ten years younger than him and Otto. He would've known that best himself, who he was spending his time with."

Then Otto picked up the phone.

"Ingvar was exploring the terrain, he wanted to know if Otto had talked to journalists," Ingrid recalls.

After the conversation, Otto was ill at ease. It had been their first contact in twenty-five years. But did Ingvar apologize?

Otto's son Peter is sure of it. He visited his parents the day after Ingvar's phone call, and they spoke about the matter.

Eva, Otto's oldest daughter, is also sure. Otto revisited that conversation a few times, Ingvar calling to apologize. As though that were possible. She recalls Otto's voice ringing with disdain. If someone asks for forgiveness, you ought to give it to them, she'd thought, and this irritated her. That's why she remembers it.

But Ingvar can't remember. All he can say for certain is that he called thirty-some people around that time to apologize, and sent his letter asking for forgiveness to another hundred.

"Darn nerve-wracking," he says today.

The memory gap opens up, and one falls into the next question.

Had Otto been unaware? Had he lived alongside Ingvar off and on for more than a decade, and not understood? Had he taken care of Master Feodor, walked side by side with rifle and hounds into the woods, and never realized?

How could he not have seen what every local knew?

When Ingvar's Nazi heritage was brought to light, Otto was deeply disappointed. Ingrid and her children agree on this point. He hadn't been aware, hadn't understood, and felt sad and angry. Ingvar, on the other hand, says the two of them had discussed the matter at some point and that was that. But where is the border between recollection and reconstruction, between what he would have wanted and what actually happened?

Ingvar sings the praises of friendship. He fell in love with Otto and they always stood by each other. Ingvar the loner, who'd always felt like the odd one out, who sought out the Nazis' anti-Semitic community for this reason. He says this himself. Was his longing for friendship finally satisfied with Otto?

Otto was a loner, too, and displaced, a migratory bird in the Smålandish landscape. Was it remarkable that the ties became tight and life did in fact become fun for two young men who loved moonshine, girls, and their friendship? It's no big deal if one is a Jew, and spending time with a fascist leader is nothing to discuss, nor are the meetings with the New Swedes worth bringing up. And why should Otto even think to ask? Otto didn't think to ask.

The best times of Ingvar's youth were in the warmth of their friendship. He didn't see a connection between his ideology and the Jewish refugee toiling at his side. Barns were barns, dance pavillions were dance pavillions, and immigration laws, a hatred of Communists, and strong leaders were something else. Friendship was friendship, the opposite of being alone.

When Ingvar's past floated to the surface like an old corpse, he went public with prayers for forgiveness—most notably he penned an emotional apology to his employees. He has reiterated his prayer for forgiveness in interview upon interview. Who wants to be remembered as a Nazi, when you've created IKEA? He made calls, he wrote to people. He called Otto that evening in 1998. "I'm sorry," Ingvar Kamprad said.

In Vienna the traffic rushes by. Buildings are torn down, others are erected. On early spring days people stroll through Prater in their free time, or take Sunday trips to the Vienna Woods, where they can find a grassy hillside on which to kick a ball and have a bite of the picnic they brought with them. Everything continues. The trees are still standing. Under them the greening shadow.

Only in his fifties did Otto manage to use the German language again. He rarely spoke of his childhood or his parents. He put those five hundred letters from Pepi, Lisl, and other murdered family members in chronological order and tied package string around each bundle, and at the end of his life he passed them on.

At Otto's funeral in 2005 one of his sons-in-law gave a speech. He recalled the time his car engine died and Otto had to help tow it to the workshop. Everything was going fine until they came to a traffic circle and the rope between the cars snapped. The son-in-law was left sitting in his broken-down car in the middle of traffic, while Otto kept calmly driving on, oblivious. Because—as the son-in-law said—Otto didn't turn around. He never looked back.

A nd my story?

We've all seen pictures of the tracks that led to Birkenau, laid strip by strip for the Jews from Hungary. Domestic Nazis split the country into five zones in order to empty it of Jews systematically, and the capital Budapest was left for last. The boy who became my father survived because he happened to be there. Because he walked to the left. To the right. Because it was raining. Because of the shade. Because. For no reason. Hear how his heart pounds inside of me.

Someone asks me: why you, this text, these words?

Because my pockets are full of stones, and I'm visiting graves that don't exist. Because the girl from London said no when I asked. Because she is eighty-two now, but still doesn't want her father's words about a reed bending in the wind to be written—because the family's Jewish heritage still has to be kept secret.

Can you hear the beating hearts?

And those that have been silenced.

Josef Ullmann

Born April 3, 1893
Last known address in Vienna: Robertgasse 2/12
Prisoner 1110 in Transport IV/12 from Vienna to Theresienstadt, October 2, 1942
Prisoner number 992 in Transport Juniper from Theresienstadt to Oswiecim, September 28, 1944
Status after the war: dead
Age 51

Elise Ullmann, née Kollmann

Born November 10, 1891
Last known address in Vienna: Robertgasse 2/12
Prisoner 1111 in Transport IV/12 from Vienna to Theresienstadt, October 2, 1942
Prisoner number 975 in Transport Oak from Theresienstadt to Oswiecim, October 4, 1944
Status after the war: dead
Age 53

Margarethe Kollmann, Aunt Grete

Born August 9, 1890
Last known address in Vienna: Robertgasse 2/12
Prisoner 712 in transport from Vienna to Maly Trostinec,

White Russia, August 31, 1942
Died September 4, 1942, in Maly Trostinec, White Russia
Age 52

ADOLFINE KALMAR, NÉE KOLLMANN, AUNT NUNY
BORN FEBRUARY 20, 1893

Last known address in Vienna: Löwengasse 49/15
Prisoner number 487 in transport from Vienna to Opole, February 26, 1941
Status after the war: dead, possibly 1942
Age 49

PAUL KALMAR

Born November 14, 1886
Prisoner 486 in transport from Vienna to Opole, February 26, 1941
Status after the war: dead, possibly 1942
Age 56

To you, and all the others. A stone on your unknown graves.

Thanks

I want to thank the Ullman family, who generously gave me their full trust to research and tell their family story.

Guido Petz, for the first translation of about 350 cards and letters.

Lena Hammargren, for her complementary translation of the letters and their final versions.

Dr. David Winterfeld, Archiv der Israelitischen Kultusgemeinde Wien, and Lars Hallberg, Swedish National Archives, Stockholm, for invaluable contributions and great patience.

Jan Samuelsson, who shared his research on Nazism in Småland.

Richard Herold, Björn Linnell, and Lena Albihn at Natur & Kultur, for the best possible support and insight.

Sources

Interviews 2010–2011

Ingrid Ullman
Peter Ullman
Eva Ullman
Åsa Ullman
Ingvar Kamprad
Kerstin K. Johansson
Hellis Sylwan, one of the children in the Swedish Israel Mission's children's transport 1939
Heinz Breslauer, one of the children in the Swedish Israel Mission's children's transport 1939
Carin Ehrenberg, daughter of Mrs. Carola Eklundh
Martin Lind, bishop
Heléne Lööw, historian

The interview with Ingvar Kamprad is a transcript of an audio recording from August 9, 2010. After that, he politely declined to participate in supplementary interviews. Sections composed of small talk or repetition have been redacted and marked with [. . .]. Ingvar Kamprad and his assistant Johannes Stenberg read all of the excerpts from the interview eight months prior to the publication of the first Swedish edition. Kerstin K. Johansson declined an equivalent offer.

Unpublished Sources

Eidem, Erling. Letters from Archbishop Eidem to Sigfrid Hansson, 1938, as well as Hansson's notes in the 1938 almanac, the Labor Movement Archives and Library in Stockholm.

Eklundh. Letter from Otto Ullmann to Mrs. Eklundh, in the Eklundhs' family archive, the Kronoberg Archive in Växjö.

Engdahl, Per. Documents in the Press Archive of the Sigtuna Foundation.

Germany's Concentration Camps. The British Government's Secret Documents.

Kalmar. Documents relating to the Kalmar family, Municipal and Provincial Archives of Vienna.

Kamprad, Ingvar. File at the Swedish Civilian Security Service up to and including 1949.

Kollmann. Documents relating to the Kollmann family, Municipal and Provincial Archives of Vienna.

Nazi meetings in Småland during the war. Register collected and compiled by journalist Jan Samuelsson.

The New Swedish Movement. File at the Swedish Civilian Security Service up to and including 1949.

Swedish Israel Mission. Documents relating to the mission's children's transport and Pastor Birger Pernow's correspondence, in the Swedish church's archives in Uppsala.

Swedish National Archives, Stockholm. Documents relating to Swedish diplomacy and refugee policies.

Ullman. The family's private collection of letters, other documents, and photographs.

———. Documents relating to the Ullman family in Vienna, Archives of the Austrian Resistance.

Ullmann. Documents relating to the Ullmann family, Municipal and Provincial Archives of Vienna.

Ullmann, Josef. Documents relating to Josef Ullmann's deportation to Ulanow in 1939 as well as his work in Vienna in 1942, Archive of the Jewish Community Council of Vienna.

Yad Vashem, Jerusalem. Archive and database of the victims of the Holocaust.

Published Sources

Aftonbladet, Svenska Dagbladet, Dagens Nyheter, Kristianstadsbladet, Smålandsposten, Jordbrukarnas Föreningsblad, Moderna Tider, Läkartidningen. 120 newspaper articles.

Åmark, Klas. *Att bo granne med ondskan. Sweden's förhållande till nazismen, Nazityskland och förintelsen* [Living next door to evil: Sweden's relationship to Nazism, Nazi Germany, and the Holocaust]. Albert Bonniers Förlag, 2011.

Andersson, Lars M., and Karin Kvist Geverts, eds. *En problematisk relation? Flyktingpolitik och judiska flyktingar i Sverige 1920–1950* [A problematic relationship? Refugee policies and Jewish refugees in Sweden 1920–1950]. Uppsala University, 2008.

Arendt, Hannah. *Den banala ondskan* [The banality of evil]. New ed. Daidalos, 1996.

Berkley, George E. *Vienna and Its Jews.* Madison Books, 1988.

Blomberg, Göran. *Mota Moses i grind* [Meeting Moses at the gate]. Hillelförlaget, 2003.

Carmesund, Ulf. *Refugees or Returnees.* Uppsala University, 2010.

Den svenska Nationalsocialisten/Folksocialisten [The Swedish National Socialist/People's Socialist]. 1939.

Engdahl, Per. *Fribytare i folkhemmet* [Hijackers in the Swedish welfare state]. Cavefors förlag, 1979.

Friedländer, Saul. *Utrotningens år 1939–1945* [The years of extermination: Nazi Germany and the Jews 1939–1945]. Vol. 2 of *Nazi Germany and the Jews.* Translated by Nille Lindgren. Natur & Kultur, 2010.

Frohnert, Pär I. "*De behöva en fast hand över sig*" [They need a firm hand to guide them]. *Missionsförbundet,* Israelmissionen och de judiska ykting-arna 1939–1945. In *En problematisk relation? Flyktingpolitik och judiska flyktingar i Sverige 1920–1950* [A problematic relationship? Refugee policies and Jewish refugees in Sweden 1920–1950]. Uppsala University, 2008.

Hammar, Tomas. *Sverige åt svenskarna* [Sweden to the Swedes]. Stockholm University, 1964.

Hedenquist, Göte. *Undan förintelsen. Svensk hjälpverksamhet i Vienna under Hitlertiden* [Escaping the Holocaust: Swedish relief work in Vienna during the time of Hitler]. Verbum, 1983.

Hilberg, Raul. *The Destruction of the European Jews.* 3rd ed. I–III. Yale University Press, 2003.

In spite of it all!, 1939. The English White Book, vol. 2.

Kamprad, Ingvar, and Bertil Torekull. *Historien om IKEA* [The history of IKEA]. New ed. Wahlström & Widstrand, 2006.

Kan judafolket räddas? [Can the Jewish people be saved?]. Swedish Israel Mission, 1943.

Koblik, Steven. *The Stones Cry Out:. Sweden's Response to the Persecution of Jews 1933–1945.* Holocaust Library, 1988.

Kristendomens historia [The history of Christianity]. Bibelfrågan. www.alltombibeln.se

Kvist Geverts, Karin. *Ett främmande element i nationen. Svensk flyktingpolitik och de judiska flyktingarna 1938–1944* [A foreign particle in the nation: Swedish refugee policies and Jewish refugees 1938–1944]. Uppsala University, 2008.

Larsmo, Ola. *Djävulssonaten* [The Devil's sonata]. Albert Bonniers förlag, 2007.

Lindberg, Hans. *Svensk flyktingpolitik under internationellt tryck 1936–1941* [Swedish refugee policies under international pressure 1936–1941]. Allmänna förlaget, 1973.

Lodenius, Anna-Lena, and Stieg Larsson. *Extremhögern* [The far right]. 2nd ed. Tiden, 1994.

Lööw, Heléne. *Nazismen i Sverige* [Nazism in Sweden]. Ordfront, 2000.

Missionstidning för Israel [The Mission newspaper for Israel]. 1933, 1938–1942.

Nationell Tidning [The national newspaper]. 1940.

Roth, Joseph. *Judar på vandring* [The wandering Jews]. Translated by Bo Isenberg. Atlantis, 2010.

Rürup, Reinhard, ed. *Topography of Terror.* Arenhövel, 1989.

The Sentencing Adolf Eichmann (e-book). "The Nisko Chapter." www.nizkor.org.

Sjöberg, Thomas. *Ingvar Kamprad och hans IKEA* [Ingvar Kamprad and his IKEA]. Gedin, 1998.

Svanberg, Ingvar, and Mattias Tydén. *Sverige och förintelsen* [Sweden and the Holocaust]. Bokförlaget Arena, 1997.

The Swedish Israel Mission's Yearbooks. 1936–1945.

Szymborska, Wisława. *Could Have.* Translated by Anders Bodegård. FiB:s Lyrikklubb, 1996.

Thorsell, Staffan. *Mein lieber Reichskanzler! Sveriges kontakter med Hitlers rikskansli.* [*Mein lieber Reichskanzler!* Sweden's contact with Hitler's Reich Chancellery]. Bonnier Fakta, 2006.

Tidskriften Judisk Krönika [Jewish Chronicle magazine]. 1938–1945.

Vägen Framåt [The way forward]. 1942, 1943.

. . . How long did the packed lunch last, is there any of it left?

And what about the suitcase. Did you get it, are your things unpacked and organized? Write to us—not just about the bag, but about the sports available to you, the weather, in short, what you do during the day and how you spend your time.

It will do you good to eat properly. It doesn't matter if you put on a couple kilos, there are plenty of famous sportsmen who've packed it on when abroad. But you're still growing, so I'm guessing your weight won't change. But I beg of you, make sure your stomach is in order. And take care of yourself. Now that you're free, we also want you to always be healthy. So we needn't worry about you. Let's agree on that, shall we?

ELISABETH ÅSBRINK is a Swedish journalist and the author of *1947: Where Now Begins*, published by Other Press in 2018. Her second book, *And in the Vienna Woods the Trees Remain*, received worldwide attention for revealing new information about IKEA founder Ingvar Kamprad's ties to Nazism. It won several awards, including the August Prize for Best Swedish Non-Fiction Book of the Year, the Danish-Swedish Cultural Fund Prize, and Poland's Ryszard Kapuściński Award for Literary Reportage. Åsbrink made her debut as a playwright with *RÄLS*, based on the minutes taken at a meeting convened by Hermann Göring in 1938, and has since written four plays.

SASKIA VOGEL is from Los Angeles and lives in Berlin, where she works as a writer and literary translator. She has written on the themes of gender, power, and sexuality for publications such as *Granta*, *The White Review*, *The Offing*, and *The Quietus*. Her translations include work by leading Swedish authors such as Katrine Marçal, Karolina Ramqvist, and the modernist eroticist Rut Hillarp.

Also by **ELISABETH ÅSBRINK**

1947: Where Now Begins

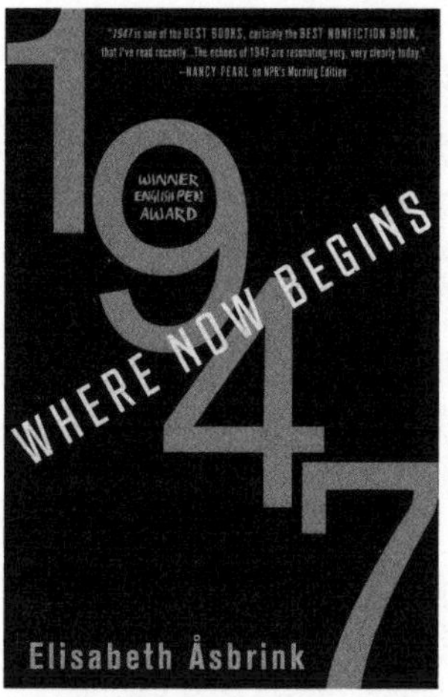

An award-winning writer captures a year that defined the modern world, intertwining historical events around the globe with key moments from her personal history.

"[A] gripping history . . . [Åsbrink's] careful juxtaposition of disparate events highlights an underlying interconnectedness and suggests a new way of thinking about the postwar era." —*The New Yorker*

The year 1947 marks a turning point in the twentieth century. Peace with Germany becomes a tool to fortify the West against the threats of the Cold War. The CIA is created, Israel is about to be born, Simone de Beauvoir experiences the love of her life, an ill George Orwell is writing his last book, and Christian Dior creates the hyperfeminine New Look as women are forced out of jobs and back into the home.

"*1947* is one of those books that makes you want to major in history. It is one of the best books, certainly the best nonfiction book, that I've read recently. I think the subtitle, *Where Now Begins*, really speaks to one of the things that makes this book so important: The echoes of 1947 are resonating very, very clearly today."
—Nancy Pearl, on NPR's *Morning Edition*

"An extraordinary achievement." —*New York Times Book Review*

OTHER PRESS

You might also enjoy these titles from our list:

BERLIN 1936 by Oliver Hilmes

A lively account of the 1936 Olympics that offers a last glimpse of the vibrant life in the German capital that the Nazis wanted to destroy.

"[*Berlin 1936*'s] publication earlier this year felt like a gift. Historian Oliver Hilmes has created an almost miniaturist narrative of the most controversial Olympics ever staged." — *The Guardian*

HITLER, MY NEIGHBOR: MEMORIES OF A JEWISH CHILDHOOD, 1929–1939
by Edgar Feuchtwanger and Bertil Scali

An eminent historian's account of the Nazi rise to power from his unique perspective. Feuchtwanger was a carefree five-year-old when Adolf Hitler, leader of the Nazi Party, moved into the building across the street.

"Vivid . . . An intimate look at the horror wrought by Hitler." — *Kirkus Reviews*

NOT I: MEMOIRS OF A GERMAN CHILDHOOD
by Joachim Fest

NAMED IN THE *NEW YORK TIMES BOOK REVIEW*'S 100 NOTABLE BOOKS OF 2014

A portrait of an intellectually rigorous German household opposed to the Nazis and how its members suffered for their political stance.

"*Not I* shrinks the Wagnerian scale of German history in the 1930s and 1940s to chamber music dimensions. It is intensely personal, cleareyed, and absolutely riveting." — *New York Times*

Nr .163

Liebster

sehr gefreut. Wi
Du gesud bist u
Du uns sobald Du
aber manchmal geht
keine Beunruhigu g

Denn zwei Stunden sp
dem Vater der Hedi,
dass Hedi mit Schar

15.13.

Mein liebes guter Junge,

jetzt wäre eigentlich wieder Post von Di

fällig, ich nehme aber an, dass sie bereits

5 h

Theres